Enhancing adoptive parenting

Enhancing adoptive parenting
A test of effectiveness

Alan Rushton and
Elizabeth Monck

with contributions by
Morven Leese, Paul McCrone,
Mary Davidson and
Helen Upright

BAAF
ADOPTION
& FOSTERING

Published by British Association
for Adoption and Fostering
(BAAF)
Saffron House
3rd Floor, 6–10 Kirby Street
London EC1N 8TS
www.baaf.org.uk

Charity registration 275689 (England and Wales)
and SC039337 (Scotland)

British Library Cataloguing in Publication Data
A catalogue record for this book is available
from the British Library

ISBN 978 1 905664 64 1

Editorial project management by Shaila Shah
Designed by Andrew Haig & Associates
Typeset by Avon DataSet Ltd, Bidford on Avon
Printed in Great Britain by Athenaeum Press

BAAF is the leading UK-wide membership
organisation for all those concerned with
adoption, fostering and child care issues.

5.3	Mean scores for SDQ sub-categories from social workers and parents for girls and boys	66
5.4	Recruitment of families into study	68
6.1	Outcomes at immediate post-intervention (Time 2)	78
6.2	Outcomes at six months post-intervention (Time 3)	80
6.3	Parents' estimates of their children's improvement in three dimensions using Visual Analogue Scales	83
6.4	Mean SDQ emotional symptoms sub-scores and "improvement" recorded by parents on the Visual Analogue Scale	83
6.5	Means and standard deviations on child-based measures at T1, T2 and T3	86
6.6	Means and standard deviations on parent self-report measures at T1, T2 and T3	88
8.1	Number (%) of participants using services and total (mean) service costs: baseline	114
8.2	Number (%) of participants using services and total (mean) service costs: T2	116
8.3	Number (%) of participants using services and total (mean) service costs: T3	118
10.1	Children showing problems in three key domains at each time point	135
10.2	Parents' report of using new methods of handling their child's emotional distress at T2 compared with T1	137
10.3	Parents' report of using new methods of handling their child's emotional distress at T3 compared with T2	137
10.4	Methods of handling misbehaviour – combined intervention group and control group at T1, T2 and T3	142
10.5	Frequency of types of relationship problems reported	143
10.6	Total personal relationship difficulties	144
11.1	The index child's problems targeted by special services	155
11.2	Family members who were receiving special services	155
11.3a	Satisfaction with the timing of post-adoption support: combined intervention group	166
11.3b	Satisfaction with the timing of post-adoption support: control group	168

List of figures

Fig 5.1	Families entering the study	69
Fig 6.1	Adopters' satisfaction with parenting their child	76
Fig 6.2	Parents' satisfaction with advice offered in the two interventions	77
Fig 8.1	Mean service costs at baseline, T2 and T3	119
Fig 8.2	Median service costs at baseline, T2 and T3	120

Notes about the authors

Alan Rushton spent many years as a social worker in both child and adult mental health services. Until recently, he was Director of the MSc programme in Mental Health Social Work at the Institute of Psychiatry, King's College, London where he continues as a Visiting Professor. He has been engaged in follow-up studies of older children adopted from care, the outcomes of sibling placements and contact arrangements. He has published many research papers and six books, including Rushton and Dance (2002) *Adoption Support Services for Families in Difficulty*, published by BAAF.

Elizabeth Monck is based at Thomas Coram Research Unit, Institute of Education, London where she conducted an evaluation of concurrent planning in the placement of very young children from care. Her previous work, at the Institute of Child Health, concentrated on outcomes of treatment for abused children. Recent publications include Monck, Reynolds and Wigfall (2003) *The Role of Concurrent Planning: Making permanent placements for young children*, published by BAAF.

Acknowledgements

We wish to thank the Nuffield Foundation and the UK Department of Health (subsequently the Department for Education and Skills and now the Department for Children, Schools and Families – DCSF), which funded the study and especially Sharon Witherspoon (Deputy Director, Nuffield Foundation) and Caroline Thomas (Manager of the DCSF Adoption Research Initiative) for their support and continuing interest in its progress. Our particular thanks go to our Research Advisory Group, chaired by Professor Roy Parker, for its sustained interest and good advice during this long-running project. We also thank our parent advisers and the research interviewers and the Clinical Trials Unit at the Institute of Psychiatry for conducting the randomisation. We thank our colleagues Morven Leese and Paul McCrone, who advised respectively on the statistical analysis and the economic analysis. Julie Smith provided excellent administrative support, especially in settling the parent advisers' complicated fees and expenses claims. We are especially grateful to Mary Davidson and Dr Helen Upright, who helped to write the parenting manuals. We also wish to thank the social workers and administrative staff who provided support for the researchers in their areas.

Our greatest thanks go, of course, to the adoptive families themselves who participated in the study.

The study was approved by the Research Ethics Committee of the Institute of Psychiatry, King's College, London: Reference number: 036/02; and registered as International Standard Randomised Controlled Trial Number: ISRCTN04448012.

March 2009

Executive summary

Background

It is now recognised that many families adopting older children from care need professional help to deal with the more severe behavioural and emotional problems that the children may present. However, concerns have been raised by adoptive parents, by professionals and researchers about inadequate provision and unevenly spread post-adoption services. Failure to recognise the extent and severity of problems of the placed children has been apparent in health and social services, and adopters feel that when they report problems, these are underplayed or dismissed. Furthermore, staffing and skill levels have been a barrier to the families' acquiring accessible therapeutic help.

The Adoption and Children Act became law in 2002 and introduced a right for adopters to be assessed with a view to receiving support services. In order to make the identification of needs and service planning more systematic, local authorities are now required to draw up an adoption support service plan and to monitor its implementation. These are welcome developments, but not enough is known about what post-adoption services need to offer, how intensive they should be, and when they should be delivered and by whom and with what level of skill. Little is known about the effectiveness and cost of helping adoptive parents to deal with the difficulties presented by some placed children. The few UK studies that have tried to evaluate the outcomes of adoption support have lacked a non-intervention comparison group and the specific post-placement adoption support has not been well defined.

The aim of the randomised controlled trial presented here was to test the cost effectiveness of two programmes designed to support adopters who were parenting a child recently placed from care and to conduct a qualitative analysis of the intervention process. The strength of a randomised trial is that with equally balanced characteristics of the intervention and control groups, any difference in outcome is likely to be due to the interventions and not to other differences between the groups.

1

Sample and method: An introduction to the research was given to 26 authorities but only 15 finally participated; these varied in size from large county councils to small unitary authorities. Four more cases were recruited from an advertisement on the Adoption UK website. Adoptive parents, looking after children between three and eight years who were screened to have serious behavioural problems using the Strengths and Difficulties Questionnaire (SDQ), participated in the trial. Thirty-seven families participated: nine headed by single parents, four by same-sex couples and the rest by married couples. With their consent, the adoptive parents were randomly allocated to one of two interventions:

(a) behavioural parenting advice with a cognitive element (n = 10)
(b) a tailored adoptive parenting education programme (n = 9)
or to a "service as usual" control group (n = 18).

The two interventions consisted of ten weekly sessions of home-based parenting advice. Each programme was based on a manual and was delivered by trained and supervised family social workers. Interviews with the adopters revealed that none of the control group parents had received a service that was at all similar to the individualised parenting advice delivered via the research. The interventions were focused on the child with the highest SDQ score at the screening stage (the index child).

Information about the children and the family was collected through interviews with the adopters and by standardised questionnaires (child-based and parent-based measures) at entry into the research study, immediately after intervention (or 12 weeks later for the control group), and six months later. Adopters in the control group were offered the choice of one of the parenting interventions after the six-month follow-up interviews.

Economic costs were calculated using an established procedure. All but one of the adopters receiving the parent advice completed the 10 sessions and research interviews were completed for 100 per cent of the sample at all points.

The parent-based questionnaires included the Parent Sense of Competence Scale, Daily Hassles and Satisfaction with the interventions. Child-based measures completed by the parents were the Strengths and Difficulties Questionnaire, the Expression of Feelings Questionnaire, a

2

Post-Placement Problems questionnaire and a Visual Analogue Scale representing the index child's progress. Adopters and parent advisers independently completed weekly feedback forms after each session.

We hypothesised that changes in the parenting and in the index child's psychosocial problems would be greater in the combined intervention group than in the control group.

Results

- At the six-month follow-up, parenting changes were more apparent in the intervention than the control group. A significant difference ($p<0.007$) and modest Effect Size (ES d = 0.7) were found on "satisfaction with parenting" in favour of the interventions over the controls as detected in the Parenting Sense of Competence scale.

- Research interviews with adopters showed that some negative parenting approaches to misbehaviour (threats, shouting, telling off) had significantly reduced in the intervention group compared with controls.

- Small post-intervention improvements were found for the mean level of child problems for the whole group (mean SDQ scores: combined intervention group: 18 to 17; control group: 19 to 18) but with no significant differences between groups for baseline compared with post-intervention or for baseline compared with six-month post-intervention. There were no significant differences between the combined intervention group and control group, adjusting for baseline scores. No differences were found on SDQ sub-scale scores or on the other child-based measures.

- A contrast of the two parenting interventions was restricted due to the small sample size and consequent low statistical power. However, parent satisfaction with the parenting advice was high and equivalent in both interventions.

Qualitative analysis showed that the parents especially valued regular, home-based interventions tailored to their specific concerns. Parents stressed the need to not simply receive advice but to work through problems and strategies with a trusted, skilled practitioner. However, parent advisers reported that some adopters' needs extended beyond the scope of the parenting advice programmes. Parents' views on the relevance and usefulness of "preparation for adoption" indicated that preparation was frequently inadequate to manage these children's behavioural or emotional difficulties.

Cost effectiveness

The children and families in this study used a wide range of services before, during and after the interventions were received. The costs of specialist services used by participants in the month before baseline, immediately after the intervention and in the six months before the final follow-up interview were measured. The mean costs at baseline for the combined intervention group and for the control group were similar (£3,058 and £3,001 respectively). At first follow-up, the mean costs were £3,186 and £1,641: that was substantially higher for the combined intervention group, but this was mainly due to the inclusion of the intervention costs. At the six-month follow-up, mean costs were again similar (£1,511 and £1,738).

Combining overall costs with differences in outcomes showed a cost of £731 per unit improvement in satisfaction with parenting in the short term and £337 in the longer term. However, in terms of reducing the children's problems/improving behaviour, the costs of the intervention were higher without improvement. For a relatively modest investment in post-adoption support, evidence can now be cited from this study to show that this money would be well spent in aiming to enhance parenting.

Limitations of the research

The planned sample size proved impossible to achieve even when the number of participating authorities was increased and the timescale of the research extended. This reduced the statistical power of the study. As about half of the parents whose children had high SDQs did not finally join the study, the sample is not therefore fully representative of the target sample. We must therefore conclude that this trial, in only achieving a sample size comparable to a pilot study, requires a larger sample replication before the results can be used as more than a pointer for changing practice in post-adoption support.

Local authorities with high representation of black and minority ethnic looked after children were invited into the study, but in the event did not participate: these children and their adoptive parents are therefore under-represented in the study sample.

For ethical reasons, all the adopters were free to seek what further services they wished throughout the research period. The trial therefore did not have a true non-intervention control group. However, very few control group adopters received an intervention comparable to the ten parent advice sessions, although four attended the six-session group-based training, *It's a Piece of Cake?*

These findings should not be generalised to all adoptions, but only to families in which children are placed between three and eight years and who show substantial problems in the first 18 months, and the findings only apply when the manuals are used by experienced practitioners.

Finally, we remain ignorant of what longer-term effects there might be beyond the six months after the parent advice sessions ended.

Other lessons learned

Apart from the main outcomes from the trial, a number of other lessons were learned from the research:

- Not all adopters wanted the free parenting advice offered by the study. We were a little surprised by this, especially when we knew they were struggling with severe difficulties (at least one child in the family had a high SDQ score). There are clearly complex help-seeking issues for adopters. Some may have preferred to struggle alone or to see if improvements would occur; some may have been waiting for a CAMHS appointment or other specialist help; possibly some were content with the level of help being delivered, or promised, by their post-adoption social worker. We suspected that some families were uncomfortable with the "intrusion" into family life they thought would be associated with the parenting sessions.
- Conducting a trial in a "real world", rather than in a clinical setting, poses considerable difficulties. Much research time and effort have to go into enlisting the help of adoption social workers and recruiting the

adoptive parents. A sound understanding of the purpose of a random-ised controlled trial is essential to obtaining the full co-operation of local authorities.

- This study attempted to define and standardise the parenting support by the use of written manuals. The parent advisers found the manuals sound and appropriate and the adopters found them relevant and of practical help. Some parents and advisers commented that there was too much material to cover in the ten sessions and some would have preferred the sessions to be about two weeks apart.

Conclusions

The randomised controlled trial design, as used here, is a stronger method of evaluation than the one group, before and after study. Furthermore, information gathering from the follow-up interviews of both intervention and control group parents was virtually complete.

The findings suggest that a home-based parenting programme for adopters caring for difficult children in the first 18 months of placement produced, at the six-month post-intervention follow-up, positive changes in parenting satisfaction and less negative parenting approaches. Satisfac-tion in parenting their child rose after receiving the advice sessions, while the satisfaction of the control group fell slightly. For the combined intervention group, raised parenting satisfaction could be seen as a better platform on which to stand when looking to the future stability of, and satisfaction with, the adoption.

The parenting advice did not prove more effective in reducing the children's psychosocial problems within the timescale of this evaluation. This lack of change in the children might be explained as a consequence of their extremely adverse pre-adoption histories. The children in the study had experienced maltreatment, separation from birth families, a period in care, multiple changes of placement, and then a relatively late placement in an adoptive family. Perhaps the beneficial influence of a longer period of stable, positive family life would be necessary before one could see significant behavioural change. Furthermore, some effects of earlier maltreatment might not readily be remedied, even in the longer term.

As both manuals were equally appreciated, as neither showed superior results and as parents generally wanted both "understanding" and "strategies", there is a strong case for combining the manuals into a single document.

Further research is needed using larger samples and improved outcome measures. However, we hope the study will be of use to providers and commissioners of adoption support services in being able to refer to an advice programme to adoptive parents that has been empirically tested.

Introduction

We have gradually increased our knowledge of the problems of children placed for adoption from the care system and the challenges they present to their adopters. We have a better idea now of what adopters say they want from services. A number of studies have indicated what helps in parenting difficult children. It seemed the right time to take an experimental approach to the question: What works in adoption support?

This study was originally part of the "Quality Protects" initiative. Objective 1 was to achieve the secure attachment of children to safe and effective carers. With the emphasis on placing into adoptive families more children in care who could not return to their birth parents, it was seen as imperative to discover how best to support and thereby increase the security of these placements. The strategy (2002–07) of the British Association for Adoption and Fostering (BAAF) stated at the time that 'Children and carers need access to a range of services including education, health and other support to enable families to parent children separated from their family of origin'.

An ambition for this study was to help health and social services to achieve a major policy objective: that is, to secure adoptive families for children who need this type of placement in order to give them the experience of ordinary family life and to enhance their life chances, despite a poor start. It is now recognised, although this was not always so, that some adoptive families need well-timed professional help to deal with the more severe problems. If normal development can be promoted, these children are more likely to become confident, well educated and psychologically healthy adults. As a consequence, they should have less need later on for adult health and social care services and will be less likely to be caught up in the criminal justice sytem.

However, studies evaluating outcomes of adoption support have mostly been uncontrolled and small scale. At the time of submitting the research proposal, no scientifically conducted trials of specific post-placement adoption interventions had been conducted in the UK. At the completion of the study this remains the case.

We hope the findings will be particularly helpful in using limited resources as efficiently and cost effectively as possible and in contributing to evidence-based training of social workers charged with supporting the placements.

This book is an attempt to give a much fuller description of a randomised controlled trial than is normally found in journal articles. Chapters 6, 8, 10 and 11 have most of the quantitative findings. The other chapters focus on the interventions and the practice issues. Chapter 1 provides a brief description of the background to developing a randomised controlled trial of adoption support, followed by a discussion of the benefits of using such an approach (Chapter 2). Chapter 3 outlines the method, the sample and the measures we used to assess progress. Chapter 4 describes the material on the adoption preparation programmes gleaned from the first research interview. Chapter 5 gives details of the recruitment and Chapter 6 presents the key findings on the outcomes of the two parenting advice interventions. In Chapter 7 we present the material from the feedback forms which the parents and the parent advisers completed each week after the advice sessions. Chapter 8 gives details of the cost effectiveness analysis. Chapter 9 presents case vignettes to illustrate the progress of the families in meeting their child's needs, and Chapter 10 focuses on the ways in which parents handled the difficulties their children showed in three key domains: emotional distress, "misbehaviour" and personal relationships. Chapter 11 provides further information on the specialist services which the parents had received to support the placement. In Chapter 12 we discuss the implications of our findings.

1 Background to adoption support and literature review

A small surge of interest in the concept of adoption support appeared in the UK in the 1980s. A series of articles in the child welfare literature began to draw attention to the needs of those adopters who had chosen to take children from care into their homes (Argent, 1985; Macaskill, 1985; Phillips, 1988; Rushton, 1989). Researchers were documenting adoption disruption rates, the high levels of mental health problems in the in-care population, and the enduring problems of some adopted children (Rushton, 1989). This concern grew into a call for better support in the 1990s (Logan and Hughes, 1995; Mulcahy, 1999). Appeals for better services came from social workers, familiar with the struggles of adopters, and acutely aware of the consequences of a failed placement. Adoptive parents themselves became more vocal and began to overcome their natural reticence and weak sense of rights to make demands for services.

The move towards better quality and more relevant adoption services

Ten years have passed since the publication of *Adoption: Achieving the right balance* (Department of Health (DH), 1998) which encouraged greater use of adoption for those children in care who could not return home. It was becoming recognised that, if a wider range of older and more challenging children were to be adopted, risks to the stability of the placements might increase. Meanwhile, government inspections began to raise concerns about inadequate provision and unevenly spread adoption services (Social Services Inspectorate, 2000).

The White Paper on Adoption (DH, 2000) had led the way on legal reform and acknowledged research which had shown that little support had been available to adoptive families, particularly over the longer term (Lowe *et al*, 1999). The Adoption and Children Act then became law in 2002. Many aspects of adoption were attended to in this first piece of domestic adoption legislation since 1976, but of particular interest here is the introduction of a *right for adopters*: not for a service as such, but to an assessment for a post-adoption service. This qualification came as a disappointment to many in the field who were hoping for something more generous and unrestricted. Accompanying the new legislation came the National Adoption Standards, the Adoption Register, targets to encourage greater use of adoption and a Task Force to help local authorities develop their services. The government then published the Adoption Support Services Regulations in 2003 (DH, 2003) and the *Practice Guidance on Assessing the Support Needs of Adoptive Families* in 2005 (DfES, 2005). In order to make the identification of needs and service planning more systematic, local authorities are now required in law to draw up an *adoption support service plan* and to monitor its implementation.

Around this time, Rushton and Dance (2002) were funded by the Nuffield Foundation to conduct a mapping of all adoption agencies in the UK, both statutory and voluntary. Reporting on services for adoptive families in difficulties, they found that specialist services were much more available in the large cities and that inadequate staffing and skill levels were a barrier to the families acquiring accessible therapeutic help. Lack of information about the number of placed children with serious psychosocial problems was also an impediment to planning. Failure to recognise the extent and severity of problems of the placed children appeared to be true in many quarters, and the attitudes of some GPs, teachers and social workers tended to underplay or be dismissive of problems reported by adopters. However, they found that some local authority adoption teams were making strides in developing their own services or contracting for more specialist therapeutic services or buying membership of a post-adoption support organisation for their adopters. Accessibility to such services was, however, very uneven.

Rushton (2003a) pointed to the lack of evidence of cost-effective interventions in helping adoptive parents to deal with the difficulties presented by their recently placed children. There was no question that many children present serious challenges to their parents in the first year of placement, but access to useful services was often problematic.

Sturgess and Selwyn (2007) recently conducted a survey of the support provided in non-infant adoptions. Their study reported on the complexities of help-seeking where many adopters were reluctant to ask for help for fear of seeming to have failed, or not wanting to feel blamed, or because they preferred to struggle alone. The adopters were not satisfied with the behaviour management advice available through the placement team and were disappointed when Child and Adolescent Mental Health Services (CAMHS) failed to provide sustained and effective help and appeared to have poor understanding of the adoption context. These two studies show that, at least during a period that saw a substantial increase in late placements from care, adopters had very mixed experiences of services and some looked in vain for genuine understanding of their needs and for support that would prove to be effective in their family.

This acknowledgement of the complexities of ex-care adoptions needed, of course, to be matched by an expansion of post-adoption services. The development of support services was taking place in permanent placement teams through workshops and post-adoption support groups, although the local authorities pleaded that they were too stretched to provide comprehensive and long-term support, even though some funds were provided specifically for expansion. Important service developments came from voluntary adoption agencies (VAAs) and independent providers (especially the Post Adoption Centre, Family Futures, Parents for Children, Barnardo's, The Children's Society, Coram Family, and After Adoption, to name but a few). VAAs have specialised in providing direct services (individual, group and family work and telephone helplines). Various theoretical approaches have been extended to the special circumstances of adoptive families, especially psycho-dynamic and family systems models with an emphasis on attachment issues and cognitive behavioural therapy models.

The growth of self-help in this field is represented by the activities of Adoption UK, which functions as an important source of adopter-to-adopter support and advice. Although much innovative work has been developed in voluntary and statutory agencies, rigorous evaluation of "what works" has lagged far behind. However, the well known adopter support training programme called *It's A Piece of Cake?* has recently been evaluated by The Hadley Centre team (The Hadley Centre, 2007).

Literature review on the problems of children placed from care and support for adoptive parents

Current knowledge of the behavioural, emotional and social relationship problems of late placed children is drawn from two groups of UK studies (The Maudsley Family Research studies and the Hadley Centre studies) which have documented the problems of children adopted in middle childhood. It is important to know not just the range of problems children demonstrate, but which ones are likely seriously to challenge the stability of the placement, or are at least likely to contribute to continuing family stress and dissatisfaction. These studies have consistently shown that conduct, overactivity and relationship problems are the ones most likely to predict poor adoption outcomes (e.g. Quinton *et al*, 1998; Selwyn *et al*, 2006).

Conduct problems might involve refusal to comply with parental requests, long temper tantrums that last for hours, extreme expressions of anger and rage, and serious aggression. Over-activity, poor concentration and restlessness have proved to be common in in-care populations and in children in adoptive placements. Such problems can persist and interfere with learning and with establishing positive social interaction both within and outside the family. Difficulties for adopters in forming a satisfactory relationship with a child can be a central problem. This might show itself as the child maintaining an emotional distance, being socially undiscriminating, being unable to trust others and expressing feelings in a distorted way. In one of the longer-term follow-ups conducted on late placed children (Rushton and Dance, 2006), 28 per cent of the continuing placements had substantial difficulties even after six years of living in the adoptive family. These included continuing developmental, behavioural and social difficulties. In the study by Selwyn *et al* (2006) of longitudinal non-infant adoption, only two-fifths of the children followed up at an average of seven years after placement were found to be free from behavioural problems.

Adopters' responses to support services

Quinton *et al* (1998) investigated post-placement social work support provided by the local authority in the first year of placement. Considerable variation in the quality of service was found in the social workers' own accounts, from very infrequent support through to detailed discussions with the parents about the problems leading to advice on using specific parenting tactics. There was evidence that by the end of the first year a more intensive service was being offered in cases where the child was showing many psychosocial problems or was not developing an attachment to the new parents. A study by Lowe *et al* (1999) recorded adopters' difficulties in having the seriousness of their child's problems recognised, frustration at being given misleading information and difficulty in accessing appropriate services for themselves or their children.

Evidence from the US comes from a recent survey of 800 adopters by Zosky *et al* (2005) who gathered the views of adopters who had 'adoption preservation services'. The adopters were found to favour free, home-based support that was sensitive to the unique and complex needs of the family. They appreciated help in understanding the behaviour and feelings of the child and wanted to develop better parenting strategies for dealing with difficult behaviour, anger and lack of trust.

The factors that emerge from such surveys tend to emphasise the need to understand the specific problems of adopted children, how to manage behavioural difficulties and how to encourage commitment to the child, especially when the child is unrewarding or has a weak or distorted attachment. Zosky *et al*'s study (2005) was published after the current research began but the findings confirm impressions gained from smaller UK samples.

The effectiveness of interventions to support adoptive parenting

A range of interventions is currently being developed to support adoptions (see Scott and Lindsey, 2003), including child-based interventions (play therapy, music and drama therapy) and adopter-based help through group support, parenting workshops and, more recently, a focus on adopter attachment styles.

A great deal of interest has been shown in community parenting programmes, especially where children have conduct problems. In a recent update, Scott (2008) emphasises the importance of changing the environment for the child in order for an intervention to be effective. Approaches targeted at the parents have also been developed in relation to adoption. However, as rigorous evaluation of support for non-infant adoptions is still largely lacking, it is useful to consult the closest examples, namely, support for foster families looking after maltreated children in care. Minnis *et al* (2001) were the first to conduct a randomised controlled trial of a group-based programme to improve foster carers' ability to communicate with children. McDonald and Turner (2005) tested, also with an RCT design, a cognitive behavioural programme with foster carers. In both cases, the foster carers reported on benefits from the programmes, but no statistically significant differences were found at follow-up on the primary outcome measure of change in the children. It is possible that the content of the programmes was not well enough targeted, or was not intensive enough or the participants had not acted on the advice sufficiently to have an effect.

New US-based studies in foster care are currently evaluating more intensive interventions. Fisher *et al* (2005) and Fisher and Kim (2007) have conducted a trial with older children (3–5 years) in foster care. They focus on the importance of a responsive caregiver who can assist with the child's stress regulation. The sample of 117 foster children was randomly assigned to the multi-dimensional treatment foster care programme for pre-schoolers or to regular foster care conditions. The experimental intervention was designed to support the foster carers in providing consistent and contingent responses to the children. Foster parent consultants worked intensively with the foster carers to encourage positive behaviour and to set limits for problem behaviour. Based on carers' reports, increases were shown in secure behaviour and decreases in resistant and avoidant behaviour. The authors claim that this is a first step in showing that attachment-related behaviour can be modified. The research base is so far mostly concerned with brief interventions. Longer-term therapeutic help may be needed for some adopted children with enduring behavioural problems and attachment difficulties. Cost-effective data are needed on such interventions.

The Rushton and Dance survey (2002), referred to earlier, made a plea for *both* accessible *and* evidence-based services. They concluded:

> *Few benefits will accrue to adoptive families if the delivery system improves greatly but the interventions are mis-targeted or inexpertly delivered. Few benefits will accrue to families if the effectiveness of certain interventions has been established but they are not equitably distributed.*

The research to be presented here was designed to test the effectiveness of accessible, readily provided and modestly priced interventions.

Summary

- The Adoption and Children Act 2002 introduced a right for adopters in England and Wales to an assessment for a service.
- Despite the call for better services for adopters of children from care, little evidence has been available on cost-effectiveness.
- The strength of a randomised trial is that with equally balanced characteristics of the intervention and control groups, any difference in outcome is likely to be due to the interventions and not to other differences between the groups.
- Controlled trials have recently been conducted with foster carers.
- This randomised controlled trial with adopters was designed to test the effectiveness of accessible, readily provided and modestly priced interventions.

2   Designing and setting up the study

It is increasingly clear that the professionals involved in supporting adoptive parents need to have a stronger evidence base for their work. Social work research relies a good deal on consumer opinion as a test of the usefulness of an intervention. Of course, the views of all the parties to adoption, especially if gathered in large scale representative surveys, are extremely valuable. However, consumers' views by themselves are not enough to improve services. Descriptive surveys will not answer the "what works" question, only what consumers think is a good idea. And without strong evidence, some consumers may opt for radical interventions promoted by persuasive therapists – while such interventions may, in fact, do harm.

The outcomes of any "before and after" study of a single intervention with families can be very misleading. If positive change is recorded, it is all too tempting to assume that the improvement is necessarily due to the intervention. Clearly, many other factors may have led to the change, not the least of which is the passage of time and the children's increasing maturity. In order to rule out these other possible explanations, it is essential to compare the intervention group with a different group experiencing no intervention, or perhaps a different intervention. Simple "before and after" studies are often conducted by practitioners evaluating their own innovations without independent assessments. Such studies are known to be more likely to report positive results than studies independently assessed. It also tends to be true that the tighter the methodological demands imposed on the trial, the less likely it is that strong evidence of effectiveness will be found.

But it is not sufficient simply to compare two groups, one with and one without an intervention, in order to discover whether the intervention is superior to no intervention. Although this may show that the intervention group gives better results, it still leaves open the question of whether this is genuinely due to the intervention or to other, perhaps unrecorded, differences between the groups. For instance, the intervention group could have less serious problems at the outset and this might be the reason for better outcomes, or some unknown factor may be the cause of better outcomes in one group. There is clearly a need to ensure that both groups are as alike as possible in order to make the inference that it is the intervention, or largely the intervention, that makes the difference.

One method of equalising the groups is to match the participants case by case (a case/control study). In a study of adoptive families this would be an attempt to ensure that the groups of children are roughly equivalent on factors like age, sex, ethnicity and level of problems. However, there is a limit to how many items can be truly matched and the possibility will always remain that some aspect that has not been measured is being left out of the equation. For example, among looked after or adopted children, one group may have had more mothers taking drugs during pregnancy, or one group may have suffered more emotional abuse. In both cases, the records may not be detailed enough, or reliable enough, to be certain about which children were exposed to these factors. Without this type of information on which to perform the matching, the groups may remain unbalanced.

The case/control design is often employed when the preferred method of random allocation is not feasible for some practical or ethical reason. The best way to make the groups equal is to randomise the allocation: that is, to decide who goes into which group on the basis of chance: this is the randomised controlled trial (RCT). Any differences, both known and unknown, should then be equally distributed across the groups. This gives greater confidence to say that any difference in outcome, having equalised out other possible causes (confounders), can be put down to the effect of the intervention alone. In other words, it is the "best shot" at a fair test of effectiveness. RCT methodology makes an attempt to eliminate bias in testing theories about intervention, but by the same token, such a well controlled trial may be much more challenging to execute.

It is important that trials of different interventions should be made publicly accessible. Current practice is to register a trial before starting the intervention. By registering a trial, the hypotheses are set out before it begins. It is then not possible to "cherry pick" the outcomes. All trial results are then recorded, whether or not they show a finding favourable to the intervention. Publication bias is a well known process whereby only successful trials find their way into print. However, nowadays trials reporting lack of effectiveness may be more likely to be published in peer-reviewed journals. A system of trial registration allows for a fairer survey of the available evidence.

Arguments about the use of the RCT with psychosocial interventions

The clear logic of this design has considerable appeal as a way of dealing with potential bias and has accounted for real progress in establishing reliable knowledge about treatment and other interventions, especially in medicine. However, the response to the use of the RCT has been more divided in the social sciences – in fact, some believe that the RCT should remain "where it belongs", in simple drug versus placebo trials. It is often alleged that the RCT is incompatible with testing complex interventions, because of the difficulty of accounting for the many interacting factors composing the interventions.

Social work commentators have argued more generously that the RCT may have its place in the social sciences, but still muster more arguments against it than for it (Corby, 2006; Gould, 2006). Those who promote their opposition to the use of the RCT in social interventions have probably had a disproportionate effect on the social work community and their views have been strongly imparted to practitioners and may have also influenced the culture of UK local authority children's services/social work services (now children's services) departments. However, it is evident that government and practitioners are increasingly concerned to establish "what works" and for whom in the field of practice and social policy and there are ethical as well as public expenditure reasons why this is important. It is unethical to offer or impose a service that is ineffectual, and it is wasteful of scarce resources to do so without seeking alternative approaches. An ethical approach requires that any intervention is properly and independently evaluated. Because of this it is important to balance the criticisms with the arguments in favour of the RCT.

Responding to arguments against RCTs

We will examine the arguments mustered against RCTs in psychological and social interventions and see what merits they have and say how we have tried to deal with them in this trial.

The ethical issues: One of the major concerns about the RCT is that it is unethical to deliver a service on the basis of chance allocation. Clearly this would be the case if it is already known that one intervention is superior. But RCTs are of most use where, crucially, the effectiveness of the intervention is not known. In our trial of two interventions, the respondent was given an information sheet saying that the interventions are believed to be helpful, but we don't know which is more helpful and which is more cost effective. Respondents were then free to sign up to the trial if they chose. Rather than argue that conducting RCTs is unethical, some have argued that it is unethical not to do so because it does not serve the respondents well to go on providing interventions that are of no proven benefit. Sometimes it can be shown that a particular well-established intervention, even when widely used, is of little or no benefit and possibly harmful (e.g. the formerly routine removal of tonsils).

It is sometimes alleged that if people are in difficulty they should not be allocated to a no-intervention option. This would certainly be true if the trial interventions were already known to be even slightly effective. And it would also be true if the participants in that non-intervention arm of a trial were being expected to deny themselves all other activities that might bring them benefit. In the current trial, it was explained to all the adoptive parents and their social workers that they could obtain other services if they wished. In addition, if they were allocated to the non-intervention or control group, they were offered a choice of one of the trial interventions after the research interviews were completed. In effect, this was a "waiting" group, which only meant that there was a delay in receiving a service.

Some objectors to an RCT state that deciding "who gets what" on a chance basis is artificial and contrived and not the way cases are allocated in ordinary practice. It is true that, in any experimental set up, the researchers may influence whether people seek other services. It can be argued that difficulties arise in trying to meet the complex and multifaceted needs of adoptive families by giving them a standardised intervention and controlling the way this is delivered. Admittedly, it would be almost impossible to separate out the effects of a specific professional contribution from a multi-professional intervention. Consequently, we have chosen here to investigate an area of family intervention that, for the most part, would fall to a single provider – the adoptive family support worker or the post-adoption worker. The intervention itself was standardised, as far as possible, by the careful selection of parent advisers with similar professional backgrounds, trained to use an intervention manual and with the availability of supervision.

It is often alleged that the measures of outcome employed in psychosocial trials are too unreliable or too simple to capture the subtle changes that are meaningful to practitioners and the recipients of the service. Such measures, some would say, fail to account for the "internal" changes which modify attitudes and perceptions that may be of longer-term value, even if behavioural change is not immediately evident. However, in the field of adoptive placements, not all outcome indicators are necessarily complex: some may be very straightforward, like placement breakdown or acceptability of the service to the respondent. It is, of course, crucial to use measures that reflect what it is that the intervention is trying to change. This is possibly the most important aspect to get right in the design of a trial. Even with a very large sample and randomisation, if the measures are not appropriate to the intervention, the method may fail to detect changes that are there to be discovered. In the current trial we used a combination of reliable and validated measures and ones tailored to the specific concerns of parenting in adoptive families.

The above considerations are about the "internal validity" of a trial. The "external validity" concerns whether or not and to what extent the results can be generalised to other contexts and other populations; in the case of the current trial, this would be other adoptive families with children of the same ages and similar level of psychosocial problems. This is indeed a worry if the samples studied have knowingly or inadvertently excluded cases that might have posed difficulties for the conduct of the trial. It may be more convenient and less complex for the analysis to exclude cases with multiple problems, or where research participation is thought to be undesirable. But such exclusions would then make the samples unlike those encountered in everyday practice. In the case of the current trial we have restricted the sample to the placement of children aged three to eight, having no major disabilities and placed in non-relative families. These restrictions were necessary so that the analysis was not challenged by too much heterogeneity, but not too restricted to make generalisation to everyday practice difficult. Any results, of course, have to be strictly confined to the sample as defined.

Some commentators object that the results of a trial of a programme of work, as opposed to a particular approach, are of limited practical value because they do not determine what to do with an individual case and they do not help in understanding the complex interpersonal dynamics that contribute to case outcomes. There may be some truth in this as the emphasis in trials has historically been on group comparisons and on inputs and outcomes rather than on exploring why the interventions work and what exactly are the processes of change (Pawson and Tilley, 1997). However, there is increasing interest in attending more to the latter (Berwick, 2007) and our trial has paid close attention to the delivery of the interventions and how they have been received by the adopters. The experienced practitioners who delivered the interventions have reported on how the programme was received by each family, and the adopters have also commented on how they experienced the helping process. Supplementing the trial with process evaluation assists in understanding the outcomes, as well as assisting with the process of subsequently implementing the findings with other adoptive families.

It is important not to overstate the case for the RCT design for addressing psychosocial problems in community samples. It is a special-ised type of enquiry designed to answer some but not all of the questions about "what works, for whom", and is not the only approach to understanding the processes associated with change (Slade and Priebe, 2001; Harrington *et al*, 2002). However, it is not ethically defensible to go on providing services without knowing whether they actually bring benefit, or at the very least do no obvious and measurable harm. In the field of adoption support, we owe it to the adopters and their children to invest in research which will guide practice. No doubt some practitioners will remain sceptical but we hold that it is only with accumulating evidence from well-designed trials that we will be able to assess the effectiveness of interventions. One randomised trial will not be able to produce answers to the complex questions surrounding the development of recently adopted children. There will need to be a succession of trials and for this to be possible there will need to be a general acceptance of the importance of this approach by the practitioners.

While the methodological skirmishes have continued, the practical-ities of designing, funding and executing RCTs in the social welfare field have resulted in very few trials of specifically social work intervention in the UK to hold up as examples. Corney's work with depressed women was a pioneering study (1981); Harrington *et al* (1998) on self-harming adolescents is a more recent one. Sample sizes in such trials have been relatively small and on the whole have not produced strong evidence for the effectiveness of the interventions. We believe many more well-designed trials are needed in social welfare. In our "real world" trial we were hoping to learn something about adoption support that practitioners will find useful, but also about how to conduct a trial in which the academic world can have confidence. The debate continues as to how best to evaluate complex social interventions (Woolf, 2000) and to improve experimental designs in the light of previous efforts (Olds *et al*, 2007).

The present study

This study was challenging to set up in that it involved collaborating with several separate groups of people: local authority managers and social workers, adoptive parents, two groups of parent advisers, our adoption consultants and a team of research interviewers. Below, we set out the considerations that went into the design of the study, testing two appro-priate and feasible parent advice programmes in the context of the current adoption scene. The method and procedures actually employed are described in the next chapter.

Our focus was on children placed from care with adoptive families where the level of problems warranted the delivery of a ten-week parent-ing intervention. We needed, therefore, to be selective as to which parents and children entered the study. We chose a sample of both boys and girls who had suffered considerable adversity before being admitted into care, and who were then placed, in middle childhood, in adoptive families. In order to make the sample as homogenous as possible, we decided not to include children who were presumably fairly well settled as they had been adopted by their existing foster carers or by relatives. We also excluded children with major disabilities as their placement needs would almost certainly not represent the needs of the majority of ex-care children.

Our aim was to test interventions that could reasonably be delivered within the local authority's financial and staffing resources. We chose local authorities rather than voluntary adoption agencies as a previous survey had shown the latter to have better developed post-adoption services (Rushton, 2003b), and we wanted to test whether an additional service could improve on the services that would routinely be provided by or arranged by the local authority.

Selection and timing of the interventions

When the study was first conceived of, although many new approaches to post-adoption support were being developed, few had been independently evaluated. Reports of the success of interventions had frequently not specified clearly enough what the interventions consisted of, and replication (an essential feature of establishing effective practice) was difficult. Many approaches to supporting these non-infant adoptions were being used, for example, through direct work with the child, or through family systems or group work approaches. Practitioners varied in their professional training and approach. Support was being provided by clinical psychologists, psychotherapists, social workers and psychiatrists, and art or music therapists to parents, to children, or to both at the same time. Such support might be in groups or in individual sessions. Multi-professional approaches posed significant difficulties for evaluation.

We chose to devise two new parenting interventions for several reasons. First, if adoptive parenting can be enhanced, and this can alter the daily home environment, it may have a positive effect on the child's behaviour and social functioning. Second, a parenting programme could be deliverable by well-trained social workers and might achieve results as good as more expensive interventions, for example, as delivered through CAMHS. Third, parenting programmes are usually delivered over eight to ten weeks and this would not be likely to prove too time consuming for the adopters, nor be too costly in staff time.

The timing of the interventions in relation to the adoptive placement had to be considered. We could have recruited adoptive families having difficulties at any stage of the placement and were aware of the need of many families for expert help during their child's adolescence. However, we chose to focus on the early stages of placement because several studies have shown that threats to placement stability tend to occur in the first year to 18 months (Festinger, 1986; Barth and Berry, 1988). Therefore, this is a crucial time for the new parents to air their doubts and difficulties and for effective interventions to be on hand. Help at this stage may not only ease the transition to becoming a new family, but also enhance parental competence for dealing with the possible emergence of problems at a later stage.

The consultants, manuals and parent advisers

Two experienced consultants helped to write the two parenting manuals. Dr. Helen Upright is a Consultant Clinical Psychologist in Fostering and Adoption, and devised the cognitive programme; and Mary Davidson is a County Adoption Adviser and devised the "educational" programme. They worked with us to write two structured manuals to act as protocols for the parent advisers. The consultants, when preparing the manual, discussed with the researchers the content of the programme, the style and language thought to be most suited to adopters, and the quality of evidence on which aspects of the manual were based. In addition to the sequence of ten weekly topics, the manuals contained handouts and "homework" – issues and strategies for consideration in the upcoming week. They also included guidance on the way the programme was to be delivered. The advisers were made aware of the need to engage the adopters in the intervention and to acknowledge the difficulties adopters often experience about seeking help. They were encouraged to build a trusting relationship and acknowledge existing parenting skills and support the adopters' commitment to the placement. They were asked to work in partnership, rather than to be didactic, and to be sensitive to the difficulties some parents may have in modifying their own behaviour or attitudes.

As the study was intended as a trial of the effectiveness of specialist social work intervention, we chose to recruit experienced child and family social workers, familiar with adoption, to act as parent advisers. The advisers were trained in groups by our two consultants to use one of the two interventions. They studied the parenting manual and guidance on its use was provided. Supervision when working with the adopters was available from one of the respective practice consultants.

Common features of the interventions

Adoption aims to create a secure base and sense of permanence for the child. The broad purpose of the interventions was to reduce the risk of subsequent placement disruption and to improve the quality of family life in intact adoptive placements. In order to achieve these goals, both interventions were aimed at promoting responsive, consistent and flexible parenting and to help the adopters to achieve better control of difficult behaviour. Where the adopters were a couple, the advisers were asked to involve both in the intervention whenever possible.

Although we assumed that the new parents were selected for possessing these characteristics, we also knew that they might react differently when these characteristics were put under severe strain. The new parents may not have been able to maintain warm feelings and a positive attitude if their best efforts resulted in an unresponsive or rejecting child. They may quickly have felt de-skilled if their efforts went unrewarded and their approaches did not appear to be working (Dance *et al*, 2002).

The two contrasting interventions

The study was designed as a three-arm trial in order for maximum benefit to be drawn from the evaluation. We reasoned that more could be gained about the relevance, acceptability and effectiveness of the parenting interventions if two approaches were contrasted with each other and with service-as-usual. Adopters would therefore be randomly allocated to one of three groups. (See Appendix 7 for abridged versions of the two manuals.)

The cognitive behavioural intervention

The most direct influence in writing the manual for this approach was the work of Carolyn Webster-Stratton and colleagues in the parenting clinic at the University of Washington, whose work has included interventions with foster and adoptive families (Webster-Stratton and Hancock, 1998; Webster-Stratton, 2003). Recent UK-based studies using this programme have shown largely positive effects of parent training for birth families

(Scott *et al*, 2001; Gardner *et al*, 2006). In this programme, adoptive parents are shown how to decrease unacceptable and increase acceptable behaviour by using praise and rewards, by ignoring inappropriate behaviour, by setting firm limits and by using "logical consequences" and problem solving.

The content of the cognitive behavioural programme was as follows:

Session 1 – Getting to know the parents and introducing the programme
Session 2 – Using positive attention to change behaviour
Session 3 – The value of play for establishing positive relationships
Session 4 – Using verbal praise
Session 5 – Praise and rewards
Session 6 – Learning clear commands and boundaries
Session 7 – Using "ignoring" to reduce inappropriate behaviour
Session 8 – Defining for the child the consequences of undesirable behaviour
Session 9 – "Time out" and problem solving
Session 10 – Review and ending

Our adaptation of this parenting programme involved even greater emphasis on the need for parents to conduct daily play sessions with their child. The manual explains the importance of playing with the child for developing attachment relationships and also considers how the parent adviser should proceed if the child does not respond well to the parents' attempts to play. This is particularly important as many adopted children may resist the parents' direct attempts to develop a relationship due to their prior negative experiences of close relationships or ambivalence about being with a new family. Play can provide a setting for developing relationships without un-nerving closeness.

The cognitive behavioural parenting programme was adapted to deal with the specific needs adopted children are known to have. Greater emphasis was placed on how parent advisers should respond if the parents reported that their child rejects their praise and/or their rewards. This was added because children placed for adoption may have been deprived of praise from their birth parents, or may have received varying amounts of praise from different carers, or may have been treated negatively and not see themselves as worthy of praise.

The value of clear communication and commands was given special emphasis because recently placed children are very likely to have been exposed to inconsistent discipline by multiple previous carers where expectations may have been unclear and the consequences possibly punitive or abusive. They may be more likely to protest and to respond with angry outbursts or show traumatic responses like withdrawal, fear or freezing. Therefore, the manuals emphasised the importance of parents being clear about commands and setting appropriate boundaries and the advisers helping the parents to understand why their child might find it hard to respond in a co-operative and timely manner.

Learning to ignore inappropriate behaviour is an important part of the programme and especially relevant in the face of confrontational, insistent behaviour by the child. The manual acknowledged the difficulty of "ignoring" behaviour if it was not the parent's natural style to do so. The adviser helped the ignoring to be done in a way that does not convey rejection of the child and assists parents in using ignoring consistently and with a jointly agreed approach between the parents. The adviser followed the implementation of the approach week by week to allow for re-con-sideration as the parents fed back their experience of using new strategies.

This intervention included a cognitive element because parenting behaviour is influenced by how adopters come to see their child (White et al, 2003). Perceptions and attributions were to be challenged if they seemed unhelpful. Adopters without previous parenting experience might have unusual or mistaken ideas about the origin of problems, or inappropriate expectations, while experienced parents might carry over attributions that really belong to their "home-grown" children. Negative thoughts were to be discussed (e.g. 'My child doesn't like me and will never become close to me') and more adaptive cognitions offered in their place. Negative thoughts often lead parents to withdraw from their child, further decreasing the chance of developing a secure attachment. The programme tried to replace the idea that the child was rejecting the parent with acknowledgement that this child may have experienced chaotic and disturbed parenting so that developing new relationships may be exceptionally slow. Altering the parents' thoughts in this way could enable them to overcome a sense of disappointment or failure and continue to behave in a positive way towards their child.

Lastly, although this programme discusses the "time-out" strategy, parent advisers were asked to caution parents in its use and to encourage them to rely on alternative strategies such as "logical consequences" and "problem solving". Practitioners have raised concerns that time-out could be damaging if it reminds the children of aspects of their previous abusive or rejecting experiences, which could affect developing relationships and the child's self-esteem.

Behavioural approaches have sometimes been challenged as being too superficial or likely to be inadequate unless the intervention focuses on the adoptive parents' deeper feelings and their own possible attachment difficulties. Such an approach is not the focus of this "early in placement" study, although there may be special aspects of the new adoptive parent–child relationship that are distinct and require different treatment.

The "educational" intervention

The "educational" approach was designed specifically for the study with the aim of improving the parents' understanding of the meaning of the children's current behaviour. For many practitioners with therapeutic ambitions, working with the person's "construction of meaning" is a major aim. This intervention was designed to help the parents to see how the child's past and present might be connected. The intention was to throw light on the possible origin of problems rather than to attempt to identify specific causes of problems – it is accepted that many interacting influences combine to shape the current behaviour. The intervention explored what meanings the parent had attached to the child's experiences and current behaviour and strove to arrive at the best-informed interpretation of how they may be linked.

This intervention was concerned both with the constructions the adopters placed on the child's behaviour and with enhancing their ways of handling challenges to their parenting. In helping parents to enhance their understanding of the possible reasons for the child's behaviour, they should be better at anticipating events and thereby increase their ability to manage the difficulties.

In contrast with the behavioural intervention, this approach is more "historical": that is, links are made to what is known of the child's history. The amount and accuracy of the information about the child's pre-placement history given to adopters can vary considerably: it can be incomplete, unreliable or even withheld. Supplying accurate information can help the adopters think about the kind of parenting the child has received in the past, which, in turn, could help them to have more realistic expectations, and develop a more empathic, flexible parenting style attuned to the child's history and current needs.

This intervention was also more social and environmental as it included the adoptive parents' experience with schools, family and friends. It was more theory driven in its concern with broken and distorted attachments, with the child's adaptive and coping mechanisms in the face of adversity, and with aspects of parenting, like the capacity for self-reflection, sensitivity and responsiveness. Some of these topics do have a research base, but less has been established on how to intervene effectively to improve "understanding". The content of the "educational" programme was as follows.

Session 1 – Getting to know the parents and introducing the programme
Session 2 – Understanding insecurity
Session 3 – Helping parents understand their own reactions to disturbed children's behaviour
Session 4 – Understanding how "bad experiences" affect learning and behaviour
Session 5 – Understanding how "bad" and broken relationships affect development
Session 6 – Children's survival strategies and defensive reactions: the outward show
Session 7 – The expression and control of feelings
Session 8 – Understanding how children develop new relationships
Session 9 – Surviving in the wider world
Session 10 – Review and ending

This approach bears greater resemblance to methods widely used by British adoption social workers, although such work is rarely so formalised. In this case we wanted the intervention to be selective, sequenced and set out in a more structured format. It is generally thought that if the child's behaviour can be better understood, problems can be better tolerated, and the child can develop trust and allow expression to their positive as well as negative feelings. Reliable knowledge of the major pre-placement circumstances and events in the child's life should help in enhancing understanding which, in turn, should reduce reactions like impatience, frustration, or bewilderment. Parents should be able not only to "read" the child better but also devise parenting strategies more rationally and not only consider new approaches if their own methods are not succeeding.

In this intervention, the parent advisers were required to consult the local authority adoption files prior to meeting the parents, in order to brief themselves on the new family and the child's history. The Form E[1], in the version produced at the time by the British Association for Adoption and Fostering (BAAF), records the number of moves the child has experienced and specific incidents in their history. Form E was used by nearly all adoption agencies to inform adoption panels that adoption was in the best interests of a child and, thereafter, as an adoption record that was passed on with the child to inform both them and their adoptive family of their background history and justifications for key decisions. This can be an invaluable tool in aiding the understanding of adoptive parents as to which genetic and biological risk factors and life experiences have had an impact on the child's current psychosocial functioning. How, for example, has living in chaotic surroundings, or with inconsistent or rejecting parenting, or constantly having to adjust to new carers, influenced current behaviour? The Form F[2] (presented to adoption panels to inform their decision making as to whether or not to recommend applicants as suitable to adopt) is often discarded after the adoption panel and not used as a working tool to assist adopters in parenting their children. This information, which is a combination of analysis by the assessing worker and self-analysis by the prospective adopter, includes assessments of how prospective adopters will parent and how they are likely to respond to children with developmental and emotional problems. Together, the contents of Forms E and F can provide valuable information as to the current level of functioning of both sides in the parent–child partnership,

---

1,2 The BAAF Form E and Form F were in use at the time of the study but subsequently replaced by the child's permanent report and the prospective adopter's report.

why specific areas are difficult and how they can address them together.

The role of the parent advisers involved in delivering the educational programme was to discuss and reflect together with the parents on how the difficult behaviour might best be interpreted and how parenting strategies and responses might change accordingly. We wanted the advisers to avoid simple explanations linking single events to certain consequences, and instead to emphasise the coping styles frequently shown by abused and neglected children. We noted that, in most cases, it will be useful to see a pattern of behaviour as adaptive in the previous abusive situation (e.g. withdrawal, hyper-vigilance or distractibility). In the new family, such behaviour may well be dysfunctional because the emotional and social contexts have changed. The parent advisers were informed that they should not think that they have to produce definitive answers about the specific origin of problems – this will rarely be possible. We also asked that they acknowledged to the parents that some difficulties would require much more specialist advice. Research efforts are ongoing to disentangle the relative contribution of adverse genetic and environmental factors and their complex combinations (Rutter, 2006).

Summary

- There is increasing evidence that social care programmes should be tested for effectiveness in order to establish "what works" and for whom in the field of practice and social policy.
- It is unethical to continue to offer interventions the efficacy of which is unknown.
- The most useful method is by using randomised controlled trials (RCTs), whereby confounding factors are reduced to the minimum.
- RCTs can only be used when the relative merits of the experimental interventions are genuinely not known.
- There is increasing interest in the process underlying effective intervention as well as the outcomes.
- The rationale and content of the two parenting support programmes are set out for a cognitive behavioural approach and an educational approach.

3   Method

The sample

The eligible families

The families included in the study were those with a child placed for adoption between three and 18 months previously. All the children in the study were between the ages of three years and 7 years 11 months at the time of placement and were not suffering from severe physical or learning difficulties, and had not been placed with relatives or with existing foster parents. A previous study had suggested that about 50 per cent of these children would still be showing serious problematic behaviour a few months after placement (Quinton *et al*, 1998, p 118).

The local authorities

Local authorities were contacted through the Directors of Social Services or Children's (and Families') Services. When an initial expression of interest was received, the research directors held meetings with the managers of adoption services and their teams. Although researchers made it clear they would welcome the early involvement of front-line social workers in these meetings, authorities varied in the extent to which they drew them in at this stage. The researchers used these meetings to describe the aims of the study and invited staff to raise any questions. Local researchers who would have responsibility for interviewing the families frequently attended these introductory meetings. At a late stage of the research and because recruitment from the local authorities had dried up, an invitation was posted on the Adoption UK[1] website. This led to responses from six families, four of them living in the areas covered by the researchers and the parent advisers. These four agreed to participate in the study.

When it was agreed that the local authority would collaborate in the

---

[1]   Adoption UK is an organisation that aims to support parents after an adoptive placement; it is not a placement agency and has no statutory responsibilities towards parents or children.

study, a letter of agreement was signed by the research directors and senior adoption officers. The study committed the social workers to liaising between the researchers and the eligible families in order to preserve the family anonymity until the parents had agreed to join the study. The first stage of the research programme required social workers to ask the parents to complete a child behaviour questionnaire (see below), to complete the same questionnaire themselves and to send both to the research team. The second stage required social workers to forward the letter of invitation to join the study to selected parents. The researchers and the parent advisers who were delivering the "educational" intervention programme (see Chapter 2) were given access to the adoption records for the identified children.

Each local authority was asked to identify eligible families, using the criteria outlined above. An initial identification would include several children already placed, but social work teams were asked to review the lists regularly so that newly placed children could be included as the research continued. A very small number of local authorities gave special support to the research at this stage, by circulating information about the study to parents via their adoption newsletters. By and large, however, there was no authority-wide dissemination of information about the research. Most adoptive families therefore did not know that their authority had become a partner in the study. This left social workers to introduce families to the aims of the study. Unfortunately, it was clear from the introductory meetings between researchers and social work teams that a complete grasp of the purposes and implictions of a randomised controlled trial in this field was not widespread. The team prepared a short brief for the social workers to use to explain the study. Social workers were encouraged not to embark on a complicated explanation when they first asked parents to complete the screening questionnaire, but to tell the families that, if they agreed to join in at the first stage, which only involved completion of the screening behaviour questionnaire, they would be able to withdraw later if they wanted.

Random allocation of the parents was organised independently by the Clinical Trials Unit at the Institute of Psychiatry. The randomisation procedure was designed to produce equal numbers of cases in the intervention and control arms of the trial and between the two interventions. The researchers could not be unaware of the group to which the adopters were allocated at follow-up interviews, as the adopters' involvement in the intervention or control condition was the focus of questions in the interview. The choice of which child from the selected families to include in the research sample is described below.

Selecting the screening questionnaire

The instrument that was selected to record the children's psychosocial symptoms was to be used both to select the children and their parents into the study and to track the children's progress during the course of the study. The criteria for choosing which questionnaire to use were that it should be short, cover behaviours and moods that would be familiar to all parents, and be expressed in language that was clear and non-technical. The results should also be capable of interpretation in terms of overall severity of symptoms, distinguishing children who are at risk of having major problems from children in the "normal" range.

The Strengths and Difficulties Questionnaire (SDQ) (Goodman, 1997; Goodman, 2001) was chosen. Among other advantages, this measure is recommended in the central government guidance on assessing support needs in adoptive families (DfES, 2005), and would be familiar to many of the social workers who would be asking parents to complete it for the research team. The SDQ has been shown to be effective as a screening instrument for detecting psychiatric problems in community samples of children (Goodman et al, 2000) and looked after children (Goodman et al, 2004). The SDQ has also been used to track the progress of children in intervention studies (e.g. Minnis and Devine, 2001; Pallett et al, 2002; Mathai et al, 2003; De Wit et al, 2007). The SDQ has been compared to the Child Behavior Checklist (CBCL) (Achenbach and Edelbrock, 1983): Goodman and Scott (1999) found that scores on the SDQ and the CBCL were highly correlated and equally able to discriminate psychiatric from control sample cases. The SDQ was significantly better at detecting inattention and hyperactivity, and at least as good at detecting internalising and externalising problems.

The four sub-scales (recording conduct problems, emotional symptoms, peer relationship problems and hyperactivity) sum to a Total Difficulties score; a fifth sub-scale measures Pro-Social behaviour. The cut-off points are slightly different for parents and teachers for each sub-score and for the Total Difficulties score; in the current study, social worker reports were rated as if for teachers, as we had specifically asked that only social workers with close and recent knowledge of the child should complete the SDQ. In the present study, children were included as having a high score when parents reported a Total Difficulties score of 14 or more, and/or social workers reported a Total Difficulties score of 12 or more. At the screening stage the impact scales were not used.

The SDQs completed by parents and social workers were sent by social workers to the research team for rating. At this stage, the child's date of birth and initials, and the social workers' names and authorities were the only identifying details for researchers. When a child had a "marginal" or "high" Total Difficulties score on either the parent's or the social worker's questionnaire (or both), the parents became eligible to join the study. However, only one child in each family could be the focus of the interventions by the parent advisers. If, therefore, two or more children in the same family had high SDQ scores, the child with the highest score was selected for study. The letter of invitation, an information leaflet and consent forms (see Appendix 4) were sent by the researchers to the social workers and forwarded to the selected parents. The parents who agreed to join the study returned a signed consent form, and only at this late stage could researchers have direct communication with the parents; a telephone call was then made to check whether parents had any further questions before their final agreement.

Before the first interview, the local researcher studied the child's file to collect data on the child's history. This provided a record that was independent of the parents' perceptions, and had the added advantage of shortening the first interview.

Sequence of interviews with parents

The first interview took place before the family was allocated to a particular arm of the trial. The parents were notified of the results of the random allocation soon after the first interview. At this stage the local parent adviser who would provide the allocated programme for the parents was contacted by the researchers. The parent advisers organised their own visits to the parents. The second interview was held within about two weeks of the end of the parent adviser completing the intervention, or (for the control group) about 12 weeks after the first interview. The third and final interview was held with parents at the end of nine months, that is, roughly six months after the second interview.

Hypotheses

The hypotheses set out before the trial began were as follows:

1. That improvement of the children's psychosocial difficulties six months after the parent advice intervention would be greater in the combined intervention groups than in the (control) group receiving only the standard community services.
2. That the extent of the improvement would be similar in both intervention groups.
3. That parenting skill and confidence in their role would show more positive change at Time 3 (six months after the intervention) among the parents in the combined intervention group (nine months after the first research interview) compared with the control group.

The content of the three research interviews with parents and the selection of measures were guided by these hypotheses as well as by a desire to learn more about the preparation for adoption and the provision of post-adoption services.

Selecting and training the family interviewers

The research interviewers were selected for their previous experience and their geographical base. All the interviewers had previously been involved in research that included a substantial element of community-based family interviewing, almost all of them with parents. Each interviewer was responsible for at least one of the widely spread local authorities; in addition, one of the research directors conducted 17 of the 114 interviews that were held with parents. The interviewers were introduced to the research aims and design in two centrally organised meetings, and were closely involved in the development of the interview protocols. Nearly all of them also attended the meetings with the local authority placement teams.

File searches

Before the first interview with adoptive parents,[2] researchers looked through the local authority case files for information on the background of the index children about whom the research interviews would be held. This enabled the first interview to be substantially shorter than if parents had been asked to supply all the pre-placement history, and had the advantage of avoiding any "effort after meaning" (making sense of something retrospectively) bias in a parent's account. Information was specifically sought on the age at first entry into care, length of time in care and number of moves between households and/or carers (both before and after coming into care), and the home circumstances that led to the child becoming looked after. A checklist of factors commonly associated with significant harm to children was used (Adcock and White, 1998). The list included some pre-birth factors such as maternal drug abuse in pregnancy or prematurity, but largely concerned the conditions within the child's life such as domestic violence or marked parental rejection. However, it should be noted that the information in case files may not always provide a complete picture of the adverse factors in the child's life, but simply provides sufficient evidence for the children's services and the courts to take the child into care. We also attempted to collect evidence on the length of "good enough" physical and emotional parenting in the child's first two years; again, this may not always have been an accurate picture. Making these points is not necessarily a reflection on the quality of the case notes, which were frequently of an exceptionally high order; it reflects, rather, the different needs of research and practice – ideally, researchers require all the information on a case while social care services only require enough information to make a case for action.

---

[2] Henceforward, we will largely refer to adoptive parents as "parents" unless there is danger of confusion with birth parents.

Subsequently, most local authorities also provided access to the files of children with low SDQ scores at the time of the screening survey. This enabled a comparison to be made of the circumstances of the high and low-score children either in the experiences (such as abuse or neglect) that had brought them into care in the first place or their subsequent experiences in care before the adoptive placement.

Content and aims of the interviews

Parents were interviewed using a semi-structured format. The three interviews each lasted about one-and-a-half to two hours. Interviewers were asked to record as closely as possible the parents' verbatim answers; tape-recorders were not used. All the interviews contained a section on the child's current behaviour and/or mood, and the parents' ways of handling any problems. Open-ended questions concentrated particularly on three issues: the child's emotional state (grief and sadness, anxiety and fearfulness), "misbehaviour", and appropriate (attachment) relationships within the family and with strangers. Each of these areas was covered by specific questions; for example, three issues around attachment were discussed – "false warmth" to family members, indiscriminate and inappropriate friendliness to others, and a complete absence of warmth to the parents. We acknowledged in the interview that some of these issues produced overlapping problems for the parents.

In the second and third interviews, parents were asked if they had changed their method of handling any of the problems presented by their child in each of these three areas of concern. In the third interview, parents were asked to record their view of their child's progress in these three areas of concern using Visual Analogue Scales (see below).

Some aspects of behaviour that have been reported in adopted children but are not tapped by either the SDQ or the EFQ (Expression of Feelings) were included as questions in the parents' interview. This technique is not uncommon when the behaviour or needs specific to looked-after children is the subject of the research (e.g., Roy *et al*, 2000). All the interviews ended with a question on the parents' view of the future for their child; on the basis of their replies they were rated as "very optimistic", "fairly optimistic", or "pessimistic".

In addition, each interview contained questions specific to the stage of the research. The initial parent interview included a section on preparation for adoption and the impact of the child's arrival. During the second interview, those parents who had received the parent advice were also asked in detail about how relevant it had been to their needs, and whether they would recommend such a programme to other parents.

At the time of each interview, parents were asked to complete three questionnaires on their own concerns and three on the child's current difficulties (see below, *Measures*). With their agreement, some parents were sent these questionnaires in advance of the interview; for one or two families questionnaires were left with them to be posted to the researchers in their own time. Parents were also asked to sign consent forms to allow the research team to approach the child's school or nursery teachers to complete the SDQ.

For the parents who had received advice sessions, the second interview included questions about their views on the helpfulness of this advice and on the method of delivery. In the third interview, detailed information was collected from both intervention and control groups about special services that the parents or the index children had received that specifically addressed the issues associated with the placement, and their opinion of the usefulness of those services in meeting their family's needs.

Measures

Parenting skills and attitudes

Parents also completed two questionnaires on their own attitudes to and experiences of the task of parenting the index child.

Parenting Daily Hassles

The Parenting Daily Hassles questionnaire is designed to capture the frequency and impact for parents of events that routinely occur in families (Crnic and Booth, 1991). Parents indicate how frequently the "hassle" has arisen for them in the previous six months: "rarely", "sometimes", "a lot", or "all the time". They separately record the impact or intensity of each event on a 5-point Likert scale from low (1) to high (5): a high score indicates that they felt greater impact.

Parenting Sense of Competence (PSOC)

The PSOC was first developed for new mothers by Gibaud-Wallston and Wandersman (1978), but later adapted for use with parents of children aged 4–9 years by Johnston and Mash (1989). The PSOC produces two sub-scales reflecting (a) Efficacy – skills and knowledge, and (b) Satisfaction – a sense of being comfortable in the parental role. It is based on 17 statements with Likert scaling from "strongly agree" to "strongly disagree". For some questions the scores are reversed so that for all items a higher score indicates higher parental self-esteem. Ohan *et al* (2000) have more recently confirmed the validity and stable factor structure. The questionnaire is given in full in Appendix 3.

Client Service Receipt Inventory

At the time of each interview, parents were asked standard questions about the number of specialist services (e.g. speech therapy) or routine services (e.g. visits to their GP) that they or the index child had used during the previous six months. Service use was measured using a version of the Client Service Receipt Inventory (Beecham and Knapp, 2001). Services were only included when the purpose of the consultation was to address problems identifiably related to the child, e.g. the parent's attendance on a course on child development. The completed questionnaires were used to prepare a cost analysis of service use over the period of contact with the research team.

As in other areas of social and health care, the provision of services and support for adopters is constrained by resource scarcity. Therefore, it is crucial to ascertain whether new interventions are cost effective compared to existing practice. This entails (a) estimating existing service use and costs and (b) linking cost data with those on outcomes. Comprehensive measurement is desirable so that the broad impact of the interventions can be determined – it may be the case that the interventions offered to adopters are relatively expensive but these extra costs might be offset by reduced costs elsewhere in the system. The Client Service Receipt Inventory includes contacts with social workers and other local authority professionals, use of mental and other health services, and specialist educational support. In addition, the schedule records any time which adopters have lost from work due to difficulties with the placement.

Unit costs, obtained from a recognised source (Netten *et al*, 2001) and from local information, were attached to the service use data in order to generate total service costs. The costs associated with each of the parent advice interventions and with the "routine care" were compared, controlling for baseline differences as necessary using an incremental cost-effectiveness ratio.

Consumer satisfaction with the parent advice sessions

The clients' satisfaction is regarded as an important component of the delivery of a service in order to prove that it is at the very least acceptable, and at best positively welcome to the recipients. At the time of the second interview, the parents who had received the research advice sessions completed a questionnaire on their satisfaction with the advice offered in the interventions. Reviewing available measures of parents' views of support and training, it was apparent that there was no single widely used/accepted tool. None of the measures developed ad hoc for different studies had been tested for validity or reliability; many were relatively simplistic (e.g. responses limited to "helpful"/"not helpful") and did not discover why it was that a service had proved satisfactory or unsatisfactory for a particular parent. We selected the Parents' Satisfaction Questionnaire (Davies and Spurr, 1998), which allowed the parent to say why they had or had not appreciated the advice sessions.

Parenting techniques for correcting "misbehaviour"

Parents were invited to say which, from a checklist of strategies, they usually used to control any unacceptable behaviour. They were handed the list given below at each interview (Maxwell, 1993). They were then asked to say which of these strategies regularly worked with their child:

Which of the following actions have you found yourself taking in the last month to deal with your child's misbehaviour?

a) Explained or discussed why s/he should not do it
b) Told him/her off
c) Threatened a punishment
d) Made him or her go without something or miss out on something

e) Made him or her go to their room or somewhere else on their own for less than five minutes

f) Made him or her go to their room or somewhere else on their own for more than five minutes

g) Found yourself bribing him or her

h) Shouted or yelled at him or her

i) Pushed or shoved or shaken him or her

j) Smacked him or her with your hand

k) Anything else?

Parents were encouraged to name any number of techniques for behaviour control if they wished.

Children's symptoms and behaviour

At the time of each research interview, parents were asked to complete the SDQ, a questionnaire on the child's Expression of Feelings (EFQ) (Quinton *et al*, 1998), and a list of nine questions reflecting behaviour observed in children recently placed for adoption from care, and which were not part of the SDQ (Post Placement Problems). Psychometric data are only available for the first of these, which was chosen as the key variable in assessing improvement. With parental permission, the child's teacher was asked to complete the SDQ at each data collection point.

Expression of Feelings Questionnaire (EFQ)

This questionnaire, derived from an earlier study and intended for completion by adoptive parents (Quinton *et al*, 1998), was designed to capture the nature of the relationship with the new carers and to tap the child's ability to show feelings and seek comfort and affection appropriately. It covers distorted ways of expressing emotion as in the "bottling up" of feelings, or over-expressiveness, or exhibiting affection lacking "genuineness". There are 50 questions employing a five-point response scale (rated 0–4); a higher score indicates better adjustment. Responses are summed to give an overall score and scores on four sub-scales. The questionnaire has been shown to discriminate between a recently placed late adoption sample and a matched general population never-in-care sample (Quinton *et al*, 1998).

Post Placement Problems (PPP)

The PPP is a brief questionnaire designed for this study by the researchers and includes common problems of maltreated children when placed in a new home, e.g. rejecting new parents, lacking trust, needing to control the actions of others. None of these items are present in the SDQ or EFQ. Each of nine items is scored "never", "sometimes", "often", "very often", or "always" (0–4; maximum score 36) where a high score indicates more problematic behaviour.

Visual Analogue Scales (VAS)

At the third interview, parents were asked to complete three analogue scales for the issues on which we also had substantial qualitative material: the extent of the child's distress, the child's misbehaviour and the family attachment relationships. The visual analogue scales were used to record the change that had occurred since the first family interview. Each scale was identified as showing to what extent the child's behaviour or mood had got worse or better; the mid-point indicated that there had been no change – labelled as "stayed the same". The parents were asked to put a cross on the line showing what progress, if any, there had been. The distance along the line from "got worse" to "got better" was converted into a percentage for analysis; these percentages were, in turn, converted to quartiles for further analysis.

Summary

- 37 adoptive parents, looking after children between three and eight years who were screened to have serious behavioural problems participated in the trial.
- With their consent, they were randomly allocated to one of two interventions: (a) behavioural parenting advice or (b) a tailored adoptive parenting education programme (n = 9), or to a "control group". Adopters in the control group were offered the choice of one of the parenting interventions after the six-month follow-up interviews.

- The two interventions consisted of ten weekly sessions of home-based parenting advice. Each programme was based on a manual and delivered by trained and supervised family social workers.
- Information about the children and the family was collected through interviews with the adopters and by standardised questionnaires (child-based and parent-based measures) at entry into the research study, immediately after intervention and six months later. Economic costs were calculated using an established procedure.
- It was hypothesised that changes in the parenting and child psycho-social problems would be greater in the intervention groups than in the control group.

4   Preparation of adopters

Introduction

As more has been learned about the short-term problems of children placed from care and the persistence of some difficulties long after placement (Rushton and Dance, 2006), it is clearly sensible, not to say essential, that all adopters receive appropriate preparation. Preparation for adoptive parenting can cover numerous interlinked aims and activities. It may include, for example, discussing adoptive parenting; providing information about legal responsibilities and financial support; advising on the common problems of children who have been in care and currently awaiting placement, and exploring expectations and anticipating difficulties.

However, the nature of an agency's "preparation for adoption" service is usually only loosely prescribed. Guidance about preparation, as set out in the Adoption Agencies Regulations (2005), is mostly concerned with providing information about the nature of the adoption process and the legal procedures and only brief mention is made of the skills necessary to be an adoptive parent (para 24, 2(d)). The details are left to the discretion of the agency. Not surprisingly, agencies deliver a different balance of advice, information, training, and psychological exploration. BAAF has published an eight-session manual (Beesley *et al*, 2006) with the aim of creating a common curriculum to assist applicants in considering the implications of adoption. It will take time before we know how widely it is being used and whether it is achieving its aims of preparing adopters.

In terms of systematic research, only a handful of studies exist that specifically concern preparation of adopters of children placed from care in middle childhood. Little is known about the typical content, methods and quality of the preparation and training on offer in the UK. Most of the research is descriptive rather than evaluative and many questions remain unanswered. For example, does adopter satisfaction at the time of the preparation have an influence on satisfaction once the child is placed with them? What is the relevance of the preparation and training to the needs of the adopters or of the child in relation to the specific child arriving in their home? Is the time and cost devoted to preparation justified in terms of outcomes, both short and long term?

The Maudsley Adoption and Fostering study, based on a sample of mid-childhood adoptions placed a decade ago (Quinton *et al*, 1998), showed that, although most of the adopters expressed general satisfaction with the preparation, by no means were all of them positive and most expressed criticisms with some aspect. Many adopters found the training too global, not sufficiently focused on the issues that they would eventually need to parent their child, and with too little input on the specific skills that they would need. Lowe *et al* (1999) examined support for the adoption of older children and found that agencies varied considerably in the way they prepared adopters. Some adopters in their study found the social workers extremely helpful, but others thought the agencies failed to recognise their previous parenting experiences. Some complained of selective imparting of information about the child to be placed. In this study too the researchers found a lack of information about practical parenting strategies. They recommended greater tailoring of the preparation to individual needs and less use of fixed practices. Adopters have a range of characteristics (single or a couple, ethnicity, sexuality, class, education, etc) and have different understandings and expectations of adoption and the preparation process should acknowledge this.

One study on preparation for being the parent of a child in care is of interest in its use of a comparative design. Puddy and Jackson (2003) measured the effects of a parenting training programme for potential foster carers aimed at teaching them to manage undesirable behaviour and build the children's life skills compared with a "no training" control group. The results were disappointing in that the experimental group improved on only a small minority of the goals of the intervention. The researchers concluded that the programme improved *knowledge* of the behavioural approach, but improved parenting *techniques* very little.

Sar (2000), in a survey of preparation for adoption from care, mailed questionnaires to adoptive mothers on average six years after the adoptive placement, inviting their recall of preparation, and attempted to relate this to features of the subsequent placement. The mothers found training to be an adoptive parent the most useful preparation task, but learning about adoption and adoption procedures proved not to be related to outcome. The study showed one of those initially puzzling findings that more learning about strategies for coping with problems was associated with higher stress, lower satisfaction and more frequent problem behaviours in the child. It is, of course, possible that adopters took up more "parenting strategy" opportunities when they knew they were expecting to have a difficult child placed with them and the outcome reflects not so much the preparation, but the enduring difficulties of the child and the related effects on the carers. However, the low response rate (30%) suggests a highly selected group of parents whose experiences may not reflect adoptions where preparation had led to better outcomes or where preparation more usefully matched the parents' needs.

In a study by Wind *et al* (2006) of adoption preparation, parents were asked about 18 different kinds of information that might have been provided before the placement. The greater the amount of either general adoption information or biological/medical information about the child the parents received, the better prepared they felt. Where children had a history of pre-placement adversities, the adoptive families were more likely to receive preparation services focusing on the child's past experiences and caretaking history. We do not learn, however, how effective these services were in meeting subsequent difficulties.

In summary, many of these studies have concluded that the preparation activities offered can be very variable and adopters have found that information could have been better tailored to the unique circumstances of the placed child and the characteristics of the adoptive family. The studies cited show the difficulties in tracing clear causal links between variations in the type and content of preparation and subsequent developments in the placement. The studies were mostly based on placements made in the 1990s and it is important to know whether the shortcomings identified then have persisted.

The preparation task has different elements: the first is obtaining general information, for example, about the law and finances; the second is finding out about the adoption process and about the kinds of children needing adoption and then, at the linking and matching stage, understanding the characteristics and history of individual children. We took the opportunity to investigate preparation to be an adoptive parent as part of the current study.

Interviews with adopters

Information was gathered from the parents in the first home-based research interviews once they had consented to being in the trial, but before random allocation to the parenting programmes. We wanted to build a picture of the pre-placement preparation offered to these parents and then to ask them to reflect on the services they had received in the light of their experiences once the child had been placed. We were particularly concerned with the salience of the preparation for the individual child and not simply the generalised satisfaction with the preparation.

We began by asking what expectations they had had about becoming an adoptive parent. Some recalled that they had anticipated difficulties, but had thought they were up to the challenge. One parent said, 'I expected hard work and a complete life change, with limitations on our freedom to do as we want'. Another said, 'We knew it would be difficult and that the children would need a clear structure, but we were not prepared for quite how difficult it would turn out to be'. They also recalled thinking that they had received all the information they needed, and admitted to feeling well prepared at the time, so it was particularly striking that they still found the child's arrival a shock. Many were taken aback at the contrast between the problems they had been warned about and the reality when the child was placed. 'I thought it would be a lot rosier than it was,' said one parent. 'I thought it would be easy, and we would skip off into the distance together. It's not how I thought it would be.' This latter view suggests that this parent was unusually optimistic and poorly informed, and that the preparation course was not providing firm enough information about the strong likelihood of children coming from care having serious and possibly continuing difficulties.

The content and quality of the preparation to adopt

In the presentation of findings, all proportions are given as a percentage of n = 38 unless otherwise stated, because 38 families were interviewed at

Time 1. (Some questions did not apply to those without partners or without other resident family members.)

The parents were asked what type of preparation they had been offered by the placing agency. The common pattern was for initial group sessions with other potential adopters with a social work leader, followed later at the linking and matching stage by individual social work visits to the home focusing more on an individual child or children. On average, three group sessions were offered, varying between one and five, and usually lasting several hours. Written preparation materials were generally provided, but a few (13%) said these had not been offered. Just over half (53%) were shown videos designed to help them to think about what would be involved in adopting from care, and experienced adopters had contributed to nearly all (87%) of the training sessions. Parents received, on average, four social worker home visits. However, as the visits often had several functions, it was not possible to say that these were entirely devoted to preparation for adoptive parenting.

Satisfactions and dissatisfactions with the preparation process

We were interested in whether any aspects of the agency activity, from initial contact through to group meetings, linking and matching, introductions to the child and social worker visits had proved helpful in the light of their subsequent experience as adopters. Frequently, the assessment and approval process would be running alongside, or thought of as part of, the preparation.

When asked if the specific preparation elements of the process had suited them, 50 per cent were satisfied that it had, 42 per cent said it had suited some of their needs, but eight per cent had not been at all satisfied. Most parents (90%) said the preparation had helped them understand the likely problems of looked after children, but 65 per cent thought that the courses had not been particularly helpful in developing the parenting skills they would need for a child coming to them from foster care.

The satisfied parents

The satisfied, or mostly satisfied, parents found the training well done and useful to them, particularly discussion of the difficulties in the child's behaviour that might confront them. One family found the social worker's home visits to be the most useful and described her as "brilliant" and "very supportive".

> *The more experienced social workers explained the psychology and potential difficulties and were good and useful. We met his [the child's] foster carers three times and that was the most useful thing.*

> *We were very impressed with the course and the 10-day lead-in to meeting our child. The course was "real" and dealt with possible issues. They "laid it out straight", nothing was held back.*

> *The training definitely suited our needs. Looking at the child's needs from different angles: being asked to say what would you do if . . . ? We were encouraged to think about the importance of food, bed, warm clothes – all things to make you feel secure.*

For this family, the training seemed to expand their horizons and promoted a lot of reflection:

> *We came up against things we hadn't even thought about, that is, the children come with baggage and you need to think about it. One session explained issues to do with different sorts of abuse – this was an eye opener. This made us think in a different way.*

Other parents emphasised help in understanding the child's past:

> *The course helped us to understand the problems and highlighted the issues around understanding the context of the birth family.*

> *The most useful bit was discussion of the consequences of abuse and how emotional abuse leaves the most permanent damage.*

The dissatisfied parents

One of the most commonly and strongly expressed dissatisfactions was that the impressions parents formed from attending the training could be very different from the reality once the child was placed. The following quotes illustrate the point.

The talks didn't seem real without knowing the children. Hypothetical situations aren't useful to new parents to learn to deal with future problems. It would have been better to do that on the home visits as then we would have been able to talk specifically about the children. A lot of issues are more significant afterwards when confronted by the real thing.

Preparation was helpful on one level but nothing can prepare you for the emotional drain, nor for how hard it is. We cried together at the end of some days.

You don't know the full impact until it happens. We were helped to understand, but until it hits you, you aren't fully aware.

As general training it was fine, but we wish we had trained for the specific needs of the children. They told us about abuse, but not about how children react to abuse. Nothing can prepare you for the real thing.

In what other ways was the preparation not suitable?

Mixed views were expressed on the benefits of meeting other families who had adopted as it did not, of itself, always guarantee enlightenment. One couple felt the adopters had nothing special to add: 'The other adoptive parents didn't say anything useful except how lovely it was and gave us no idea of how to cope'.

Some wanted better information on how long the difficult behaviour was likely to last and what other problems might emerge, as the following quotes describe.

We weren't warned that it would take him three months to settle in, and us not to feel like babysitters, but start to feel like a family.

It didn't suit us as it offered little on the practical side of being an adoptive parent. Too much time was spent on detailed discussions about disability, race and so on and not enough on behaviour manage-

ment. No advice was given on the possible effects on other children in the family, and how to deal with the new sibling relationship.

Classes were useful in talking about what to expect, but didn't really prepare us for how to cope with the behaviour. We were helped to see what the problems might be but not really how to deal with them. Social workers have not really lived with it so they don't know how to deal with it.

These illustrative quotes all point to the need for a more skills-based approach that goes beyond describing potential difficulties to recommending sound parenting strategies.

Matching the type of preparation to the parents' needs

One of the themes that emerged was that the preparation may have been good in its own right, but did not meet the needs of particular parents and particular children. Several adopters who already had parenting experience were frustrated by what was offered. One couple said: 'It was not suitable as we were the only ones who had other children; the course was biased in favour of people without kids'. This couple's concerns were different and they wanted to know how the attachment process might compare with their birth children and wanted more on the impact of the new arrivals on their resident children.

Another family said: 'We had to attend a course for young children because we wanted an under-five-year old, but there was too much nappy changing and bottle mixing and first aid for tiny children'.

One couple, who had adopted previously, were not invited to the preparation classes and were sorry to be excluded and said their need was for 'a more meaty, in-depth, concentrated course'.

We asked all the parents what else they would have liked to be told about: 40 per cent mentioned more on child development issues, especially what to expect of the children who would be placed with them. More than half the parents wished they had been told more about how to deal with aggressive behaviour and more than half wanted more information on attachment problems, while one-third wanted information about handling their child's peer relationships.

Understanding adoption and managing problems

We asked the adopters to look back and say whether the classes and social work visits had been useful in thinking about being the parent of the child subsequently placed with them. There was a spread of opinion, but the parents largely responded positively: 26 per cent said they found them very useful, 42 per cent useful, 26 per cent mixed and six per cent not useful.

We then asked whether the preparation had helped the parents to understand the kinds of problems children placed from care might have. A third (33%) said very fully, two-thirds (62%) said well enough, and only five per cent said their understanding had not been helped at all. However, in relation to the more specific question as to whether any of the classes or social worker visits offered help with managing difficult behaviour, only 16 per cent said they had been helpful, 35 per cent said not very helpful, 30 per cent said not at all helpful, and the remainder (19%) could not remember. It was surprising that so few said that they had been helped with this central task. One dissatisfied couple said:

> We didn't feel that the course covered possible problem areas and was more concerned with getting us approved as adopters. There was a suggestion that behaviour problems may be an issue – but nothing in particular was mentioned. We drew on our "common sense" to realise there would be problems.

Topics well covered or inadequately covered in the preparation

We asked the parents to think about what had been the important issues for them that had been covered in their pre-placement training. Parents were given a list and asked to tick as many topics as applied. Table 4.1 summarises the frequency with which the topics were chosen, in descending order from the most important.

The parents were then asked to report any topics they would have liked to have been told about or which could have been better addressed in the preparation. Table 4.2 shows, in descending order, beginning with the most frequently named, the issues the parents would have liked better covered in the preparation process. Strategies for dealing with aggression and attachment difficulties were the most commonly requested topics. One couple added:

> *We would have liked to have been told more about how to deal with anger, about bereavement, and the child's fear of people close to him dying.*

Only a few asked for more on the question of contact with the birth family, but this issue may not have had a great impact by the time we saw the families in the first year, or perhaps little birth family contact was planned in these cases.

We were interested in the parents' reactions to the child's arrival in the first one or two weeks after their child came to live with them – Table 4.3 shows the range of responses of the main carers and their partner and other family members.

Table 4.1

Important issues covered in preparation

Topic	% of parents rating these as the important issues
Problems of ex-care children	76
Health issues	50
Sources of help for adoptive parents	42
Legal information	34
Parenting skills	34
Financial information	24
Effect on own children*	32

* Of those who had their own children still resident in the family, a third thought it was important to cover the effect of the placed child on the family in preparation.

Table 4.2

Topics thought to be missing or inadequately covered in the preparation course

Topic	% of parents thinking this item poorly covered
Anger/aggression	55
Relationships with adopters (attachment issues)	53
Child development issues	40
Relationships with peers	34
Withdrawn behaviour	24
Identity issues	10
Contact with birth family	8

Table 4.3

General adoptive family reactions in the first weeks after placement

% responses	Wholly positive	Mixed	Wholly negative	Can't remember or not applicable
Self	37	53	10	–
Partner (n = 31)	51	42	7	n/a
Adopter's view of child's reaction	29	55	11	5
Other resident family member (n = 15)	40	53	7	n/a

Although the first reaction was wholly positive for some respondents (37%) and their partners (when there was one – 51%), it was clearly not unalloyed pleasure for the remainder. Half reported a mixed reaction and a few had a wholly negative response. This may be expected from the sheer novelty of the situation for both the parents and the newly arrived children.

Parents' expectations and reactions to the children's arrival

On the assumption that the preparation process could have helped prospective adopters to put their expectations in line with the common experiences of receiving children from care, we asked how the experience of the early days of placement matched up with what they had been expecting. The parents were given a list of possible reactions and asked to indicate which ones applied to them (see Tables 4.4, 4.5 and 4.6). The categories are not mutually exclusive.

It was fairly surprising to discover that, even after agency preparation, 24 per cent of the main carers, and 16 per cent of their partners, said that the reality of the presence of the child in their home was a totally unexpected experience (Table 4.4).

Table 4.4
Expectations and reactions to the arrival of the child

	Much as expected (%)	Totally unexpected (%)
Self (n = 37)	58	24
Partner (n = 31)	47	16

Their arrival was chaotic. First few days were awful: C was rejecting, hiding under the table, trying to trip me up. At first they slept and ate well and then started rejecting food that we had been told they liked. C was screaming and crying and talking to herself and very angry at being taken from the foster carers with whom they had been for two years. We (had been) under the impression that the children were "ready to move", so we were very shocked. We were particularly shocked by the children's anger; we could have coped with sadness, but found it very hard to deal with anger.

She was very distressed and volatile; testing the boundaries about our routines. Very tiring (and) I was exhausted.

The first few days were "wild"! He wouldn't settle; no smile; no laughter; no concept of playing. He followed me (mother) everywhere. Very aggressive. We hadn't expected him to be so wild. I suppose I was shocked.

One couple summed it up as:

Our child was not as we expected, for example, his aggressiveness and how to cope with it – so we weren't well prepared for him.

Feelings of exhaustion were very common (Table 4.5). Few were disappointed, but a substantial minority reported feelings of inadequacy. It was perhaps less surprising that the main carer was more likely to feel exhausted and inadequate than the partner (where one existed), although most partners had taken at least a week off work to help settle the children in.

Table 4.5
Negative reactions of parents to the child's arrival

	I/we felt exhausted (%)	I/we felt disappointed (%)	I/we felt inadequate (%)
Self (n = 37)	52	8	24
Partner (n = 31)	32	8	18

Just under half felt pleased and in control, with their partners having very similar reactions (Table 4.6). However, parents not infrequently used the term "honeymoon" to describe the first days in the household, after which problems would emerge.

Table 4.6
Positive reactions to the child's arrival

	I was/we were pleased/happy (%)	I/we felt on top of things (%)
Self (n = 37)	47	42
Partner (n = 31)	47	39

A honeymoon period and an absolute angel. He couldn't wait to stay here. We were all very happy and felt on top of things.

Honeymoon for two weeks then her first tantrum in Tesco. There were "mixed" reactions from relatives but I felt wholly positive myself.

The first few days were wholly positive for us and for her. She was chatty and amiable, responsive, pleasant, a fussy eater but no bedtime problems. There was a honeymoon period before everything went wrong.

Conclusions

This study of preparation for receiving a child who had previously been in care has the advantage of being based on a defined group of adopters and their recently placed children rather than a heterogeneous sample of adoptive families. All the children had been identified either by their parents or by their social worker as showing significant problems on the Strengths and Difficulties Questionnaire at the time they entered the research study. The results might have been different with children of different ages or with less severe difficulties than those in this sample.

In the research interviews we asked about the satisfactions and dissatisfactions with the pre-placement process, both introductory sessions as well as individual meetings, with a special focus on whether it had proved useful for taking on an individual child. Most of the parents thought the preparation was generally relevant and that it had helped them to reflect and to improve their understanding at the time but few of these adopters thought the sessions had prepared them for the parenting challenge that their child brought or had trained them in the necessary skills and strategies to manage the behavioural difficulties. This is a reminder that any feedback taken at the end of preparation sessions may well be positive, but a more telling picture emerges when initial benefits of the preparation are compared with parents' experiences and reflections after the child has been placed with them.

The responses of these parents can be compared with information collected for the Maudsley Adoption and Fostering study a decade ago (Quinton *et al*, 1998). Adopters in that study found the training too global, with too little emphasis on parenting skills. The current findings were similar, in that experienced parents were the most dissatisfied and insufficient attention was paid to the impact on the families' own children.

The main question thrown up by this study appears to be how to deliver a service which meets the need both for general preparation and for preparation to parent the child eventually placed. Only so much can be achieved by the introductory group model, and providing the skills to handle the likely difficulties of the child to be placed has clearly proved hard to achieve in advance of the placement. Fresh consideration needs to be given to the best means, and timing, of a skills-based parenting programme. Some UK agencies are encouraging more active learning from personal contact with recently formed adoptive families with whom the applicants have been matched, and applicants are encouraged to learn about the real life experience of the challenges children from care might present by links to Family Centres.

A number of alternative options are worth considering for developing a skills-based approach. First, adoption social workers could have more training in preparing the adopters to deal with specific problems; the two which stand out from the current study are the child's challenging behaviour, especially anger, aggression, and defiance (present in all 38 families who were interviewed at Time 1) and distorted attachment behaviour (present in two-thirds of the children). Second, greater use could be made of behaviour management specialists to advise social workers and adopters in selected cases during preparation. However, this still leaves the question as to whether behaviour management skills can be usefully taught in advance of the arrival of the child(ren). Third, it is possible that the transfer of information from the foster carers to the adoptive parents could be arranged as a series of supervised meetings, so that every aspect of the child's current behaviour could be shared by the "new" parents and the social workers on whose advice they may have to depend in the next few months. This information would then form the basis of discussions about how best to help the child to settle in his or her new family. Fourth, and probably the most useful for the adoptive parents, professional resources could then be shifted forward to the early months of placement where *continuing assessment of the interaction* between parents and the placed child can be more closely observed, and more tailored parenting advice can be offered. This last option could reassure adopters taking on a child with difficulties that are either already known or may develop in the new placement that effective practical help will be at hand in the crucial early stages of the placement. There are important implications for the training of post-adoption social workers.

Summary

- The parents were asked to reflect on the preparation services they had received in the light of their experiences once the child had been placed.
- Many were taken aback at the contrast between the problems they had been warned about and the reality once the child was placed.
- Most parents (90%) said the preparation had helped them understand the likely problems of looked after children, but 65 per cent were not helped in developing the parenting skills they would need for a child coming to them from foster care.
- Preparation was thought generally relevant but often did not meet the needs of particular adopters and particular children.
- Parents thought the least well covered preparation topics were: dealing with anger and aggression, relationship with the adopters and childhood developmental problems.

5 Recruitment into the study and the background of the children

Introduction

This chapter presents the results of the recruitment and screening process, the rating of the children's difficulties at the screening stage, and the characteristics of the final sample entering the trial. We also give some data on the experiences prior to being placed for adoption of all the screened children.

The first point to make is that the sample from which the parents were invited into the study was smaller than had been planned for. Based on returns to the (then) DfES, authorities were selected which had made a large number of adoptive placements in the course of three previous years. We calculated that these 12 authorities could theoretically produce about 100 cases in the age group selected for study. In the event, these authorities produced insufficient cases in the time expected. Subsequently checked against detailed returns from two of the larger authorities, it became clear that the criteria governing inclusion to our sample slightly reduced the number of potential cases. In each of these authorities a small number of children had severe disabilities, and a further small number had been placed with relatives or their current foster carers. Both these groups would have been excluded from the start. In addition, local authority returns give the total number of children placed for adoption; within this, each child in a sibling group was counted separately, but the researchers selected only one child from each family. In an attempt to overcome the low recruitment rate, the funding bodies agreed to the extension of the timescale of the research to recruit more authorities.

The screening stage

Over the lifetime of the project, the adoption teams in 34 local authorities were approached to take part in the study; eight did not reply. Meetings between the research team and the adoption placement teams were held in

26 authorities; 11 subsequently decided not to participate; with one exception these were all in Greater London. Reasons given for non-participation included forthcoming inspections, staff shortages and staff turnover. At a late stage, a recruitment invitation on the Adoption UK website led to responses from four families living in the areas covered by the project's parent advisers, giving the researchers 16 sources of cases. Some smaller unitary authorities were included if they were linked in placement consortia with larger county councils. Table 5.1 shows that six authorities referred fewer than five children; one county adoption service referred 44 eligible children, while another similar-sized county referred 17. A detailed analysis of the figures from two geographically large authorities suggested that the researchers had received completed behaviour checklists on only one-third of eligible children in one area but 93 per cent in the other. The reasons for this difference were unclear.

Table 5.1

Sources of Strengths and Difficulties Questionnaires (SDQs) at the screening stage

Referring authority	Low SDQ score	High SDQ score/non-case	High SDQ score/case	Total
1	0	2	4	6
2	0	1	2	3
3	1	0	0	1
4	0	1	0	1
5	4	0	1	5
6	5	2	4	11
7	1	1	1	3
8	9	10	6	25
9	9	5	3	17
10	9	14	3	26
11	7	8	2	17
12	4	1	0	5
13	18	19	7	44
14	0	1	1	2
15	3	3	2	8
16	2	1	1	4
Totals	72	69	37	178

In total, SDQs were returned for 178 children at the screening stage.

Of the 178 completed SDQs, 152 were filled in by parents, 150 by social workers and 124 by both informants. Of the 28 children for whom there was no social worker's SDQ, seven no longer had a social worker close enough to the family to be able to report on current behaviour and mood; six social worker responses were exact replicas of the parents' ratings, and were discarded as possibly reflecting lack of independence of view; and for 15 children no social worker SDQ was returned to the research team. Parents' responses were missing for 26 children, but the reasons were not available to the research team: some parents may have refused to complete the SDQ, but it is also possible that some social workers chose not to ask them. More than half the cases where there was no parental SDQ occurred in one authority.

For the 124 children for whom there were two informants, there was a high level of agreement between social workers and parents on the extent of the children's psychosocial problems at the screening stage (Table 5.2).

Parents reporting on 152 children were more likely to categorise the boys as showing serious problems in peer relationships (Pearson $\chi^2 = 6.84$. 1df, p<.01) compared with the girls. Social workers, reporting on 150 children, were more likely to categorise the boys as showing hyperactivity problems (Pearson $\chi^2 = 4.18$, 1df, p<.05). Table 5.3 shows that the parents gave significantly higher mean scores for conduct

Table 5.2

Parents' and social workers' ratings of Total Difficulties on the SDQ: selected sample with ratings from both informants: N = 124

| | | Parents' SDQ | | Total Difficulties scores | | | |
| | | Low | | High | | Totals | |
		N	%	N	%	N	%
Social workers'	Low	50	85	23	35	73	59
SDQ Total	High	9	15	42	65	51	41
Difficulties scores							
Totals		59	100	65	100	124	100

Pearson $\chi^2= 31.1$, 1 df, p<.001

problems (t = 2.17; p .031) and hyperactivity (t = 2.61; p .01), indicating that they perceived more of the children as showing these particular problems than the social workers did.

Table 5.3

Mean scores for SDQ sub-categories from social workers and parents for girls and boys. Total screened sample N = 178

SDQ sub-score	Parents' ratings		Social workers' ratings	
	Boys (74)	Girls (78)	Boys (n = 70)	Girls (n = 80)
Emotional disturbance	2.70	2.67	3.11	2.69
Conduct disorder	2.72	2.35	2.33	2.10
Peer relationships	2.82*	1.71*	2.47	2.00
Hyperactivity	6.12	5.46	5.69**	4.63**
Total difficulties	14.38	12.19	13.69	11.41
Pro-social scores	6.89	7.32	6.21	6.58

* 2-tailed significance F 2.85, 150df, p<.003;

** 2-tailed significance F 7.07, 148df, p<.02

For 54 of the children, there was only one SDQ; of these, 22 (41%) had low SDQ scores. The parents of these 22 children (in 18 families) would therefore have been invited to join the study only if there was a sibling with a high SDQ score. In these 18 families, the absence of a second informant may have led to an under-estimate of potential cases. Twelve of these children had no siblings in the study population, and six more only had siblings with low SDQ scores. However, assuming approximately the same rate of potential cases as was reported when there were two informants (roughly half, see below) the second informant might have identified another nine parents of children with high Total Difficulties scores.

Since the reasons why the second SDQ was not available were largely unknown, it is more appropriate when considering the differences between informants' reports to compare results for the children with two informants. The test of any differences of opinion about the children's problems is derived from the 124 cases where the parents and the social workers, clearly working from an independent perspective, rated the same child.

This comparison showed that both on the Total Difficulties scores and on the sub-scores of the SDQ, parents were significantly more likely than social workers to give the children scores over the cut-off point. For Total Difficulties, 60 per cent of parents compared with 41 per cent of social workers gave the children high scores (Table 4: $\chi^2 = 31.12$, 1 df, p<.001). On emotional problems, parents rated 32 per cent of the children and social workers 22 per cent of the children over the cut-off point ($\chi^2 = 3.98$, 1df, p<.05); for conduct problems, the figures were: parents 61 per cent, social workers 40 per cent ($\chi^2 = 42.2$, 1df, p<.001); for peer relationship problems, the figures were: parents 35 per cent and social workers 24 per cent ($\chi^2 = 11.2$, 1df, p<.001); and for hyperactivity, the figures were: parents 53 per cent and social workers 41 per cent ($\chi^2 = 6.28$, 1df, p<.01).

Although it is not possible to state how many of the children with high SDQ scores had a mental disorder, since no clinical interview took place, it is of interest that both parents and social workers identified high proportions with problem scores on the SDQ sub-scales. In a community population the expectation is that roughly 80 per cent of the children will fall into the "normal" range. From the 150 valid SDQ returns from social workers, 22 per cent of the children were identified with emotional problems, 23 per cent with problems in peer relationships, 40 per cent with conduct problems and 44 per cent with hyperactivity problems. Social workers reported no significant gender differences except for the hyperactivity scores noted above. It appears therefore that the social workers were perceiving the sample to be close to a community population on emotional or peer problems, but distinctively more likely than a community population to have conduct and hyperactivity problems.

From 152 SDQs returned by parents, 33 per cent of their children were identified with emotional problems, 35 per cent with problems in peer relationships, 44 per cent with conduct problems and 55 per cent with hyperactivity problems. Gender differences were only recorded by parents for peer problems, as noted above. From this it would appear that parents see substantially more problems across all four categories of behaviour and mood than would be expected in a community population, but – like social workers – rate conduct problems and hyperactivity as the main difficulties.

From these data it was possible to identify the parents who should be invited into the next stage of the study. Table 5.4 gives the figures on the potential study population, showing that although 80 parents were invited to join the study, only 38 (48%) accepted. The reasons why parents declined to join the study included moving house, changing jobs, emigrating and 'having too much to do'. Some parents gave no reasons, and 14 parents did not respond. Further possible reasons are put forward in Appendix 6. The following chart illustrates the recruitment procedure.

Table 5.4
Recruitment of families into study

Children's SDQ scores	SDQ scores and sibling status	N. of children	N. of eligible families	N. of families entering study
High	Singletons	49	80 parents invited into study (25 refusals; 3 disrupted placements; 14 non-responds)	38 (One withdrew after the first research interview)
High	Highest scoring sibling	31		
High	Siblings of higher scoring sib	26	n/a	
Low	Low scoring siblings	27	n/a	n/a
	Low scoring singletons	45	n/a	
Totals		178	80	37

Figure 5.1
Families entering the study

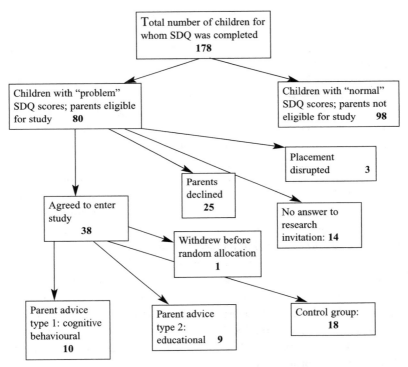

Case note material on screened sample

Information on the children's experiences before being placed for adoption was obtained from case files. Permission was granted by local authorities to look at case files of children with low SDQ scores at the screening stage. This enabled us to test whether the children with high SDQ scores differed significantly in their earlier experiences from those with low SDQ scores. Even within sibling groups the experiences of children can be quite different; for example, the arrival of a new baby may trigger final entry into care for the whole family. Three years later, the "baby" would be eligible to be screened into the current sample, but might have spent all her life with one foster family, whereas older siblings might have been moved in and out of care several times before the baby's arrival.

Information from case files was obtained for 57 of the 72 low-score children. Permission to see the case files for the other 15 children was not granted. The reasons for not being given access to the files were not explained. However, there were no significant differences in the mean SDQ Total Difficulties screening scores between the 57 children for whom a case file search was subsequently made and those for whom it was not possible, suggesting that the former were reasonably represent-ative of the whole low score group. Among these 57 children with low SDQ scores, there was a tendency, which did not reach significance, for there to be more girls than boys.

Comparisons were carried out on the background experiences of the 37 (high SDQ score) children in the research study and the 57 low score children who did not enter the study. There was a significant difference in the number of months between coming into care and the adoption placement: the low score children had a mean of 25 months (SD 13.0) in care compared with a mean of 34 months (SD 18.8) for the high score children ($t = 2.51$, p .014). Comparison of the age at placement in the adoptive family was also significantly associated with the screening SDQ scores: the low score children were more likely to have been placed before the age of five years ($\chi^2 = 8.98$, 1df, p<.003). The difference between the number of moves between carers the child had experienced at any time in their lives (i.e. not just after coming into care) approached significance, with the low score children experiencing fewer moves than the high score children ($t = 1.87$, p.064). These three variables are probably not uncon-nected, but it certainly looks as though a high SDQ score not long after the eventual adoptive placement is associated with more movement between households before that event, and longer total time spent in care. However, it is important to add that the more disturbed children may take longer to place, so a causal link is not suggested here.

Pre-care birth family problems

One possible further source of difference between children with high and low SDQ scores is their experience of serious problems associated with dysfunctional parental care in their original families. Case notes were searched for a record of the reasons why children came into care in the first place. The data on background circumstances were probably not exhaustive; provided that sufficient evidence could be drawn together to support the Care Order application, it is possible that further factors might not have been fully investigated. There may also have been varying definitions behind the use of terms like "non-organic failure to thrive", where there have been significant shifts in diagnosis (Batchelor, 2008). For that reason, the figures on pre-care circumstances should be treated with care.

The mean number of major problems (e.g. parental alcoholism or mental health problems) did not differ between the low and high score children (low score children, mean = 7.07 serious problems, SD 2.77; high score children in the research study, mean = 7.73, SD 2.8). It should be noted that "neglect" was recorded for all the children; there was very little detail associated with this, so it was not possible to determine whether the neglect was of basic needs like adequate food and clothing, or of more complex issues like the absence of loving attention or toys or the experience of playing creatively.

Taking this universal problem into account, however, it seemed possible to differentiate three main types of dysfunctional parental care. The first group is relatively small – 10 (18%) of the 57 low SDQ score children and two (5%) of the 37 cases in the intervention study – where the main reason for taking the child into care was the addiction and/or severe mental health problems of the main carer, predominantly mothers. The second group was where the reasons for taking the child into care included one or more aspects of violence in the household: domestic violence, sexual abuse, physical abuse or the presence of a Schedule 1 offender in the household. In total, 82 children (87% of the combined groups) had experienced or witnessed extreme violence: 47 (82%) of the low score children and 35 (95%) of the high score children. There was a non-significant tendency for this to have been absent in the low score children's lives before coming into care ($\chi^2 = 2.98$, 1df, p =.117).

The third group experienced both violence and rejection within the core family. Rejection by parents had been noted in the files for 15 children (7–19% of cases in the intervention study; and 8–14% of low score children); this difference was not significant.

Using evidence from the case notes, a rating was made of the child's experience of positive physical and positive emotional parenting in their first two years, whether or not that had been with their family of origin or a substitute family. The evidence of "some" positive parenting did not differentiate between the children with high SDQ scores and those with low SDQ scores.

These data suggest that experiences associated with coming into care and while in the care system may be more influential than experiences before coming into care in determining children's behaviour in the first few months of an adoptive placement. However, it is important to note that the question of the children's resilience was not investigated; it is a complex issue and perhaps not surprisingly was not systematically commented on in the case notes. It may well be that the lack of significant differences between high and low-scoring children in their pre-care circumstances is in part affected by differential resilience. However, to set against that, it does appear that the subsequent in-care experiences have an effect on the SDQ score shortly after placement. It would be necessary therefore to posit that high resilience to pre-care experiences did not carry over into effective resilience to events during the children's time in care.

Conclusion

Recruitment proved to be more difficult and slower than had been planned, and the refusal rate was unexpectedly high. The researchers had made an assumption that the offer of ten sessions of parent support in the home would be attractive to parents with very troubled children, but this proved to be too optimistic.

In line with other studies of ex-care children, neither parents nor social workers identified gender differences in the level of difficulties (e.g. Quinton *et al*, 1998). This stands in contrast with studies of children in community samples where there is a significant tendency for parents to rate boys as showing higher problem scores than girls (e.g. McMunn *et al*, 1997).

Summary

- Recruitment proved to be more difficult and slower than had been planned. Local authorities varied widely in the proportion of eligible children who were referred into the study.
- There were almost no children from black and minority ethnic families.
- The refusal rate of eligible parents was unexpectedly high.
- Comparison of the backgrounds of the children with high SDQ scores and low SDQ scores suggested that experiences associated with coming into care and while in the care system may be more influential than experiences before coming into care in determining children's behaviour in the first few months of an adoptive placement.

6   Outcomes of the interventions

This chapter presents the key findings from the study, the aim of which was to test the outcomes for the two different approaches to parent support.

The first point to make is that although the sample is relatively small, the data are complete. In terms of the parenting interventions, nearly all the adopters completed the 10-session parenting programme to which they had been allocated. One family asked to stop at Session 5 as they felt that they had achieved what they wanted. Two families had double sessions at the end to fit in with family or adviser holidays, and one family asked to have five two-hour sessions. Except for one placement which broke down very quickly, making all data except the first interview irrelevant, all the placements initially screened remained intact at both follow-ups (n = 37) and the researchers collected data from all cases at all three time points. Very little data were therefore missing and an "intention to treat"" analysis was not necessary. In this main analysis, most of the comparisons are made between the controls and the two intervention groups with their scores combined in order to have a more powerful test of the differences. The presentation of results was carried out using the CONSORT guidelines for behavioural and psychotherapy interventions (Boutron *et al*, 2008).

For ease of reading, the tables with the raw questionnaire scores can be consulted at the end of this chapter (Tables 6.5 and 6.6). These show the scores for the three child-based measures and two parent-based measures, with means and standard deviations for totals and sub-scale scores, separately presented for the intervention group and the control group and at three time points:

Time 1 (T1) = baseline;

Time 2 (T2) = immediately post-intervention, or for the control group roughly 12 weeks after the first interview; and

Time 3 (T3) = 6 months post-intervention follow-up.

Between-groups analysis

The main analysis of differences between the combined intervention group and control group at T2 and T3 can be found in Tables 6.5 and 6.6. Linear regressions were run entering the baseline score as a covariate. It is important to include any differences in baseline scores because the finding of a significant difference at outcome can disappear when these are taken into account. The test for a significant difference (the adjusted p value at the 5% level) and the Effect Size appear in columns 4 and 5 of the tables. The Effect Size is an indicator of the magnitude of the difference between Interventions and Controls (calculated as the mean difference divided by the Standard Deviation (SD) of the baseline score). This "standardised mean difference" permits a comparison of the Effect Size across different measures (0.2 is indicative of a small effect, 0.5 a medium and 0.8 a large effect size). The final column shows which group of families (intervention group or control group) is favoured by the observed difference in scores regardless of whether the differences are statistically significant.

Results from the parents' self-report measures

Parenting Sense of Competence scales (PSOC)

As described in Chapter 3, the PSOC is composed of two sub-scores reflecting Satisfaction with the Parental Role and a sense of Efficacy as a Parent. In the combined intervention groups, the Parenting Satisfaction score increased at T2 and stayed high to T3, whereas for the controls the level of Satisfaction stayed fairly constant. At the six-month follow-up, a highly significant difference (p<0.007 (<0.05 Bonferroni corrected) and large Effect Size (d = 0.7) was found in favour of the combined intervention group over the control group. The Parenting Satisfaction scale is composed of items reflecting feelings of parenting being rewarding and not a source of anxiety or frustration. The scale has items like: having a sense of accomplishment, doing a good job, having some talent as a parent, not being frustrated or made anxious. Nearly all the "Satisfaction" items had higher scores in the intervention groups, but only one item i.e. "feeling in control and not being manipulated" had a significantly higher score (F 5.9, df 1, p<0.02). It is reasonable to regard these changes as attributable to the parenting interventions as they were not reported by the control group parents. The Parenting Efficacy score on the PSOC did not show a significant difference as both scores rose over time (i.e. both groups were feeling more competent and familiar with parenting).

Figure 6.1 illustrates this point for all three arms of the trial. The adopters' Satisfaction with the Role of Parenting (measured on the PSOC) was compared and showed mean scores rising in both intervention groups, while a fall in Satisfaction is evident for the controls. The small group sizes did not allow for statistical testing.

Figure 6.1

Adopters' satisfaction with parenting their child (for all three arms of the trial at T1 and T3)

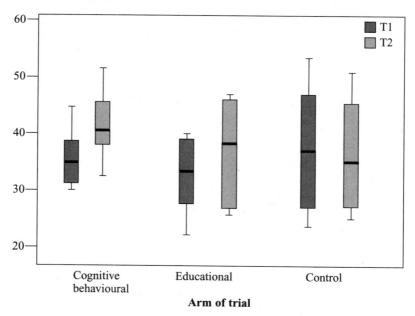

"Daily hassles"

Mean scores for the combined intervention group and the control group rose and fell over time on both the Frequency and Intensity scales. Scores were higher on the intensity scale for the control group at T2 (p<0.09), indicating more problems, but at T3 differences were not significant.

Parent satisfaction with the advice offered in the interventions

At the time of the second research interview we also asked parents to complete a questionnaire on how satisfied they were with the advice offered in the parenting intervention sessions. The questionnaire was completed only by those who received the interventions. Figure 6.2 shows that the summary scores indicate high satisfaction levels and there were no differences between the groups. More information on the parents' experience of the two interventions was also obtained from the research interviews at Time 2 and this will be reported in a later chapter.

Figure 6.2
Parents' satisfaction with advice offered in the two interventions

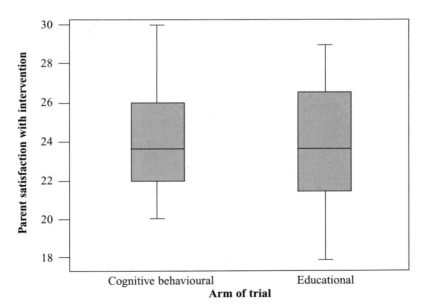

Table 6.1
Outcomes at immediate post-intervention (Time 2)

Outcome measures at T2	Mean differences at T2 and 95% CI	Adjusted mean differences (B) and 95% CI	Effect size Cohen's d	P value adjusted	In favour of . . .
SDQ Total Difficulties T2	-0.18 -4.4 to 4.0	-2.13 -5.72 to 1.45	0.35	p = 0.23	Control group
Conduct	-0.08 -1.74 to 1.57	-0.46 -1.70 to 0.78	0.2	p = 0.45	Control group
Emotional	-0.02 -1.69 to 1.63	-0.76 -1.9 to 0.41	0.3	p = 0.19	Control group
Hyperactivity	-0.14 -1.8 to 1.5	-1.09 -2.46 to 0.28	0.45	p = 0.11	Control group
Peer relations	0.07 -1.46 to 1.3	0.02 -1.11 to 1.16	0.45	p = 0.96	Intervention groups
Pro-social	-0.23 -1.45 to 0.99	0.10 -0.76 to 0.96	0.05	p = 0.81	Intervention groups
Impact score	0.57 -1.17 to 2.31	0.10 -1.37 to 1.57	0.03	p = 0.88	Intervention groups
Expression of Feelings Questionnaire Total scores	-14.7 -29.9 to 0.49	-10.4 -23.4 to 2.5	0.49	p = 0.11	Intervention groups
EFQ openness	-4.08 -10.8 to 2.6	-3.13 -7.7 to 1.4	0.32	p = 0.17	Intervention groups
EFQ attention-seeking	-5.5 -12.2 to 1.11	-3.8 -10.0 to 2.4	0.36	p = 0.22	Intervention groups

Outcome measures at T2	Mean differences at T2 and 95% CI	Adjusted mean differences (B) and 95% CI	Effect size Cohen's d	P value adjusted	In favour of...
EFQ showing affection	-2.7 -7.9 to -2.3	-2.1 -4.1 to -0.10	0.19	p = 0.53	Intervention groups
EFQ trusting	-2.3 -4.3 to 0.26	-2.1 to -0.10	0.7	p = 0.04	Intervention groups
Post Placement Problems	1.23 -2.6 to 5.1	0.08 -3.25 to 3.0	0.01	p = 0.95	Intervention groups
Parenting Sense of Competence: Satisfaction with Parenting Role	-1.05 -5.84 to 3.73	-2.09 -5.94 to 1.75	0.31	p = .27	Intervention groups
Parenting Efficacy	-2.03 -6.49 to 2.41	-1.3 -4.93 to 2.32	0.20	p = 0.46	Intervention groups
Daily hassles: Frequency	4.3 -1.67 to 10.4	1.81 -2.55 to 6.19	0.25	p = 0.4	Intervention groups
Daily hassles: Intensity	7.04 -2.2 to 16.03	7.01 -1.16 to 15.19	0.53	p = 0.09	Intervention groups

All differences calculated as Control minus Intervention scores

Adjusted mean differences at T2 (B) controlling for T1 (linear regression)

Cohen's d calculated on the basis of adjusted mean differences

Table 6.2

Outcomes at six months post-intervention (Time 3)

Outcome measures at T3	Mean differences at T2 and 95% CI	Adjusted mean differences (B) and 95% CI	Effect size Cohen's d	P value adjusted	In favour of . . .
SDQ Total Difficulties T3	1.04 −3.15 to 5.24	−0.79 −4.45 to 2.85	0.13	p = 0.66	Control group
Conduct	0.76 −1.70 to 1.08	0.35 −0.80 to 1.52	0.15	p = 0.53	Intervention groups
Emotional	0.20 −0.61 to 2.02	0.54 −2.08 to 0.99	0.21	p = 0.47	Intervention groups
Hyperactivity	0.28 −1.4 to 2.06	0.63 −2.11 to 0.84	0.26	p = 0.38	Intervention groups
Peer relations	0.27 −1.93 to 1.3	−0.23 −1.77 to 1.30	0.09	p = 0.75	Control group
Pro-social	−0.30 −1.70 to 1.08	0.12 −9.01 to 1.15	0.06	p = 0.24	Intervention groups
Impact score	−0.18 −1.96 to 1.60	−0.59 −2.20 to 1.0	0.21	p = 0.45	Control group
Expression of Feelings Questionnaire Total scores	−11.2 −26.0 to 3.5	−6.18 −17.2 to 4.8	0.29	p = 0.26	Intervention groups
EFQ openness	−3.2 −8.8 to 2.3	−2.3 −6.6 to 1.9	0.23	p = 0.27	Intervention groups
EFQ attention-seeking	−4.4 −10.9 to 2.0	−2.8 −8.1 to 2.5	0.3	p = 0.28	Intervention groups

Outcome measures at T2	Mean differences at T2 and 95% CI	Adjusted mean differences (B) and 95% CI	Effect size Cohen's d	P value adjusted	In favour of....
EFQ showing affection	−2.79 −7.2 to 1.6	−1.0 −4.3 to 2.1	0.16	p = 0.50	Intervention groups
EFQ trusting	−0.82 −2.8 to −1.16	0.91 −2.17 to 3.99	0.21	p = 0.49	Intervention groups
Post-placement Problems	−3.22 −8.8 to 2.37	−0.91 −2.17 to 3.99	0.21	p = 0.55	Intervention groups
Parenting Sense of Competence: Satisfaction with Parenting Role	−3.67 −8.4 to 1.1	−4.9 −8.4 to −1.4	0.7	p = 0.007	Intervention groups
Parenting Efficacy	−3.41 −7.92 to 1.64	−2.26 −5.86 to 1.33	0.34	p = 0.21	Intervention groups
Daily hassles: Frequency	−0.97 −5.5 to 7.4	−0.91 −5.4 to 3.5	0.13	p = 0.68	Control group
Daily hassles: Intensity	1.29 −6.4 to 6.4	1.78 −4.7 to 8.34	0.13	p = 0.58	Intervention groups

Adjusted mean differences at T3 (B) controlling for T1 (linear regression)

81

Results from the child-based measures

SDQ completed by parents

First, in looking at the whole sample regardless of group allocation, the SDQ Total Difficulties scores remained well above the cut-off for serious problems six months after the intervention for all except five of the children. Small reductions were found for the mean level of child problems for the whole group (Time 1: 19.78, Time 2: 18.6, Time 3: 17.8).

When contrasting interventions with controls immediately post-intervention (T2), Table 6.1 shows that the mean SDQ Total Difficulties scores for the combined intervention group had risen slightly and the control group's scores had declined slightly. Table 6.2 shows that, by the six-month follow-up (T3), the control children ended with slightly higher SDQ Total Difficulties scores than the intervention group. Linear regression analysis was conducted (first with T2 and T1 as a covariate and then T3 with T1 as covariate) to compare the combined intervention group with the control group. No significant differences were found between the baseline and post-intervention, and the baseline and six-month post-intervention follow-up scores, nor between the interventions groups and the control group. In addition, no significant differences were found on any of the problem sub-scales, on the pro-social scores or the SDQ impact scores at T2 or T3. Effect sizes were small.

Visual Analogue Scales (VAS)

Parents' responses on the VAS were converted to percentages indicating where on the line the parent had put their mark from "much worse" (0%) to "much better" (100%). The mid-point showing "no change" was recorded as 50 per cent. Table 6.3 shows that the parents overwhelmingly recorded their children as having made some progress: only 22 per cent recorded that their child had deteriorated in the field of emotional distress; 19 per cent in behaviour; and six per cent in attachment within the family. This means of assessing outcome has produced a more optimistic report of change than the standardised questionnaire (SDQ – see below) which showed very little movement. This may simply reflect the fact that the analogue method is tapping a sense of global change whereas the SDQ requires an item by item response in relation to psychosocial problems.

Table 6.3

Parents' estimates of their children's improvement in three dimensions using Visual Analogue Scales

Extent and direction of change	Emotional distress		Misbehaviour		Attachment within the family	
	N	%	N	%	N	%
Much worse (0–24%)	1	3	2	5	1	3
Worse (25–49%)	7	19	5	14	1	3
Better (50–74%)	22	60	18	49	14	38
Much better (75%+)	7	19	12	32	21	57
Total	**37**	**101**	**37**	**100**	**37**	**101**

Note: Percentages may not add up to 100.

Table 6.4

Mean SDQ emotional symptoms sub-scores and "improvement" recorded by parents on the Visual Analogue Scale

	Visual Analogue rating	Mean SDQ score Time 3	SD	2-tailed significance
Parents' SDQ sub-score of emotional symptoms	Misbehaviour Poor outcome	6.33	2.42	p .014
	Misbehaviour Improved outcome	2.83	2.30	
	Emotional distress Poor outcome	6.00	2.23	p .008
	Emotional distress Poor outcome	2.79	2.36	

It is also important to recognise that "improvement" may still leave the child with substantial problems and the parents with major concerns with which they need professional help (see below, *The use of specialist services*).

When we compared the progress and the direction of change on these key dimensions (apparently indicating considerable improvement), with the SDQ Total Difficulties scores at T3 it was clear that parents' report of improvement was not necessarily the same as having a score in the "normal" range. It appears that change may feel substantial to the parents but still leave the child with major difficulties. We compared the mean scores on the full range of five SDQ sub-scores and the Total Difficulties score derived at Time 3 from parents' questionnaires for two of the three major dimensions for which we used the VASs. The SDQ does not aim to record information on attachment issues, so we did not test it against change recorded on the "attachment" VAS. Table 6.4 shows that an "improved" outcome recorded on the VAS for both emotional distress and for misbehaviour was significantly related to low mean scores on the SDQ domain of emotional symptoms alone. There were no significant relationships with the other SDQ sub-scores or with the Total Difficulties score at Time 3.

There were no differences between the intervention groups and the control group on the extent and direction of change recorded on the VAS.

Expression of Feelings Questionnaires

Tables 6.1 and 6.2 (above) also show that the EFQ total scores were higher (i.e. more positive) at all time points for the combined intervention group, and the general pattern showed a rise for the combined intervention group and little change for the controls, but differences were not significant at T2 and T3 when controlling for the baseline scores.

In most of the EFQ domains, mean scores for the combined intervention group rose a little and controls remain constant, but in only one domain was the difference significant. The "Trusting" sub-score at T2 was favourable to the intervention and significant ($p = 0.04$, Effect Size $d = 0.7$). However, no great weight can be given to this finding because the difference for the total EFQ score was not significant and the "trusting" sub-score had converged by T3 and was no longer significantly different.

Post-placement problems

A higher post-placement problem score indicated a worse outcome. The control group had higher mean scores than the combined intervention group at T2 and T3 but not significantly so when controlling for baseline scores.

Response to being part of the research study

In the third interview, parents were asked if they had any comments on being part of the research study: 86 per cent had at least one positive thing to say about being a participant, but a third (32%) had at least one negative comment. These were usually about how tiresome it was to have to complete the questionnaires three times.

Conclusions

Although there are some indications of better outcomes for the intervention group (e.g. nearly all the measured differences favoured the combined intervention over the control group), nevertheless the regression analysis produced only a handful of significant findings. The adopters' Satisfaction with the Parenting Role on the PSOC scale, six months after intervention, was significantly higher in the intervention group than in the controls. By contrast, no great transformation of the child's difficulties was shown in favour of the interventions at immediate post-intervention or at the six-month follow-up. However, parents appeared confident that there had been changes "for the better" when they filled in the Visual Analogue Scales, even though their children's Total Difficulties scores were seldom within the "normal" range on the SDQ.

The methodological issues and implications concerning this finding are discussed in the concluding chapter. However, a possible explanation of the findings is that, given the children's exposure to early adversity (maltreatment, poor parenting, broken relationships and moves in the care system) and given that only those with high difficulties entered the study, aspects of parenting may have changed in the intervention group but were not sufficiently powerful or had not existed long enough to have an impact on child outcomes at the six-month follow-up.

Table 6.5

Means and standard deviations on child-based measures at T1, T2 and T3 Combined interventions vs controls

	Baseline (T1)		Post-intervention (T2)		6 months post-intervention (T2)	
	Intervention	Control	Intervention	Control	Intervention	Control
	Mean (sd) n = 19	Mean (sd) n = 18	Mean (sd) n = 19	Mean (sd) n = 18	Mean (sd) n = 19	Mean (sd) n = 17
Parents' SDQ Total Difficulties	18.32 (4.5)	21.33 (7.1)	18.74 (6.0)	18.56 (6.7)	17.37 (5.8)	18.41 (5.4)
Conduct	4.53 (1.9)	5.06 (2.79)	4.4 (2.1)	4.33 (2.7)	3.53 (1.9)	4.29 (2.5)
Emotional	3.16 (2.0)	4.17 (2.8)	3.53 (2.6)	3.5 (2.3)	3.26 (2.6)	3.47 (2.7)
Hyperactivity	6.84 (2.4)	8.22 (2.3)	7.47 (2.2)	7.3 (2.8)	6.95 (2.4)	7.24 (2.7)
Peer relations	3.79 (2.4)	3.89 (2.6)	3.32 (2.0)	3.3 (2.1)	3.68 (2.5)	3.41 (2.3)
Pro-social	6.79 (2.25)	6.28 (1.7)	6.79 (1.6)	6.56 (1.9)	6.89 (2.0)	6.59 (2.0)
Impact score	3.22 (2.5)	3.33 (2.6)	2.84 (2.4)	3.41 (2.7)	3.47 (2.7)	3.29 (2.5)

	Baseline (T1)		Post-intervention (T2)		6 months post-intervention (T2)	
	Intervention	Control	Intervention	Control	Intervention	Control
	Mean (sd) n = 19	Mean (sd) n =18	Mean (sd) n = 19	Mean (sd) n = 18	Mean (sd) n = 19	Mean (sd) n = 18
Expression of Feelings Questionnaire Total scores	114.5 (14.7)	107.0 (25.9)	117.6 (23.0)	102.8 (22.5)	120.5 (18.4)	109.2 (25.5)
EFQ openness	35.50 (9.8)	33.50 (10.0	36.42 (10.0	32.33 (10.2)	37.0 (7.5)	33.78 (9.1)
EFQ attention seeking	41.11 (7.4)	38.44 (11.3)	42.00 (11.2)	36.44 (8.6)	43.63 (7.9)	39.1 (11.3)
EFQ showing affection	26.39 (4.7)	23.94 (7.2)	26.63 (7.2)	23.83 (8.0)	27.6 (6.0)	24.89 (7.1)
EFQ trusting	11.56 (2.7)	11.11 (3.2)	12.58 (2.6)	10.28 (3.3)	12.21 (2.6)	11.39 (3.3)
Post-placement problems	10.32 (4.2)	12.39 (6.5)	10.26 (3.8)	11.50 (7.2)	9.74 (4.3)	11.7 (6.6)

Table 6.6

Means and standard deviations on parent self-report measures at T1, T2 and T3

	Baseline (T1)		Post-intervention (T2)		6 months post intervention (T3)	
	Intervention	Control	Intervention	Control	Intervention	Control
	Mean (SD) N=19	Mean (SD) N=18	Mean (SD) N=19	Mean (SD) N=18	Mean (SD) N=19	Mean (SD) N=18
Parenting Sense of Competence						
Satisfaction with parenting role	34.16 (5.3)	35.78 (7.8)	37.05 (6.0)	36.00 (8.08)	38.84 (7.1)	35.17 (7.2)
Parenting efficacy	30.68 (6.4)	29.59 (6.6)	32.32 (6.9)	30.28 (6.3)	34.47 (6.9)	31.33 (7.3)
Daily hassles: frequency	40.95 (7.0)	42.83 (7.2)	39.72 (7.0)	44.12 (10.4)	41.58 (9.1)	42.56 (10.3)
Daily hassles: intensity	47.79 (16.2)	47.72 (9.2)	43.72 (11.3)	50.76 (14.8)	44.47 (12.2)	45.76 (10.4)

Summary

It is important to summarise the results in relation to the hypotheses set out before data collection began:

- Recruitment into the study proved disappointing, with a lower than expected response at the screening stage, and a response rate of 48 per cent from parents invited into the study.
- The prediction of an improvement in the children's psychosocial scores after the parent advice sessions did not hold, as improvement in measures of the children's difficulties was no greater in the combined intervention group than in the control group six months after the intervention.
- There were no differences between the intervention groups and the control group on the extent and direction of change recorded on the Visual Analogue Scales.
- The prediction that change would be similar in the two intervention groups held. However, numbers were too small for statistical testing when controlling for baseline measures. Consequently, it was not possible to prove that one type of intervention was superior to the other in relation to the children's behaviour.
- The prediction held that aspects of parenting would show more positive change in the combined intervention group at six months follow-up compared with the control group.

7   Feedback from the adopters and the parent advisers on the parenting programmes

In this part of the study, information was gathered on the parenting interventions as viewed both by the parents and by their advisers in order to complement the quantitative analysis. A better understanding is sought of how elements of the intervention package might be linked to change in the behaviour of the children or the parenting practices of the parents. The parents and the advisers were each asked to complete session-by-session one-page feedback forms which contained seven questions, ending with an invitation to add any further comments about the intervention. The questions to the parents asked what they found most and least useful in the content of the sessions and what guidance they found easy or difficult to apply. The questions to the advisers asked how the parenting topics were covered in the sessions, whether they achieved their aims and what aspect of the intervention seemed to make a difference. It should be remembered that the contemporaneous written feedback by the parents may well offer a different perspective from the information gathered by the independent research interviewers following the intervention. (This included a rating of satisfaction with the parenting advice, a measure of the Parenting Sense of Competence and a record of Daily Hassles – described in Chapter 3.)

The weekly feedback forms were returned by all the parent advisers who delivered an intervention (19) and by the advisers of those control families who accepted the offer of an intervention after the research interviews were completed (6). It seemed sensible to profit from the feedback available on *all* the interventions (25), although the post-control cases are not included in the main outcome analysis. In relation to parent feedback, three families out of 19 receiving the service did not return their forms and another only partly completed the task. The parent advisers tended to write much more fully than the parents, who tended to be less expansive, especially when they were very positive about the interventions. Some parents, however, provided very carefully considered feedback in their detailed responses.

How was the parenting help received?

The parents' feedback shows clearly that the sessions were well received. None of the parents had difficulty understanding the advice programmes and all thought them well explained, highly relevant and acceptably delivered. They were very positive about both parenting advice programmes and generally about the parent advisers themselves. Some said it was the most useful support they had received so far.

The parents often gave high praise for the intervention, saying, for example:

A big thank you for everything you have done to help us. As much as we felt we were just coping with his extreme behaviours, we finally had to say we needed some guidance and your offer came at just the right moment.

And further positive testimony:

One particular benefit has been that by understanding more about what our child may be thinking and feeling, we are able to respond to particular situations in a calmer, relaxed and more measured way. The course has been immensely valuable to us. It has enabled us to take stock of how far we have come in creating a warm, loving and supportive home for our child. Where we have experienced difficulties, our adviser has helped us to work out strategies and tactics for dealing with these in a sensible and practical way. Thank you.

Another parent wrote:

I would have liked more sessions simply because they were so useful. We were able to be completely open with [parent adviser], and value her advice and confidentiality.

A single parent with three adopted children:

I felt I was treated as an equal, which was really good. I did get enough time, but only because we "over-ran"; an hour would not have been enough. The homework was "mixed"; I have some psychology knowledge so some of it I knew; when I couldn't manage (to do it) it was because of lack of time. I definitely plan to use the advice but I wanted more hands-on advice on how to deal with misbehaviour. Gained insight into causes, but could still do with clear advice. Would definitely recommend to others – it was a support for me, not just the kids. Ten sessions is fine, but maybe a few sessions in six months or so would be useful. The issue of lying and stealing was not properly dealt with. Now I feel more relaxed and confident in what I'm doing. I was encouraged to try new strategies. I learnt new insights and with regularity and consistency (they have worked).

The advisers said most of the parents had been welcoming and had become committed to the programme. Parents said they appreciated the intervention being home-based, because of convenience for them and so that the adviser could have a better understanding of the family setting. On one occasion the adviser witnessed challenging behaviour "in the raw" when the child produced a prolonged temper tantrum in the house.

The parents appreciated the focus on the common problems of children placed from care in middle childhood (for example, inattention, poor concentration, exaggerated attention seeking) rather than general behaviour difficulties, and many reported on the benefit of learning that the parenting problems they struggled with were not unique. Some difficult behaviour diminished; more than one child was said to show an overall attitude and mood change, to begin to show more affection and to be more enjoyable company. Some examples of these changes in personal relationships are also given in Chapters 9, 10 and 11.

In both interventions, help in reviewing their parenting style had led to more reflection and negotiation in place of instant and habitual reactions to difficult behaviour. Parents were often helped to learn that their own reactions to difficult behaviour (exasperation, uncertainty, fatigue) are common among parents of ex-care children. Some reported a change from tense, exasperated parenting to more relaxed interaction (see also Chapter 8).

Overall, the parents reported on the benefit of the intervention being centred on their own specific experiences with the child with advice tailored to their age and developmental level. They were helped to separate out the negative effects of the child's past from the possible effects of their current parenting behaviour. In the research interviews, some parents contrasted the receipt of this family-specific advice to the much less useful general advice they had had from the "training" before the child arrived. And one couple, who had followed a cognitive behavioural parenting course before the children arrived, were very appreciative of the opportunity to go over this approach again but, this time, focused on the index child's personality and needs.

Two specific issues received frequent comment from both advisers and parents: "special play" and "praise". Reviewing patterns of parenting led to a recognition of how little relaxed time was spent, in some cases, with the child each week. Simply persuading parents to find more time in their busy lives for relaxed play has been one of the more significant interventions, often leading to an immediate beneficial impact: warmer responses from the child and more enjoyable interaction. This sometimes needed a re-scheduling of the family routine, perhaps getting up earlier, to make space for "special play". One family incorporated focused playtime away from the other siblings as part of family life. Interestingly, more than one family linked the difficulty of getting good babysitters with the difficulty of finding time that they could spend with one child alone: they often wanted to do this but found it hard to separate the children. Some children were said to have "loved the special time" set aside while some were avoidant and/or resistant initially. In some cases, the play materials were too sophisticated or did not lend themselves to eye contact but parents saw the point of using simpler toys. Some parents were sceptical at first, ill at ease with play themselves, or too eager to be directive, but in general were surprised at the benefits of relaxed play, especially in helping parent and child to feel closer.

Learning to give clear, specific praise and commands was a feature of the behavioural intervention and often resulted in the child becoming calmer almost immediately, or at least reducing extreme behaviours. Some aspects of the educational intervention in encouraging "understanding" of the child's behaviour in relation to the past produced immediate results. In one case, a family was struggling with their daughter's reluctance at bath time. In discussion with the adviser, it emerged that this could be linked to newly-discovered information that this was the context in which she had been sexually abused. Armed with this information, bath time was handled differently from then on and with less protest.

New understandings emerged when parents were encouraged to see the world from the child's perspective. One family realised that when asked to do something the child seemed to see this as being told off and reacted resentfully. This helped the parents to think more carefully about their behaviour and language and to take this into account when making requests of her.

Of course, variations existed within the generally positive responses. When parents were asked what was most difficult for them, strong emotions were sometimes evoked as they realised the extent of the problems they had been experiencing with the children. Some felt they were losing their way during the intervention or having to sort out some confusion about the best approach, which involved attending to disagreements with their partner. In addition, some parents told the researchers that they had not got much out of the advice sessions:

Homework was only sometimes useful. The notes did help to go back and focus on things, but very obvious statements. I preferred to go through my own notes – more useful than notes provided. The "homework" was an extra chore I didn't need; the questions were not helpful. It did make me look at my parenting style – overall a positive experience. But after each session I felt quite "drained". Sometimes, I look through the notes for a reminder; good tips on managing behaviour.

It is an interesting comment on this case that the mother did not cite the parent adviser as a source of changed ideas on how to manage bad behaviour; the sources she listed included herself, her parents, the family social worker, friends, other adopters, books etc., and adoption organisations – practically the longest list of anyone asked about sources of ideas, but she did list the parent adviser as a source for encouraging closer attachment: 'She said to me: "Be there; praise more".'

Some reflections on parenting, by the advisers, also revealed high expectations by parents of their child. Having to revise these initial ambitions and "fantasies" was difficult and time-consuming, and was frustrating for those impatient for quick solutions. But some parents were enabled to see that, although progress might be slow, the rewards would be there in the end. One couple saw considerable change in their child:

I feel more confident; we use praise and play more than we did, and we use the rewards system more carefully. I think we are more patient, happier waiting for change; more understanding about the child's defensive reactions, and about the effect we are having.

Some appreciated being asked to keep record sheets and to do "homework", while others felt it a chore and that it "got in the way of" thinking about parenting. Some parents took time before putting the learning into practice, but became more positive when they saw it working and once the new approach had been fully implemented. Some wanted a more selective approach to the contents of the manual if they wanted to concentrate only on one or two very specific problems while others were interested in all the topics.

How was parenting being "enhanced"?

These parents, in agreeing to join the trial, were motivated to parent more effectively, but nevertheless said they benefited from being praised for their efforts and often needed a boost to their confidence and self-esteem. They said they appreciated the one-to-one contact with advisers, working through problems together, being given new ideas and seeking reassurance about their parenting. One adviser commented that the mother naturally used verbal praise a great deal and she was gratified to hear this acknowledged. It was generally the case that the parents had tried to inform themselves about how to help a difficult child, via books and the internet, but needed assistance in applying this to their particular child. They may have attempted to use a technique, like a star chart, in the past but had devised too complicated a system and abandoned it, or they may not have used it effectively or enthusiastically previously but were willing to try it again now with expert help and ongoing support.

The role of the adviser was often not so much about providing new techniques or insights, but about carrying forward the existing skills and understanding and making sure these were fully applied and absorbed. The advisers commented that some couples were already very skilled and thoughtful and that they were aiming more for "tweaking" the parenting than seeking fundamental change. Sometimes parents had not fully grasped how to use what they knew to maximum effect. They were reassured that, if a changed approach appeared not to be working straight away, it might well prove to be helpful in the longer term. In both manuals, much of the programme was taken up with discussion as to what might be the best approach, the best construction to put on the child's behaviour, and the best type of reward or choice of "consequence" for the child, drawing on the parents' current practices. This individual "working through" of a problem was evidently one of the most valued aspects of the parenting help.

Aspects of the cognitive behavioural intervention

The CB intervention manual contains a role play element with the parent adviser acting as the "interfering parent" and asking the parent to role play the child. Some parents reported initial embarrassment or reluctance at role play, but then said it helped to demonstrate the problem of an intrusive or over-prescriptive parenting style. Some parents who tended to let their child play alone, or only joined in with computer games or watching TV, learned the benefits of giving the child their undivided attention. One family had started with the parents playing with the child, but had moved to encouraging her to play by herself for some of the time – which she had not been able to do before. The mother said she was always there while her daughter played, but not always actively involved unless the child wanted it. Applying this with a child who is afraid to play imaginatively sometimes proved difficult but persisting with special play could help to free the imagination and encourage self-confidence.

Again, some parents reported that their praise was used to better effect after the advice sessions:

The advice was good and very useful. I thought the course was brilliant. I was not sure what to expect but I got the more practical advice and plan to go on using it. I've probably changed as a parent as a result, I'm more confident, more patient, I use more praise, more play, and I use rewards more carefully. And I think [she] is better.

Many sessions were concerned with reversing negative parenting responses and turning them into positive encouragement. The focus on the parents' reactions encouraged them to "open up" about their parenting style and to examine its possible effects. When one parent was asked to count how many times she used "telling off" over a half-an-hour period, this proved revealing.

Some children did not know how to react when first praised and the praising behaviour needed to be refined. Parents who were not accustomed to it, became more used to giving frequent praise, praising more quickly after the behaviour and ignoring some behaviours while continuing to praise others. They were encouraged to go beyond generalised praise (good boy/girl) to specifically naming the desired behaviour (labelled praise) and to consider carefully what sort of reward matched the chosen behaviour.

Time 2: *There are no (attachment) problems now. She still loves attention, but doesn't have to be the centre of attention any more. She does "withdraw" from us, if she's in trouble, but we make her laugh or ignore it. We have been building the bond with lots of praise; we spend more time with her; are more affectionate to her. Our parent adviser said, 'Simply being there will build affection', meaning that we don't have to respond every time to every single demand for attention.*

Parents learned to become more specific with commands and boundaries, not "running on" beyond what needed to be said and making sure their facial expression was consistent with the command. However, finding behaviour to praise was sometimes difficult because it was so continuously challenging or because praising came less readily to some parents. One family worried that the child would get used to being praised and not take any notice. They were reminded of the importance of being both specific and sincere in their praise.

Some parents had to work hard to modify their behaviour and especially where fixed cycles of parent–child interaction had become established. Some changes came more slowly with a child gradually coming to accept praise more readily, when at first praise was only met by crossness and temper tantrums. Helping children to be more aware of the "consequences" of their behaviour was not easy with a child who had a strong resistance to accepting that anything might be his or her fault.

Where a child had experienced extreme neglect and abuse, the ensuing temper tantrums, impulsiveness and physical aggression presented a considerable challenge. Learning about the "thoughts, feelings, behaviour" cycle embedded in this programme was often helpful to the parents and encouraged a slowing down or delaying of the parents' response in relation to the child's expression of strong emotion.

Learning to ignore undesirable behaviour appeared to be one of the hardest tasks as noted by both parents and advisers. Some had not used the technique of "ignoring" before. It could be difficult if it was not the parent's natural style and especially in the face of very confrontational, insistent behaviour by the child. One mother wanted help with the exasperation she felt at her daughter's incessant chatter ("white noise" she called it). She practised ignoring the behaviour with some success and even more so when both parents saw the need for a jointly agreed consistent approach between them. Some were aware of the principle of "ignoring" undesirable behaviour but had not felt comfortable in using it, or felt it might appear rejecting to the child, or had not managed to use it consistently. This part of the programme threw up more difficulties in implementation than others. An exasperated father found it hard to ignore the riotous behaviour of the children in the back seat of the car which was seriously distracting his driving. In another case, the child reacted to "ignoring" by continuing with the behaviour in a more and more extreme bid for attention until the mother could ignore it no longer. These are examples of how the interventions needed to be followed through week by week to allow for a re-consideration of strategies.

Aspects of the educational intervention

A major aspect of the educational intervention was to explore how the child's past and present might be connected. The parents may not have been properly informed, nor fully understood, the implications of the child's pre-placement adversity. Several parents had been fighting prolonged battles with the placing agency to fill in the information gaps in their child's earlier abuse history. Parents may not have really comprehended the links with everyday behaviour. How, for example, might the effects of insecurity or bad memories, or a sense of rejection or loss of relationships play out in the present? The opportunity to step back and to review the child's history and their current parenting was valued by many, giving fresh insight into early years' experience and adaptive behaviour. Revelations about former insecurity led one mother to see the need to build in more structure to help the child feel more contained and safe. Parents were helped to gain a better understanding of the possible origins of extreme tantrums, and puzzling or aggressive reactions when under stress and distortions in the expression of feelings. In one family quiescent behaviour at bedtime was at first seen to be desirable, but later the child was discovered to be in a terrified state, which then could be seen as related to past abuse.

Reviewing the child's history could also be a reminder of how the child has strengths to be recognised despite poor early experience. Although gaining fuller recognition of the abuse the child had suffered was instructive, parents could still be at a loss to comprehend the extreme behaviour and sudden changes of mood. Some parents made quick use of new understandings, while others were slower in acknowledging the extent of problems and had difficulties in seeing the connections with the past or generally resisted psychological explanations. Advisers helped the parents to get behind behaviour like "apparent confidence" and "false affection" to their possible origins in insecurity and attachment history.

Some parents became inventive in linking the child's past experiences with current behaviour, as in working on why a child attempts to push her mother into responding in a way familiar to her from her early abusive experiences. One parent said, 'Understanding is essential to finding solutions'.

In one case, a mother was reported to be desperate for support and for parenting suggestions. The adviser discussed the evolution of the child's lying and stealing in relation to her past and helped the mother to think about the child's previous experience of parenting, which included rejection and scapegoating, and how this may have resulted in ineffective strategies for engaging adults. In relation to another rejected child who appeared to be counter-rejecting her, the mother recognised that the rejecting behaviour 'is not about me' but arose from the child's past experience of emotional abuse.

Another family said their agency preparation was entirely "behaviour management oriented" but offered little on "understanding". The adviser encouraged them to consider the meaning of the behaviour and then to think about broadening their range of responses. They reflected together on the six difficult years the child had experienced before the placement and came to acknowledge that they had avoided certain difficult issues which caused them discomfort. They re-visited their approach and changed their style so that they "stayed with him" when he was being difficult or in a rage. This helped them to get to know their child "on the inside". The adviser explained the importance of validating the child's anger and helped them reframe "naughtiness" as "inability to cope".

A quotation from one of the research interviews gives a flavour of the same effect:

We are calmer and more understanding. But feel it is necessary to understand why the child is behaving like that before using the strategies to cope with it. The parent adviser not giving definite answers was frustrating but useful as it made us think about things more.

We have not had any support from the post-adoption support team, so having someone to "blow off steam to" was really useful. I was expecting to be told what to do, an authoritarian approach, so I was pleasantly surprised by the give-and-take nature of the sessions. I am now more aware of the reasons why E behaves as she does, and how my reactions impact on her. I am now able to identify causes. I'm more relaxed and firmer too. We used to lump all the behaviour together and give her one punishment. We now deal with things separately and in a calmer way. We used to react immediately and without a full understanding of why she behaves as she does.

We use a lot of the strategies the parent adviser suggested. They definitely made me more understanding of [child]. We use play and praise more; I'm more confident and firmer; and use "ignoring" more often.

In another case, the issue of the daughter's need for control was worked on in several sessions in the sequence. The mother was helped to see her daughter's intense need for control as a strategy to keep herself safe in a world she had not been able to trust. The mother could identify which situations seemed to bring this behaviour on and this led to a better basis on which to engage openly with her daughter. The inappropriate expression of feelings was often discussed. A child who responded with a smirking smile was causing a lot of irritation but the parents were helped to re-interpret her motive not as malicious pleasure, but as a possible need for reassurance.

Some families were helped to challenge their expectations of the child and to achieve more reasonable ambitions. This involved discussion of the nature of change and recovery from adversity. The gradual acceptance of the possibility of long-term negative effects led to a lessening of their disappointment and to greater realism, but was also accompanied by "scary feelings" about the future.

The educational model gives more emphasis to the social context of adoption. Topics like the experience of dual heritage children and people's reaction to adoption were more to the fore. The idea of creating a "cover story" appealed to some, especially in relation to the school setting, where it was important to balance the information the teacher would need to know against information that was far too intimate to disclose to someone outside the family.

Special issues arose for same-sex adopters in presenting their "unconventional" family to the world. One parent said the better understanding they had gained put them in a better position to tackle problems and challenge professionals when necessary.

Forming new attachments

Did anything appear to help with the growth of attachment to the new parents? Aspects of both interventions may have contributed to improved mutual closeness. Building relaxed play regularly into everyday life was reported by parents as a significant factor in relationship building. Also a more consistent and attuned parenting style was said to lead to a calmer mood in the child, and to more relaxed interaction with more physical affection shown. Better understanding of the child's relationship history provided a useful context for thinking about adjusting current parenting to promote attachment.

Special dynamics in seeking help and receiving help for adopters

The special dynamics of adoptive parenting in the context of providing support, advice and help need to be acknowledged. The parents' caution about acknowledging problems and their sensitivity to criticism indicate that a lot is at stake if anything but good progress seems to be being made. Parents may need to be seen to have a positive attitude to the child, and therefore to consider their negative thoughts and emotions as inadmissible. This may have dissuaded some from signing up to the trial, but even when embarked on the parent advice sessions, advisers reported that parents could minimise the problems at the start, even though they had rated the child with a high score on the SDQ. It seems that the parents needed to be reassured about the stance of the adviser and the nature of the help on offer in order to trust before making use of the intervention. Their growing trust was then demonstrated by them being more honest, being more enquiring, wanting to discuss alternative approaches and being open about their parenting struggles. Parent advisers observed that they were not able to start on the manual sequence with some parents until this initial hesitancy was understood and appropriately addressed.

It is worth keeping in mind that some of the families, when finding time for these ten sessions, had been dealing with many other challenges at the same time: some were moving towards the adoption hearing; some were planning to adopt another child with all the accompanying social work attention; some were dealing with employment difficulties, family illness or bereavement. This study focuses on one index child in each family, but in 23 families (62%) the children had been placed with siblings, or there was an older birth child in the family whose needs the parents were trying not to ignore.

Greater complexity

In some cases the intervention process amounted to far more than simply "delivering an intervention" and expecting the parent to profit: exceptions and complications arose. This is a rather specific parenting programme, and presented to the parents as such, but in some cases parents may have had much broader and deeper concerns: perhaps tension with their partner, unresolved personal difficulties, struggles with intense feelings of disappointment at unmet expectations or blows to their confidence from parenting an "unrewarding" child. When problems emerged as more deeply rooted, this posed a dilemma for advisers wishing to stay faithful to the manual. Parents may have signed up to the trial because they are glad of the offer of help, but may in fact want something more than a parenting programme.

Self-awareness can be painful. Accepting that parenting behaviour could be improved does not always come easily. The parent can be defensive or wish to find the source of problems elsewhere, or may suffer from fear of failure. Therefore, the intervention must be delivered by sensitive, experienced, skilled professionals who can balance attending to these problems as best they can while attempting to deliver the pre-designed programme.

What worked less well in using the manuals?

Many comments from the advisers suggested that the topics deserved more than hour-long sessions to do them justice, that there was too much material in the manual, and that it was frustrating not to be able to cover a topic satisfactorily. Some parents needed points explained more slowly and simply or had difficulty focusing on specific problems and aims. It can take several sessions to develop trust and establish productive work. Advisers often found that they were pondering on whether to forge on with the next topic in the sequence or to remain with "unfinished business". They had to juggle giving priority to coverage of all the material or when to stay with an important dialogue. One adviser would have preferred to take a break so that parents could work on one topic before moving on. This was more of a problem with garrulous or emotional parents or when they shifted off the topic of the index child. Some bigger parenting issues clearly cannot be confined to a session, for example, reluctance to reflect on the child's abusive past or over-avoidance of conflict with the child. Some material that appeared to have been dealt with in earlier sessions may need re-visiting.

Where parents were dealing with aggressive and even dangerous behaviour, some advisers found the manuals less useful as they didn't give relevant examples or indicate how extreme behaviour might be understood and handled. The manual could not cover all possible problems; for example, one parent was constantly faced with her daughter running away when confronted with a problem. The manual didn't deal specifically with this but key principles were applied: identifying what triggers the behaviour, thinking of how to pre-empt it, devising appropriate consequences and removing the attention that being chased provides. The mother explained to her daughter why she would not chase her in future, but that this was not a withdrawal of love.

The duration of the programmes, set at ten weeks in order to establish a test of a standard programme, appeared to suit most parents, although it may have deterred some from joining the research by appearing too long and too great an intrusion on family life. In the event, the structured, targeted programmes appealed to all but a minority who found them too regimented. One mother was persuaded that more specialist intervention was now needed for her child beyond what had been gained from the 10-week programme and that she should seek further training in managing child trauma. Another parent was made aware of the need for educational assessment to understand better her child's difficulties in learning. One family stated: 'There is still further to travel – but we use the handouts to remind ourselves of what we have learned'.

A case example illustrating the complexities extending beyond parenting help

This placement was of an eight-year-old girl and the mother was allocated to the "educational" intervention. The mother saw the child's problems as superficial attachment, over-eating, bottling-up feelings and conflict in school relationships, where the child reported that she was being bullied.

The adviser engaged with the mother's disappointment at her feelings of slow progress as an adoptive parent. The mother was encouraged to think about what continually being left with strangers in the past did to her daughter's sense of continuity and how this helped to explain her current social relationship difficulties. The mother explained how relatively small changes, like the comings and goings of family life, had disproportionate effects on her daughter's regressive, anxious and clinging behaviour. The adviser explained how a child can take a long time to be convinced of new routines and feel a sense of security.

The adviser explored the mother's own reactions to her daughter. She admitted wanting to be needed by the child, and having to be a perfect mother. She was reading as much as possible about adoption in the hope, the adviser suggested, of finding immediate solutions to problems. The adviser explored whether the mother felt very driven by what she wanted the child to be and the adviser helped her to allow the child to "be herself".

Some tension then developed with the adviser as to what "understanding" of her daughter was the "right" one. The mother wanted to pin the problem on bullying at school rather than exploring the child's past or her own parenting. Appointments were cancelled and there was a short break is the sessions. When the mother discovered that the child had been lying about the bullying, she experienced a range of negative feelings: she became angry and rejecting towards with the child, embarrassed at making a mistake, distressed and pained. The adviser began to feel that the mother's own pain was preventing her from seeing her child's pain. Tension and disagreement were growing in the marriage. The father stopped attending sessions because he did not identify the problems as the mother saw them and preferred to "get on with it".

The mother was resisting the intervention, did not see the need for change and considered abandoning her involvement in the study. But, after another break, she decided to continue. By this stage she was doing what had to be done practically for the child, but was maintaining an emotional distance. The adviser described this as 'a self-preservation course'. The child, in response, became more avoidant and "blocking" of any friendly overtures. The adviser persuaded the mother to begin to acknowledge her fear of failure and vulnerability. She became somewhat depressed, but in her ruminations realised she needed 'a change of heart' and had to risk making changes in her attitude.

On subsequent appointments she appeared calmer and more ready "to give" again and said she wanted to preserve this new confidence and good feeling. She developed a stronger identification with her child and could empathise with a child afraid of experiences which could be taken away. The parenting improved notably. In the discussion with the adviser that followed, it was acknowledged that painful self-reflection led to substantial change (although it is not known whether it is being sustained). Had this skilled and sensitive intervention beyond parenting advice not been provided, a placement disruption may well have followed.

A case example illustrating the different parent and adviser perspectives

The parallel feedback on the sessions offered the opportunity to see whether the parent and adviser accounts concurred. The following example is of a family with a five-year-old child placed with them and the allocated intervention was cognitive behavioural. The parents reported that all the sessions were useful. They said they had profited from keeping a diary to monitor progress and found the diagrams (the parenting pyramid) and building blocks very useful aids. It encouraged them to step back and observe their own behaviour. They found the handouts helpful to refer to when trying to make their praise specific to a behaviour and they learned to be more precise when giving commands and setting boundaries. They used the star chart successfully to reduce the number of times their child would wake them up each night. The feedback was positive or sometimes even more enthusiastic, for example, saying that the adviser's role-playing of the child "was brilliant".

Following this very satisfied account, the adviser's report made interesting reading. She reported some difficulty to begin with in getting the parents to name specific goals. The mother became very emotional when talking about the difficulties and the adviser had to simplify explanations considerably to get the messages across. She felt that sometimes the parents' enthusiastic response was an obstacle to identifying problems more specifically and that they needed more time to practise before moving on to the next topic and wondered if a bigger interval was needed between sessions. She was not always sure the adopters were absorbing the advice. Obtaining dual accounts guards against investing too much in the testimony of one side of the encounter.

Conclusions

The feedback forms clearly show that most of the parents had been experiencing uncomfortable feelings as new adopters: of being overwhelmed, emotional, exhausted, bewildered, disappointed, frustrated or fighting a sense of failure. In some cases they were eager to express their anger at the neglect and abandonment they experienced by the placing agency and needed to give an "outpouring" about the lack of support. Many had a hunger to talk about the difficulties and wanted longer and more in-depth sessions than the structured intervention permitted. One mother had been surprised to find herself parenting in a way abhorrent to her but found it hard to admit. She was advised not to punish herself too much over "mistakes". The parents needed to build trust before being willing to admit to a feeling of having mis-managed a situation.

It was clear that the advisers, based on their professional experience, were offering more than simply delivering the contents of the manual. One way of looking at their interventions is to see the child's expression of extreme behaviour and emotions as hard to contain by the new parents. Parents admitted to becoming angry when faced with difficult behaviour, or having to cope with uncomfortable feelings when the child was over-friendly and over-familiar with others. The adviser role frequently became one of helping the parents to tolerate or to manage these strong feelings as well as assisting them in finding a way forward. There were many examples of parents experiencing "negative moments" but they were able to discuss their uncertainties and seek reassurance from someone whose knowledge and experience they came to trust.

The last of the ten sessions was devoted to summarising what had been gained and the changes that had taken place. Although the interventions – inevitably – had not covered all the likely problems of ex-care children, nor had the parenting challenges by any means disappeared, and progress was sometimes followed by setbacks, nevertheless, their satisfaction with the parenting role and confidence as parents appeared to have grown.

This "feedback" chapter is intended as a contribution to understanding how a parenting programme was delivered and received in relation to this specific group of parents (non-related adopters of high problem, ex-care children) at a specific time (early in adoptive placement). The feedback from the advisers offered some excellent examples of professional thinking and practice. Creative solutions were frequently offered when strategies did not seem to be working as desired.

In common with other psychological interventions, non-specific factors were clearly at play: giving hope, listening and acknowledging, encouraging and reassuring. However, it was turning good intentions into sensible and practical strategies and building on the experience and knowledge of their child that the parents already possessed that seemed to be most appreciated.

Summary

- Parents and advisers completed weekly feedback forms so that we could learn more about how the interventions were related to change.
- The parents were positive about both parenting advice programmes and generally about the parent advisers themselves.
- Parents said they appreciated the convenience of the intervention being home based and this also gave the adviser a better understanding of the family setting.
- Parents appreciated the intervention being centred on their own specific experiences with the child.
- The role of the adviser was often not so much about providing new techniques or insights, but about carrying forward the existing skills and understanding and making sure that these were fully applied and absorbed.
- Individualised "working through" of a problem was one of the most valued aspects of the parenting help.
- In the cognitive behavioural intervention, learning to ignore undesirable behaviours was one of the most difficult challenges.

- In the educational intervention, parents were helped to think about how the effects of insecurity, a sense of rejection or loss of relationships might play out in the present.
- Some parents had broader and deeper concerns than were covered in the parenting programme.

8　The costs and effectiveness of services used by the families

Cost effectiveness

As in other areas of social and health care, the provision of services and support for adopters is often constrained by resources. Policy-makers have to make difficult choices about when and how much support to provide. Therefore, it is crucial to ascertain whether new interventions are cost effective compared to existing practice. This entails estimating service use and costs and linking cost data with outcomes after receipt of the services.

Method

In each interview, parents were asked about the use of services to support their child and the placement and the number of parenting advice sessions that the families received was recorded by the parent advisers. Each session was assumed to last for one hour and the hourly cost of a social worker – £80 (Curtis, 2007) – was used to estimate the total cost of this service. (This unit cost includes salary costs, overheads and training and is based on the amount of face-to-face contact time with clients. Travel costs were not included.) The use of a wide range of other services in relation to the welfare of the adopted child was measured using an adapted version of the Client Service Receipt Inventory (Beecham and Knapp, 2001). Services included contacts with social workers and other local authority professionals, use of mental health and other health services, and specialist educational input. The services included direct contact for the child (e.g. with an optician) or by parents in order to meet the needs of the child (e.g. attending parenting courses). In addition, the schedule recorded any time that adopters lost from work due to difficulties with the placement.

Comprehensive measurement is desirable so that the broad impact of the interventions can be determined – it may be the case that the interventions offered to adopters are relatively expensive but these extra costs might be offset by reduced costs elsewhere in the system. Services were retrospectively measured for the time since placement to baseline assessment and for both follow-up periods (from T1 to T2 and from T2 to T3).

Unit costs, obtained from a recognised source (Curtis, 2007), have been attached to the service use data in order to generate total service costs (the parent advice sessions plus other service costs). The costs associated with each intervention group and with the control group have been compared, controlling for baseline differences as necessary. If either of the experimental intervention groups or the control group is less expensive and more effective than all other options, then it is deemed to be "dominant" and the preferred choice. However, the interventions might be more effective *and* more expensive than routine care given to the control group. If this is the case, then differences between the combined intervention group and the control group, and between the two interventions, need to be compared using an Incremental Cost-Effectiveness Ratio (ICER), defined as the difference in costs divided by the difference in outcomes. This reveals the cost associated with an extra unit of outcome achieved by any comparator. It would then be a policy decision as to whether the extra outcome is achieved at an acceptable cost.

Results

At baseline there were few noticeable differences in service use (Table 8.1).[3] Most participants had contact with GPs and dentists for their child's needs, and most, not surprisingly, had received input from the child's or family social worker. There was a relatively high level of use of outpatient services for the children, but this included some statutory medical inspections before adoption orders were granted.

Between T1 and T2 all but one family in the intervention groups received the full ten sessions from the parent advisers (see Chapter 6). Use of some services (e.g. classroom assistant/special education needs

---

[3]   The baseline figures include one family which subsequently dropped out of the study because the placement disrupted.

co-ordinator, health visitor, dentist/optician, CAMHS,[4] after-school club) at T2 was higher in the intervention groups compared to routine care (Table 8.2). However, the small sample size means that we need to treat such comparisons with some caution. Table 8.3 shows the service use and costs during the whole research period from T1 to T3, where there was some indication of greater use by the two intervention groups of therapists and counsellors, in addition to the parent advice sessions.

The mean service costs at baseline were similar for each group (Figure 8.1). Costs at T2 were substantially higher for both the intervention groups compared to the control group, but this was mainly due to the inclusion of the intervention costs. By T3, when the interventions had ended, the mean costs in each group were very similar. Median costs (Figure 8.2) at T2 were substantially higher for the intervention groups but at T3 were similar to those for the control group.

As with the outcomes described in Chapter 6, we have combined the two intervention groups. The mean (and standard deviation) costs at baseline for the combined intervention group and for the control group were £3,058 (£2,119) and £3,001 (£3,232) respectively. At T2, the mean (sd) costs for the combined intervention group was £3,186 (£2,087) and for the control group the cost was £1,641 (£2,021). The difference controlling for baseline was £1,528 and this was statistically significant (bootstrapped 95% Confidence Interval, £67 to £2,782[5]). By T3, the costs were £1,511 (£1,352) for the combined intervention group and £1,738 (£3,532) for the control group. The difference controlling for baseline was £222 but this was not statistically significant (bootstrapped 95% CI, £2,384 to £1,182). Over the entire follow-up period, the mean (sd) costs for the combined intervention group were £5,043 (£3,309) and £3,378 (£5,285) for the control group. The adjusted difference was £1,652, which was not statistically significant (95% CI, £1,709 to £4,268).

The median costs at baseline for the combined intervention group and for the control group were £2,741 and £2,130 respectively. At T2 the median costs were £2,943 for the combined intervention group and £809

---

[4] Child and Adoptive Mental Health Services.

[5] "Bootstrapping" is a statistical technique used to make a better estimate of where the means and standard deviations might lie in a larger population.

for the control group (Pearson test, p = 0.001). At T3 the combined inter-vention group had a median cost of £992 while the median cost for the control group was £1,034 (Pearson test, p = 0.738). The median costs over the whole follow-up period were £4,669 for the combined intervention group and £1,692 for the control group (Pearson test, p = 0.004).

The combined intervention group carried higher mean costs at T2. Chapter 6 has shown that the adjusted SDQ Total Difficulties score at T2 was 2.13 points worse for the combined intervention group. Based on these results, the control group is seen to be dominant. Similarly, routine care dominates at T3 as costs by then were still higher for the combined intervention group, whilst the SDQ difference was 0.79 in favour of the control group.

However, Satisfaction with the Parenting Role was higher for the intervention group at T2 (difference of 2.09) and T3 (difference of 4.90). Combining these differences with the cost differences at T2 and over the whole follow-up period results in ICERs of £731 and £337 per point of improvement on the Satisfaction with Parenting scale.

The interventions did not result in reduced likelihood of lost production. At T2, six parents from the combined intervention group had had time off work compared to four in the control group. At T3, the numbers were seven and three respectively.

Discussion

The children and families in this study used a wide range of services before, during and after the interventions were received.[6] The combined intervention group had significantly higher costs over the post-treatment follow-up, but the longer term difference compared with the control group was not significant. In terms of improvement in the children's

---

[6] There are only limited data on service use among children in the general population. The General Household Survey (2006) indicates that 0–4-year-olds have an average of five GP contacts per year and 5–15-year-olds have two per year. This would equate to costs of £150 and £60 pa respectively (Curtis, 2007). In our study the GP costs over the entire study period were £105 for the cognitive behavioural approach group, £168 for the education programme group and £160 for the routine care group. As such, the GP costs appear to be broadly in line with the population norm for the age group.

psychosocial problems, this suggests that the interventions were not cost effective. However, outcomes for parents were improved in terms of increased satisfaction with their parenting role. It could be argued that this is a reflection of confidence, which will, in turn, form the basis of future effective parenting of troubled children. It is therefore a value judgement as to whether a cost of £731 per unit improvement in satisfaction with parenting in the short term or £337 in the longer term represents good value for money.

Table 8.1

Number (%) of participants using services and total (mean) service costs: baseline

Service	Cognitive behavioural approach group (N = 10)	Educational programme group (N = 10)	Routine care group (N = 18)
Educational psychologist	0 (0%)/£0	2 (20%)/£188 (£94)	1 (6%)/£94 (£94)
Welfare officer	0 (0%)/£0 (£0)	0 (0%)/£0 (£0)	0 (0%)/£0 (£0)
Classroom assistant/ special education needs co-ordinator	4 (40%)/£8,551 (£2,138)	3 (30%)/£2,859 (£953)	4 (22%)/£11,351 (£2,838)
Hospital – A&E	2 (20%)/£168 (£84)	2 (20%)/£252 (£126)	2 (20%)/£504 (£252)
Hospital – outpatient	3 (30%)/£276 (£92)	3 (30%)/£1,012 (£337)	5 (28%)/£644 (£129)
Hospital – operation	1 (10%)/£587 (£587)	1 (10%)/£1,205 (£1,205)	0 (0%)/£0 (£0)
School nurse	1 (10%)/£16 (£16)	4 (40%)/£58 (£14)	6 (33%)/£257 (£43)
Health visitor	3 (30%)/£387 (£129)	2 (20%)/£373 (£186)	5 (28%)/£520 (£104)
Dentist/optician	10 (100%)/£417 (£42)	10 (100%)/£509 (£51)	15 (83%)/£398 (£27)

Service	Cognitive behavioural approach group (N = 10)	Educational programme group (N = 10)	Routine care group (N = 18)
GP	9 (90%)/£403 (£45)	9 (90%)/£644 (£72)	14 (78%)/£1,014 (£72)
Paediatrician	5 (50%)/£253 (£51)	4 (40%)/£429 (£107)	5 (28%)/£552 (£110)
Child development centre	0 (0%)/£0 (£0)	0 (0%)/£0 (£0)	0 (0%) / £0 (£0)
CAMHS	2 (20%)/£516 (£258)	0 (0%)/£0 (£0)	2 (11%)/£301 (£151)
Speech therapist and hearing specialist	3 (30%)/£385 (£128)	2 (20%)/£127 (£63)	4 (22%)/£118 (£30)
Family therapist, individual therapist, and other counselling	0 (0%)/£0 (£0)	2 (20%)/£1,910 (£955)	3 (17%)/£944 (£315)
Home help/care worker	0 (0%)/£0 (£0)	1 (10%)/£4,370 (£4,370)	0 (0%)/£0 (£0)
Day care centre	0 (0%)/£0 (£0)	0 (0%)/£0 (£0)	1 (6%)/£10,822 (£10,822)
Social services nursery school place	0 (0%)/£0 (£0)	0 (0%)/£0 (£0)	0 (0%)/£0 (£0)
After-school club	3 (30%)/£3,501 (£1,167)	2 (20%)/£3,046 (£1,523)	4 (22%)/£2,821 (£705)
Other support	1 (10%)/£792 (£792)	1 (10%)/£932 (£932)	0 (0%)/£0 (£0)
Child social worker, family support social worker, and other social worker	9 (90%)/£13,319 (£1,480)	10 (100%)/£13,689 (£1,369)	17 (94%)/£23,687 (£1,393)
Total costs (excluding intervention)	**£29,571 (£2,957)**	**£31,603 (£3,160)**	**£54,027 (£3,001)**

Table 8.2

Number (%) of participants using services and total (mean) service costs: T2

Service	Cognitive behavioural approach group (N = 9)	Educational programme group (N = 9)	Routine care group (N = 18)
Educational psychologist	0 (0%)/£0 (£0)	2 (22%)/£141 (£71)	0 (0%)/£0 (£0)
Welfare officer	0 (0%)/£0 (£0)	0 (0%)/£0 (£0)	0 (0%)/£0 (£0)
Classroom assistant/ special education needs co-ordinator	3 (33%)/£5,273 (£1,758)	5 (56%)/£3,711 (£742)	3 (17%)/£2,477 (£826)
Hospital – A&E	4 (44%)/£504 (£126)	2 (22%)/£168 (£84)	4 (22%)/£336 (£84)
Hospital – outpatient	1 (11%)/£92 (£92)	1 (11%)/£460 (£460)	3 (17%)/£736 (£245)
Hospital – operation	0 (0%)/£0 (£0)	1 (11%)/£1,205 (£1,205)	0 (0%)/£0 (£0)
School nurse	2 (22%)/£26 (£13)	5 (56%)/£102 (£20)	5 (28%)/£71 (£14)
Health visitor	3 (33%)/£387 (£129)	3 (33%)/£667 (£222)	2 (11%)/£194 (£97)
Dentist/optician	8 (89%)/£397 (£50)	9 (100%)/£384 (£43)	11 (61%)/£552 (£50)
GP	6 (67%)/£221 (£37)	9 (100%)/£728 (£81)	9 (50%)/£811 (£90)
Paediatrician	2 (22%)/£115 (£58)	2 (22%)/£138 (£69)	3 (17%)/£554 (£185)
Child development centre	0 (0%)/£0 (£0)	0 (0%)/£0 (£0)	1 (6%)/£3 (£3)
CAMHS	4 (44%)/£2,243 (£561)	1 (11%)/£86 (£86)	2 (11%)/£258 (£129)
Speech therapist and hearing specialist	2 (22%)/£260 (£130)	4 (44%)/£106 (£27)	4 (22%)/£227 (£57)

Service	Cognitive behavioural approach group (N = 9)	Educational programme group (N = 9)	Routine care group (N = 18)
Family therapist, individual therapist, and other counselling	1 (11%)/£402 (£402)	2 (22%)/£1,307 (£653)	3 (17%)/£436 (£145)
Home help/care worker	0 (0%)/£0 (£0)	0 (0%)/£0 (£0)	2 (11%)/£2,546 (£1,273)
Day care centre	1 (11%)/£65 (£65)	0 (0%)/£0 (£0)	1 (6%)/£2,236 (£2,236)
Social services nursery school place	0 (0%)/£0 (£0)	0 (0%)/£0 (£0)	0 (0%)/£0 (£0)
After-school club	4 (44%)/£2,681 (£670)	4 (44%)/£3,467 (£867)	5 (28%)/£7,972 (£1,594)
Other support	0 (0%)/£0 (£0)	2 (22%)/£275 (£138)	3 (17%)/£672 (£224)
Child social worker, family support social worker, and other social worker	6 (67%)/£5,897 (£983)	8 (89%)/£11,835 (£1,479)	17 (94%)/£9,465 (£557)
Total costs (excluding intervention)	**£18,563 (£2,063)**	**£24,779 (£2,753)**	**£29,546 (£1,641)**

Note: Mean costs (in brackets) are arrived at by dividing costs per group in the trial by the number of cases in that group.

Table 8.3

Number (%) of participants using services and total (mean) service costs: T3

Service	Cognitive behavioural approach group (N = 10)	Educational programme group (N = 9)	Routine care group (N = 17)
Educational psychologist	1 (10%)/£282 (£282)	1 (11%)/£188 (£188)	1 (6%)/£94 (£94)
Welfare officer	0 (0%)/£0 (£0)	0 (0%)/£0 (£0)	1 (6%)/£50 (£50)
Classroom assistant/ special education needs co-ordinator	4 (40%)/£8,111 (£2,028)	5 (56%)/£1,623 (£325)	5 (29%)/£2,704 (£541)
Hospital – A&E	2 (20%)/£420 (£210)	3 (33%)/£336 (£112)	0 (0%)/£0 (£0)
Hospital – outpatient	2 (20%)/£460 (£230)	2 (22%)/£184 (£92)	4 (24%)/£644 (£161)
Hospital – operation	0 (0%)/£0 (£0)	1 (11%)/£1,205 (£1,205)	0 (0%)/£0 (£0)
School nurse	1 (10%)/£21 (£21)	2 (22%)/£126 (£63)	2 (12%)/£16 (£8)
Health visitor	1 (10%)/£54 (£54)	2 (22%)/£215 (£108)	2 (12%)/£237 (£118)
Dentist/optician	8 (80%)/£348 (£45)	9 (100%)/£629 (£70)	15 (88%)/£479 (£32)
GP	4 (40%)/£273 (£68)	6 (67%)/£520 (£87)	10 (59%)/£702 (£70)
Paediatrician	0 (0%)/£0 (£0)	4 (44%)/£813 (£203)	3 (18%)/£238 (£79)
Child development centre	1 (10%)/£24 (£24)	0 (0%)/£0 (£0)	2 (12%)/£162 (£81)
CAMHS	2 (20%)/£1,118 (£559)	0 (0%)/£0 (£0)	3 (18%)/£1,118 (£373)
Speech therapist and hearing specialist	1 (10%)/£10 (£10)	2 (22%)/£70 (£35)	4 (24%)/£97 (£24)
Family therapist, individual therapist, and other counselling	4 (40%)/£1,327 (£332)	4 (44%)/£1,355 (£339)	2 (12%)/£335 (£168)
Home help/care worker	0 (0%)/£0 (£0)	0 (0%)/£0 (£0)	2 (12%)/£10,526 (£5,263)

Service	Cognitive behavioural approach group (N = 10)	Educational programme group (N = 9)	Routine care group (N = 17)
Day care centre	0 (0%)/£0 (£0)	1 (11%)/£543 (£543)	1 (6%)/£4,471 (£4,471)
Social services nursery school place	0 (0%)/£0 (£0)	0 (0%)/£0 (£0)	0 (0%)/£0 (£0)
After-school club	4 (40%)/£1,377 (£344)	3 (33%)/£790 (£263)	5 (29%)/£2,363 (£473)
Other support	0 (0%)/£0 (£0)	1 (11%)/£851 (£851)	3 (18%)/£972 (£324)
Child social worker, family support social worker, and other social worker	4 (40%)/£1,889 (£472)	8 (89%)/£3,555 (£444)	12 (71%)/£4,331 (£361)
Total costs (excluding intervention)	**£15,714 (£1,571)**	**£13,003 (£1,445)**	**£29,539 (£1,738)**

Figure 8.1
Mean service costs at baseline, T2 and T3

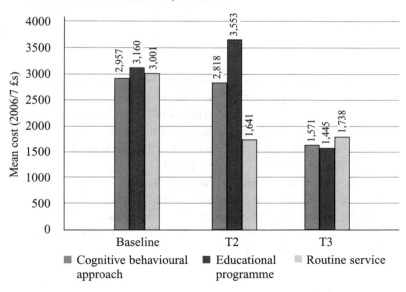

Figure 8.2
Median service costs at baseline, T2 and T3

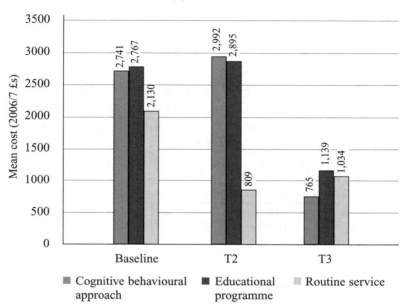

Summary

- A cost-effectiveness analysis estimates service use and costs, and links them with outcomes after receipt of the services.
- The costs of the full range of services used by adoptive parents for their adopted child or for themselves in the month before baseline, immediately after the intervention and in the six months before the final follow-up interview were measured.
- In terms of improving the children's psychosocial problems, the costs of the intervention were higher without significant improvement.
- Combining overall costs with differences in outcomes showed a cost of £731 per unit improvement in Satisfaction with Parenting Role in the short term and £337 in the longer term.

9 Case vignettes from the intervention and control groups

The point of this adoption support trial was to compare *group* outcomes and these represent the foremost findings of the study. As it turned out, by the six-month follow-up, group means on the Strengths and Difficulties Questionnaire (SDQ) were not significantly different, whether parenting advice was received or not. Falling below the cut-off point indicates a move from abnormal and borderline to the normal level of problems, but neither the intervention group nor the control group achieved this. Given that the study was designed to test the intervention on a group selected as highly problematic, these children proved resistant to change, at least in the short term.

However, we thought it of interest, having analysed the group-based data, to move to the individual case level. Closer scrutiny of the children's total parent rated SDQ scores at baseline (T1), post-intervention (T2) and six-month follow-up (T3) shows that within each group changes were indeed taking place: there was movement in scores for individual cases, both rises and falls, and lack of movement in others. One case showed improvement at post-intervention but then fell back and another was worse at post-intervention but then improved. Nevertheless, it was possible to allocate all other cases to three broad groups: "no change", "improved" or "worse". Brief illustrations of cases representing each group will follow. Information on which the vignettes are based comes mostly from the three face-to-face research interviews with the adopters.

In presenting the case vignettes, changes have been made to preserve confidential information. Adoptive families may feel they recognise their own experiences, but should bear in mind that many of the children shared the same background circumstances – for example, severe neglect and domestic violence were very common, as was care from an older sibling. In general, the types of behaviour and distress shown by the children at the time of placement were also very similar, although there were obviously some specific differences. In addition, many of the adopters shared the same sense of not having been very well prepared for these aspects of "their" child.

Three case vignettes from the intervention group

No change – started with high SDQ scores, stayed high and above the cut-off (T1: 24, T2: 25, T3: 25)

E had experienced severe neglect by her mother when the mother worked as a prostitute. She would leave her for hours in a high chair or pushchair without feeding her. E also suffered from the effects of her mother's pre- and post-natal substance abuse, severe domestic violence, physical abuse and rejection following the birth of her younger brother. The quality of both physical and emotional parenting was poor in her first two years, with lack of secure attachment figures. She behaved in a very sexualised way at age three years. Her mother attended a parenting group and social work files record "some benefits" for about six months when E was four years old. On entering care, she had poor hand-eye coordination, poor gross motor skills, attention and concentration difficulties, and was only toilet trained by age six. However, on the positive side, she was said to be sociable and friendly. She had language and learning difficulties and a Statement of Special Educational Needs (SEN). The adoptive mother was not told of the Statement of SEN before E's arrival.

Between the ages of two and six, E was frequently admitted to care and then returned home – in all, about 20 short-term placements. She was placed for adoption with her younger brother in a family with three children of their own. However, the placement broke down as she was aggressive to her own brother. Five more foster placements followed up to the age of eight years, when she was placed with her current single parent adoptive mother.

Her new mother said there was a three year gap between "preparation to adopt" and E arriving and she did not remember being told at that stage that there could be severe behavioural problems, like the frequent temper tantrums.

On arrival in her adoptive home, E was very clingy, but could also be ill-tempered when thwarted. She had tantrums lasting two to three hours.

The GP referred her to CAMHS, but the (adoptive) mother did not think they displayed much understanding of adoption. The adoptive mother was in a profession that enabled her to have considerable understanding of E's special needs. She took the parenting advice very seriously but struggled to complete the homework. Although she found the parenting sessions relevant and informative, she did not find time to practise the advice before moving on to something else and wanted more space between the sessions. E's continuing problems were her disobedience and aggressive behaviour. The adviser helped the adoptive mother to modify the "consequences" approach. This was a technique she was already employing, but the adviser enabled her to be less condemnatory and more supportive and sympathetic in its use. Apart from this, she doubted if any parenting strategy was working at this stage.

In the final interview, the adopter admitted she had been horrified by how she had been launched into being an adoptive parent: 'They just said give us a ring if you need help'. She thought her current social worker was too inexperienced: 'You know more than I do about children' was not what she wanted to hear when she asked for advice. E's tantrums had become fewer but were more intense and seemed to come out of nowhere. They had attended a CAMHS appointment but the mother felt patronised, didn't get her questions answered and after two sessions did not return. Various diagnoses were made including Anti-Social Disorder, dyspraxia and Semantic Pragmatic Disorder. Art therapy was suggested for the child.

The Visual Analogue Scales indicated that E's behaviour continued at the same level of difficulty but that attachment to her mother was better. She still had very low self-esteem and was hyper-vigilant. The mother found E's ability to understand cause and effect to be very poor and came to use "consequences" much more to emphasise the sequences of events. She used "time-out" only after a tantrum or a very angry outburst. The mother was making use of the Adoption UK website, posting problems and receiving answers.

Improved – started above and ended below the cut–off (T1: 23, T2: 10, T3: 8)

J, a little boy, was placed with a couple when aged three-and-a-half. He was first admitted to care aged nearly two and with periods of holiday care, and one of respite care, had had five moves by the time he finally came to the adoptive family. J had experienced severe neglect, sexual and physical abuse by his father and rejection by his mother. He grew up in severe poverty and his mother had learning difficulties and severe ill-health. Some of his older siblings were main carers for much of the time. His mother hit and smacked a lot and only his older sister showed warmth towards him. He had delayed development across the board, and possible Attention Deficit/Hyperactivity Disorder, was attention-seeking and rebuffed cuddles and demonstrations of warmth from adults.

When faced with the range of J's problems, the couple found that they were not well-enough prepared. They lacked specific information about him and thought they could have been given more understanding of the problems and shown how to deal with them. They found him 'a very angry little boy'.

By the second interview they had profited from the parenting advice and were using the strategies that were suggested. The adviser provided them with a great deal of welcome reassurance as they had felt very isolated after the legal adoption. The parenting sessions made them more understanding of the child and they came to use play and praise more often. The boy's father said: 'I'm more confident and firmer, and able to ignore more often'. They said they hated the "homework" but agreed that when they 'read it in black and white' it made more sense and confirmed that it was the right way to improve their parenting. They planned to go on using the advice and 'to look at things in a new light'.

The adopters felt they had become more understanding once they had time to digest the advice and begun to see the child's attitude change. This was partly put down to completion of the adoption process and consolidating the feeling of being a family. They described how J used to laugh when being told off but would now get upset and apologise. He also began to go to his new parents for comfort, which he had not done at placement. His destructive behaviour was diminishing all the time.

The couple reported a dramatic change by the third interview. J's new school was a great success. They had changed their handling of emotional problems in that, initially, if he showed signs of anxiety or behaved badly they used to leave him as they didn't know how to deal with it. But then they started to talk to him at these times and explain more to him. J was said to have improved in several ways: he was better behaved and more helpful to other children and his anger, although still there, was less obvious. There were, however, remaining problems like disinhibited attachment, as J often approached strangers and had to be called back. The adopters admitted, 'This is our biggest battle at the moment'.

On the Visual Analogues Scales they reported strong improvements in the three areas: emotional, behavioural and attachment problems. They concluded that the child was developing well and that they were running smoothly as a family unit. They thought J would eventually be able to lead an independent life, which they had not thought would be the case when he had first moved in. They had not received any other support service except the parenting advice.

Got worse – scores started above the cut off and rose (T1: 19; T2: 30; T3: 32)

R was placed, with his brother, when nearly five years old with adoptive parents. Having come into care at two years, he had had a number of moves to friends, back to his father when his mother died and to foster homes before coming to this couple. R was born prematurely, suffered neglect and domestic violence, was diagnosed as non-organic failure to thrive and possible dyspraxia. He was on the special needs register when placed for adoption.

The adopters would have liked more information on his problems as these were only briefly mentioned and generally seemed underplayed. The records they were given were not up to date, some details did not match and the medical records lacked important information. (However, some reports on the file did suggest there would be a need for specialist help.) The social worker was said not to be very supportive when they ran into problems and was not sufficiently available. Therefore, many problems took them by surprise and more problems emerged as they got to know him. He was not seen as a happy child and they did not find him genuinely affectionate, although he could be over-demonstrative with false-seeming hugs and cuddles. At first he had tantrums that lasted for three hours and he screamed when dressed or undressed. He also would not talk but simply stared at his new parents. He was aggressive towards his younger brother of whom he was inordinately jealous. They found the various techniques to improve his behaviour worked for a day or two and then tailed off.

By the second interview, the adopters thought they were starting to understand his needs but with no real change yet. He was diagnosed with Reactive Attachment Disorder and thought to be generally operating at the level of a three-year-old. They discovered that the birth mother was unable to read and had been to special school. Their social worker said she thought these were the most emotionally damaged children she had ever placed: she said this well over a year after placement!

In relation to the parenting advice, the couple offered very positive testimony but thought the issues were so great that ten sessions weren't enough. They found the adviser "pretty fantastic" as she made them think about what they did and how the children reacted: 'She was much more supportive than anyone else we have had; she left us feeling uplifted'. They had not expected the course would be as useful as it was. The advice they were keen to follow was to "play, play and play" and to practise "ignoring". The adviser gave them more understanding of "where R is coming from" and they came to shout less and give more cuddles.

They also came to use explaining, consequences and ignoring more frequently and consistently. The boy was still overly charming to strangers and might inappropriately hold their hands and his social skills were very immature. Social services had not been very responsive to mini-crises and on occasion the parents had to threaten to give the children back to get a response.

By the third interview, the adopters were complaining of poor social services support and by now were dealing with their fourth social worker. The boy was still found to be very controlling, especially since receiving "Theraplay" sessions. This was undertaken by a social worker said to be inexperienced in dealing with the strong emotions aroused in her by the child and poor at structuring the sessions. The adopters thought their son could not cope with the "freedom" the sessions offered.

Tantrums had become less extended but just as frequent and R was still argumentative, volatile and socially immature. On the Visual Analogue Scales the parents disagreed on whether he had improved emotionally but they concurred that attachment to them had grown, while behavioural problems had worsened.

In the first interview R was reported as "drawn to" strangers and this was still true at the post-intervention follow-up. He had appeared to understand why it was not safe to talk to them, but still persisted in doing so. In relation to the future, one adopter tended to expect the worst, but the partner was more hopeful. They were annoyed that the parent advice sessions ended after ten weeks and were in search of the type of therapy promoted by Dan Hughes (2004).

Three case vignettes from the control group

No change – started with a high score, remained high and above the cut–off (T1: 25, T2: 25, T3: 23)

V had lived a chaotic life in her birth family, which had moved home 18 times before her second birthday. A similar pattern continued until she was taken into care and placed with a foster family at the age of five. V had suffered neglect, physical abuse, inadequate nutrition and sexual abuse by her father and half-brother. Her mother was a drug addict and father alcoholic. Many of these details emerged after placement.

V was placed at seven years with her younger sibling. The adopters said they thought they were as well prepared as they could realistically be, but certainly weren't prepared for her behaviour, which was very alarming and overwhelming. They were not prepared for the rejection by both children, who wanted to go back to their previous foster carers', especially as they had been told that the children were "ready to move".

The parents said the first few days were awful as V was so rejecting. She slept and ate well at first and then started refusing food that they had been told she liked. She screamed and cried and talked to herself and they were particularly shocked by her extreme expression of anger. The adopters had asked for professional help, were waiting for an appointment at CAMHS and were making use of a parent support line.

By the second interview, the adopters described disobedience, dangerous behaviour and rampaging rages with biting, kicking and spitting. The child would ask for and reject affection at the same time. On the other hand, she would become anxious if taken out, sucking her thumb in silence. The adopters said it was hard to say if anything had had an impact on her behaviour.

By the third interview, improvements were noted in a number of areas: fewer rages and less impulsive behaviour, more appropriate affection seeking and expression of emotion. In talking to her more, the parents learned what prompted the rages, which then affected their handling style. However, the SDQ score on the emotional problems scale was still high and less improvement was shown on emotional problems on the Visual Analogue Scale. The adopters also felt that when V showed affection it didn't feel entirely natural or she would first ask for affection, then reject it and distance herself. The adopters had come to appreciate that the challenge would be a long-term one.

They were appreciative of the service from the local CAMHS and its specialist attachment clinic – such praise was unique from the control group parents. The parents attended eight CAMHS sessions and felt the extent of the problems was acknowledged and were encouraged by the advice that such children need to be parented differently. They received both reassurance and behaviour management advice. For instance, in relation to the controlling behaviour, they were advised to think of specific activities where their daughter could safely be allowed to be in control.

This family also devised their own methods and learned from several sources. They attempted to reward all good behaviour as recommended by their social worker and by the Adoption UK website message board. They felt that closely supervising the children in a calming atmosphere, but as though they were younger than their chronological ages, had reduced the rages.

Improved – a fall in scores but still above the cut-off (T1: 28, T2: 28, T3: 16)

S had been placed on the Child Protection Register even before birth and she was subsequently taken into care due to neglect, physical abuse and non-organic failure to thrive. Later behaviour suggested some inappropriate sexual knowledge or experience. There were multiple placement moves. Although the adopters had been given a lot of background information, they claimed that the full extent of problems had been 'played down'.

They found the preparation classes useful in talking about what to expect, but they didn't feel appropriately prepared for how to cope with the behaviour they finally faced. They would have liked to have had the expertise of a child psychiatrist straight away to help understand why the child was behaving in a certain way.

S was placed with the adopters when she was four-and-a-half. They found her very loud and intrusive to begin with as she followed her mother around all the time. Her behaviour was demanding and controlling. She had temper tantrums, was rude and bossy and screamed a lot. They used star charts, rewards, sanctions and encouragement. They had difficulty judging if she was genuinely upset or being histrionic. They reported her difficulty in showing "real" feelings; she had shallow attachments and would walk off with strangers.

By the second interview, the mother had gone back to work part-time but the child had felt 'rejected all over again' and she started to self-harm. The move to junior school led to an increase in violent tantrums. Problems with distorted relationships included risky behaviour with strangers and running off. She would talk to anybody but especially those with dogs and would wander off with them: 'We have explained about danger but she just doesn't see it'. The adopters thought that V had the ability to display affection, although it felt "false" sometimes. The main behaviour problems were lying, cheating and stealing and obstructive, controlling and aggressive behaviour. The parents said nothing worked all the time, although grounding and reward charts worked some of the time and they always tried to calm the situation.

This family were struggling without the benefit of structured parenting advice. They were able to arrange to receive social work visits but they were not thought very profitable. They drew on other sources of information and experimented. The adopters tried to distract the child or provide treats, an approach which was different from their original tactics. They got new ideas from many sources: from friends, other adopters and books. They thought they were using different techniques because of their growing understanding of the child.

By the third interview, some problems had reduced, but overall the behaviour was still very difficult: 'Anything that she doesn't want to do (is met with) a violent negative reaction'. Developing friendships with local children led to more disputes in the home, as the child wanted to be out all the time. If the parents tried to control her, she would scream and accuse them of hitting her. The Visual Analogue Scales indicated mild improvement in behaviour and distorted relationships but not in emotional problems.

The adopters had eight sessions with the Family Centre, which provided the "Parent–Child Game" but they didn't find it very effective although they felt listened to. They were disappointed at the lack of individual work with the child. Improvements in behaviour, such as they were, came about because it emerged in the Family Centre work that the child was frightened of being taken away and she revealed that: 'Being adopted is the best thing that has happened to me'.

The adopters thought they had learned through experience to be more consistent and they were dealing with the child's high level of anxiety by reassurance and affection. However, they did not think any of their parenting changes appeared to be having an effect on attachment problems or aggression. They were still hoping for a professional assessment of their child and appropriate intervention.

Got worse – started at the cut-off and rose (T1: 13, T2: 11. T3: 19)

A, a mixed heritage girl, was born prematurely with a small head circumference and was initially left in the "special care baby unit". She experienced neglect related to maternal drug and alcohol abuse problems and severe domestic violence. Both parents were drug abusers. When her mother was living in bed and breakfast accommodation, the owners alerted Social Services to her poor parenting and A was taken into care aged 21 months. After one foster home, she was placed (with her brother) for adoption with a couple with plenty of parenting experience with older children.

The adopters were well prepared for general behavioural problems but they needed to understand and have strategies for dealing with puzzling behaviour. For instance, they questioned why she would ask female visitors to attend to her in the toilet rather than the adoptive mother and why she would insert herself between other children and their mothers. She would also make inappropriate approaches to unfamiliar women.

They found her disobedient, picky about food, likely to soil herself if she didn't get her way and lacking in respect for other people's possessions. However, they came to regard her "bad" behaviour as an expression of sadness at losing her family.

By the second interview, a little improvement was reported in some areas: A was eating better at the table, following instructions more responsively and becoming more affectionate toward other children in the family. She had no more "irrational" fears, nightmares or hand-wringing. However, in other domains her behaviour appeared to be getting worse. Her behaviour was described as bordering on the uncontrollable when out of the house and disobedient in the home. She would attack her brother, especially if their mother gave him attention. She lied, was attention seeking, shouted a lot and barged into people on purpose. The adopters said they dealt with this inconsistently: sometimes shouting too much and using smacking when they had not done so before. They found the bad behaviour made them lose patience which they would not have done previously.

By the third interview, A was described as wilful, rivalrous with siblings, panicky and "hyped up". Her anger was being expressed even more strongly. The adopters found it difficult to identify whether she was feeling sad sometimes or being manipulative. They thought she was over-whelmed by having to share her parents with anyone. However, she had become less impulsive and more attached to her adoptive father. They were trying to modify their parenting techniques by giving the child a clear warning and using "consequences" more often. On one occasion she went off with another woman in the playground. The Visual Analogue Scale showed a slight improvement in emotional difficulties and attach-ment, but a deterioration in behaviour, especially over-activity.

Discussion

These case vignettes have been presented to try to gain a better under-standing of the relationship between the parenting intervention and the case outcome in a group of children selected for the study because of their high level of challenging behaviour. They had been in their adoptive families for at least 3 to 18 months and were followed up for an average of 11 months. It is probably true that these children were not very resilient to the experiences they had encountered. Their earlier adverse experiences included longer periods in care and more moves between households than the children with low SDQ scores.

Most clearly, the vignettes remind us of just how challenging the children could be. The cases contained the familiar range of problems of ex-care children: indiscriminate attachments and slow growth of attach-ment to (yet another) new parent; controlling, inappropriate and socially immature behaviour; obliviousness to risk; and distancing and "false" affection. They showed dysregulated emotional expression with very extended temper tantrums, screaming and tearful sessions. The adopters were trying to mitigate the troublesome behaviour as best they could and also to adapt their own parenting to the child's needs.

The three selected intervention group adopters were appreciative of the sessions of parenting advice and felt they were making positive changes, but the quality of intervention with the parents did not guarantee changes in the child, at least over this period of time. But even in the case that had persistent, indeed, escalating child problems, the family had been helped and felt some guarded optimism for the future.

As for the control group cases, although they were not receiving the parenting advice sessions, they were trying to take advantage of whatever help was on offer or could be gleaned from a number of sources. These adopters experimented and learned to concentrate on what seemed to work best. They made efforts to be consistent, to try to understand the "bad" behaviour and to create a calm, nurturing atmosphere regardless of the challenges. There were frustrations at the inadequate professional help on offer, although one control group family did manage to receive a more intensive support service, which they appreciated as relevant and helpful.

In general, however, few control group cases had received anything like the ten week parenting advice sessions.

Closer inspection of the individual cases revealed that outcomes were frequently not across the board but showed improvement in some domains and not in others. Attachment could be growing slowly towards the adopters but the child could still behave indiscriminately on occasion towards strangers. Temper tantrums might become less intense, but lying and stealing were still a problem. In the Maudsley Adoption and Fostering Study (Quinton *et al*, 1998), it was found that very difficult behaviour could be tolerated by new parents as long as there were signs of growing attachment to them.

The cases presented here were selected solely on the basis of high SDQ scores and the children's scores did not always correspond with the fuller parental reports on the children in the research interviews. This was to some extent expected because the SDQ is not a comprehensive measure designed for maltreated children in transition to a new family. Adopters reported changes that were significant to them but are not SDQ items. For example, if the child appeared happier, more relaxed, better able to play, more communicative or capable of more "genuine" affection, these non-SDQ items were taken as signs of progress by the adopters.

Clearly, many factors within the children (for example, their temperament and intelligence) and in their prior life experiences will contribute to, or prove an obstacle to, their developmental progress in the adoptive home. The match with the new parents, the new family environment and indeed the characteristics of the immediate and extended family, neighbourhood and school environment will also exert an influence. Considering these multiple contributory factors, it is perhaps not surprising that the children's pattern of problems took different directions in the relatively short term. In this study, positive parenting changes were shown more frequently in the intervention group, but patterns of change in their children were more divergent.

Summary

- These case vignettes have been presented to try to gain a better understanding of the relationship between the parenting intervention and individual case outcome.
- The selected intervention group adopters were appreciative of the sessions of parenting advice and felt they were making positive changes, but the intervention with the parents did not guarantee changes in the child, at least in this early phase of the adoptive placement.
- Although the control group cases had mostly not received anything like the ten week parenting advice sessions, these adopters experimented and learned to concentrate on what seemed to work best.
- The children's patterns of problems were complex and took different directions as they were subject to multiple influences in their transition to a new home.

10 Parents' approaches to handling their children's current problems

One section of each of the three face-to-face research interviews was concerned with the ways in which parents were handling difficulties the child might be presenting. We were interested in how the adopters dealt with problems known to be a challenge with this group of late placement children. In the next chapter we present the information the parents gave us about the services they had received outside the intervention study; here we present the ways in which the parents were variably able to meet their children's needs and influence their behaviour and adjustment.

In order to focus the interview discussions more clearly, we asked about any current problems in three specific domains: emotional distress, misbehaviour and problems of regulating relationships. In this latter domain, we asked about whether the parents felt that their child was averse to close family relationships or cold towards them; whether, if warmth was shown, it was – in their view – "genuine"; and whether their child tended to approach or trust strangers in ways that they thought were inappropriate. In this chapter we discuss the strategies the parents were using to help the child or to correct the behaviour in each domain. We were well aware that the children's behaviour in these three domains was often linked: the emotionally frozen child failing to respond to warmth from parents, and behaving aggressively to siblings or school peers.

Table 10.1 shows the proportions of children showing these problems at the time of each research interview.

Table 10.1
Children showing problems in three key domains at each time point

	Time 1		Time 2		Time 3	
	N	*%*	*N*	*%*	*N*	*%*
Emotional distress	24	65	29	78	32	86
Misbehaviour	37	100	36	97	36	97
Distorted personal relationships	24	65	27	68	20	55

Emotional distress

First, we asked adopters whether their child was showing signs of emotional distress with abnormal frequency, or whether their child's responses seemed inappropriate or extreme, including children who appeared "frozen" and unable to respond at all – which indicated to their parents that their responses to certain situations were completely inappropriate.

A single example will illustrate what several parents said:

> *When he arrived he seemed emotionally untouched by the loss of a happy foster family. I felt it was wrong he didn't cry. He seemed enthusiastic to go away with strangers (us). He didn't appear distressed; very quiet – unnaturally able to cope. He refused to talk about his feelings.*

As can be seen from Table 10.1, parents reported a rising proportion experiencing emotional distress over time. There are several possible explanations for this. For example, parents may have become more sensitive to the ways in which their child was showing distress; or they may have made it more possible for their child to express fears or sadness which initially appeared extreme. There were almost equal proportions in the combined intervention group and the control group at each time point. At T1, in response to upset behaviour, most parents either talked to the children to reassure them (45%) or used physical affection, like giving a hug (18%) or both (5%). A minority (8%) used distraction.

Of those reporting that their child experienced emotional distress at T1, significantly more of the combined intervention group said they were responding differently after the intervention at T2 and at T3 (see Table 10.2 and Table 10.3). The following are examples of these changed methods and their effects.

> An intervention group parent said at T2: *She is still undemonstrative – probably due to a fear that she will have to move on again* [There had been a previous breakdown of placement]. *She doesn't express it as sadness, but we are more aware of what is going on inside her head and reassure her over permanence, and how much she is loved. We can now reassure her the best way; we learnt this from the parent adviser.*

Another intervention group parent said at T1:

I cuddle her; she likes to sit on my lap; we talk about why she's upset. She loves cuddles, attention and praise. She asks for a dummy and sucks her thumb, which is quite odd for her age (c. six years).

At T3:

She is more confident in every area. She is a bit less clingy, but still more than her siblings; not very adventurous. She's more positive, happier, and less anxious. I now allow her to be clingy – I have to guide her emotionally and intellectually; (in this domain) she is much younger than her years.

Table 10.2

Parents' report of using new methods of handling their child's emotional distress at T2 compared with T1

	Combined intervention group	Control group	Totals
We handle problem differently	9	2	11
We use the same methods	5	13	18
Totals	**14**	**15**	**29**

χ^2 7.9, df 1, p< 0.005

Table 10.3

Parents' report of using new methods of handling their child's emotional distress at T3 compared with T2

	Combined intervention group	Control group	Totals
Quite differently	11	5	16
The same or a mix of old and new	5	11	16
Totals	**16**	**16**	**32**

χ^2 4.5, df 1, p< 0.03

As Table 10.3 shows, some families in the control group also started to use new approaches to help their child, and the following example shows that this led to the child being able to express distress appropriately. Control Group parent at T1 said.

We deal with his (considerable) distress with cuddles and talking about it; he is a very cuddly tactile child. Reassure that he is loved and that he is staying.

At T2:

He clings to us in new situations and with new people (unusual at his age); nowadays we just let that happen until he is happy to let go, which he does after a few minutes.

At T3:

If there were any, they are gone. He's so much more secure and happy with us and trusts us. Out of the blue last week he said he wanted to look at his life book pictures and he did this without any problems this time.

Not all the children made progress in this domain. The following is an example of a child whose parents felt that he had made almost no progress. The family were in the control group but had attended two local authority programmes designed to help adoptive parents, and the child had been with them for two-and-a-half years; they were very disappointed that he had not made more progress:

At T1:

We cuddle him and encourage him to talk about what is upsetting him. He will sit on our laps and cuddle up; doesn't "clam up", but we need to pick up on snippets of things he says. We try to prepare him for situations; give him the chance of talking about his feelings. [We have learnt that] when he is in trouble at school he "diverts" by crying and saying he is missing his mum; so we talk about that but still point out that he must face up to the consequences of misbehaving.

At T2:

Typically, his sadness or anxieties come out as bad behaviour. For example, he behaved very badly out shopping one day; I ticked him off several times until he broke down in tears and confessed to being worried about seeing his sisters. He winds us up, gets told off, cries and it all comes out, we reassure him and hug and things settle down. He still cannot tell us even though we have reassured him he can tell us if he's worried about anything. We think he doesn't know he's worried; he says 'I just feel angry'.

At T3:

We try to get him to talk to release his anger, but (he seems) petrified to start the ball rolling; he has insight but only after an event. He's only sad when we tell him off or he's feeling sorry for himself; otherwise acts out emotions like being upset when remembering his mother. He feels guilty if he feels angry with her and won't hear a word against her.

At T3, we also asked if the parents thought any of their new responses had been particularly helpful to their child and to say why. Combined intervention group parents at T3 said:

She finds it hard to share her feelings and will not come to you when she's worried about something. We can (now) assess her behaviour for telltale signs; code for needing a chat. I tended to badger her about why she felt something but now I understand how difficult it is for her to say why she's sad.

A control group couple who had been to a course laid on by the local authority and had a two-hour parent consultation with CAMHS said:

We have been taught to describe his feelings to him: 'I think you are feeling . . .' And this has been very useful. I wouldn't have thought of it myself.

Perhaps it is pertinent to add that the family had waited over six months for the CAMHS appointment, which they had found particularly helpful.

Dealing with misbehaviour

At the time of the first interview, all the parents reported that their child "misbehaved" in ways that were causing them sometimes grave concern. For a high proportion of the children this included unprovoked aggression and fighting; children were often biting and kicking their parents and other children; lying, and extreme obstinacy and non-compliance were commonly described. By the time of the third interviews all except one of the parents were still describing their child as having significant behaviour problems, but as we have seen from the Visual Analogue Scale results reported in Chapter 6, the majority thought there had been some "improvement" in behaviour. In a useful example of this apparent contradiction, several parents described their child as still having tantrums which they knew to be inappropriate and found unacceptable at the ages of seven, eight or nine years, but they were happening less frequently or with less intensity or not lasting so long. For those parents there had been definite improvement, although by any standards their child still had serious problems. However, it was also true that parents were learning to handle the difficulties with more understanding or more skill.

A control group parent at T1 said:

She lies and steals; she gets very angry and fights with siblings. Tantrums last for an hour or more before properly calm.

At T3:

Very few tantrums now and can calm down in 20 minutes, whereas it used to take hours. Still fights with her brother, who is developmentally very retarded and constantly provoking her to fight. We give her more expectations of behaviour and she realises she can choose not to behave (well), but rarely makes that choice (now).

At T2 an intervention group parent said:

There has been a big change from last year; there is not a lot (of misbehaviour) now. We use a combination of sending her to her room and talking to her about what she's done and why she shouldn't do it. I am firm but I don't shout any more; I am definitely more firm now.

At T3 this parent said: 'It comes in fits and starts but is much better.'

Tantrums were not the only way in which "misbehaviour" was expressed. Generalised aggression and fighting were common, but new ways of dealing with this also brought about some improvement.

An intervention group parent said at T1:

There is a lot of anger and bad language when he doesn't want to do something; much attention seeking; constant interrupting.

At T2 she said:

He does things when told not to, but doesn't like the consequences; we also distract him. Talk to him more about what is expected and why behaviour isn't acceptable. Talking helps to slow things down and he calms down a lot quicker than six months ago. We learnt that from [parent adviser] and he's taking control of his feelings more now.

At T3 the couple said:

We wait, speak, look and listen to him for five minutes if he acts or speaks in a certain way. There are consequences like no dessert, but there are treats for good behaviour. We did the charts and stars and it wasn't working, so we decided to ignore him for five minutes; done off our own initiative as it gives us more control. [NB. Their intervention course included "ignoring" – see Chapter 2 – so it is possible they were unconsciously drawing on it.] We lay out the options to do the right thing and he is choosing this more often now. Perhaps because he is a bit older and can see the benefit. Sometimes we don't say a word and he doesn't like that but it leaves us in control so the incidents are getting less. We understand him better now and our handling has got better as a result. Staying calm is the best way of dealing with him; shouting and smacking makes him worse – brings back memories of childhood violence maybe (they think he witnessed more than they were told about). He is disobedient and pushes his luck all the time.

Parents were asked to look at a printed card listing common ways of handling misbehaviour (see Chapter 3) and to indicate which responses

Table 10.4
Methods of handling misbehaviour – combined intervention group and control group at T1, T2 &T3

Parent response	T1				T2				T3			
	Combined intervention group		Control group		Combined intervention group		Control group		Combined intervention group		Control group	
	n	%	n	%	n	%	n	%	n	%	n	%
Explain	19	50	19	50	18	50	18	50	18	50	18	50
Tell off	15	48	16	52	15	47	17	53	14	44	18	56
Threaten	13	48	14	52	8	35	15	65	13	50	13	50
Go without	18	53	16	47	16	53	14	47	17	51	16	49
Time-out for <5 minutes	14	48	15	52	10	43	13	57	13	52	12	48
Time-out for >5 minutes	10	56	8	44	9	53	8	47	9	53	8	47
Bribes	7	50	7	50	7	44	9	56	6	43	8	57
Shouting	16	53	14	47	9	39	14	61	10	38	16	62

Note: The T1 column includes data from a family who completed the baseline interview and then withdrew.
(The percentage indicates how many used a particular response in each group.)

they had used to control children's behaviour in the last month. Table 10.4 summarises their responses. It should be noted that this list of parental options does not include "ignoring" the behaviour.

Very little difference was apparent in the way that parents from the two groups dealt with misbehaviour to begin with (T1). Post-intervention (T2) the parents were similar in their use of explaining and making children go without, but considerable differences were evident in the greater use of "threats" (χ^2 =5.9, df 1, p<0.01) and "shouting" (non sig p<0.08) in the control group. At the six-month follow-up (T3), equal proportions again used explaining. Although the control group parents were no longer using more threats, they were still "telling off" (χ^2 = 4.5, df 1, p<0.03) and "shouting" (χ^2 = 4.9, df 1 p<0.02) significantly more than the combined intervention group. Smacking was still rare across the group but was used equally frequently.

It appears that these adopters all preferred "explaining" as a strategy for handling misbehaviour which was consistent over time and independent of the intervention. More angry responses, like telling off and shouting, reduced in the intervention group and increased in the control group.

Problems of distorted and/or inappropriate relationships

Parents reported difficulties for their children in all three areas of appropriate or distorted relationships with other people (Table 10.5). They

Table 10.5
Frequency of types of relationship problems reported (%)

Type of difficulty	Time 1 %	Time 2 %	Time 3 %
Indiscriminate/inappropriate displays of affection or friendliness	57	40	34
Difficulty showing "real" feelings	30	19	22
Cool behaviour, averse to any display of warmth/friendliness	19	30	14

said that indiscriminate friendliness and the problem of showing real feelings diminished, but the problem of the children being "cool" or slightly averse to close affectionate display by their parents was reported more often after the intervention before reducing again. When the frequency of each relationship problem was compared across the combined intervention group and control group, at the three time points, no significant differences were found. These three types of difficulty with appropriate relationships were then summed to give an overall rate of those without and with several difficulties.

Table 10.6
Total personal relationships difficulties [percentages]

Number of areas in which child had relationship difficulties	*Time 1* %	*Time 2* %	*Time 3* %
No difficulties	37	38	48
Difficulty in one area	29	38	36
Difficulties in two areas	29	15	8
Difficulties in three areas	39	12	8

Table 10.6 shows that over time fewer difficulties were reported and those having two or three types decreased. However, about a third of the parents were still reporting difficulties in appropriate personal relationships at the six-month follow-up. The frequency of total personal relationship problems was compared across the combined intervention group and the control group and at the three time points. None showed a significant difference, but "indiscriminate relationships" at T3 appeared less frequent in the intervention group, with the difference approaching significance ($\chi^2 = 2.9$, df = 1, p<0.08).

Parents were asked what they had done to help their child if they did not show "real" affection or did not like being the object of affection. Not surprisingly, families were varyingly successful in achieving change:

She is not hugging everyone now, being more discriminating; under-stands the "code of closeness". Our attachment is loads better, and we have a close and genuine relationship with her now. She knows we will be there for her and is a lot more settled. However, she is still very manipulative and friendship is only useful to her if she can get something out of it.

One control group family in which there was almost no change had tried different techniques. At T1:

She has had difficulty attaching to me (new Dad), possibly due to the men in her life before foster family. We don't know what happened previously so I just back off. She has difficulty showing "real" feelings.

At T2:

She does have the ability to display affection, but it can be false; very severe attachment difficulties – she scores 20 on the internet version of the Reactive Attachment Disorder questionnaire. We try to give her space and don't force her (to be affectionate with us). We think we are (now) using very different techniques because we have greater understanding of her. We went to a conference with a child psychologist and a child welfare rights speaker. But nothing works for long.

At T3:

Attachment is our biggest problem. We don't deal with the affection issue any differently from six months ago. The plan of praising her is getting a more positive reaction but it's not changing her really.

Some improvement was noticed by parents who ascribed changes to time spent in the family. The following parents had also attended the Adoption UK course: *It's a Piece of Cake?*:

At T1:

The children all thought that if one of us was going out we might not come back. They would block our way to the front door and scream and hang on to me even though I always said I would return. They made me leave my wedding ring; they had an enormous fear of being abandoned. (But) her emotional warmth to us was almost nil.

At T2:

> *We feel she is (now) giving genuine and appropriate shows of affection to us.*

At T3:

> *Our attachment is loads better, and we have a close and genuine relationship with her now. She knows we will be there for her and is a lot more settled. However, still very manipulative and friendship is only useful to her if she can get something out of it.*

Another control group parent at T1 said:

> *She's more attached to me than to her father; she just gives him the top of her head to kiss. He ignores this as we think it will get better as she learns to trust us.*

By T2 the mother said:

> *Just before the adoption she was very clingy to the exclusion of her brother, but I had to make time for him, which made her angry. She will push Dad away only 50 per cent of the time, not all the time as before; I'm not doing anything – I'm not going to force it.*

And at T3:

> *She is more attached to her dad now and to the wider family.*

They put this change down to maturity and the time in the family and had not attended any special courses.

An intervention group couple had noticed some improvement arising from using the techniques suggested by the parent adviser; at T1:

> *She was close to the foster mother and misses her – she is struggling to attach to me. She seeks my approval for things, but I don't think she misses me when we are apart. Her affection feels forced. She also follows strangers around, but we tell her she needs to leave them alone or we may (have to) go home.*

At T2:

> *No problems now. She does "withdraw" from us if she's in trouble but we make her laugh or ignore it. We have been building the bond with lots of praise; we spend more time with her; are more affectionate to her. All this from [the adviser's] suggestions and she said "simply being there will build affection", and she seems to have been right.*

At T3:

> *It has turned into her being very shy now, and I'm not sure how to deal with it.*

Definite improvement was noticed in several families.

A control group family, at T1 said:

> *It is difficult for him to be affectionate but he has commented on affection between us (parents). He is always pleased to see us and got very upset when he was lost for a few minutes the other day. We don't force affection on him if he is obviously resisting but encourage people not to give up on him as he is getting better with hugs now.*

At T3:

> *Really no problems any more. Asks me to help when he's ill, now calls me [Mum] in the night, kisses on the lips, cuddles me in bed, holds my hand when out, asks to play with me, makes or gets things for me which he has chosen: 'I thought you would like . . .'*

The parents were also asked what they were doing when their child showed inappropriate behaviour towards strangers. Again, parents used different approaches, but commonly did not force the pace and continued to give affection and to praise.

At follow-up, this control group parent had found her daughter much improved; at T1:

> *She does talk to strangers, and it's difficult as she doesn't see it as dangerous, just friendly.*

At T2:

We continue to have concerns about inappropriate friendliness to strangers.

At T3:

She is not hugging everyone now, being more discriminating; she understands the "code" of closeness (which I have taught her).

An intervention group parent had used "explanation" to reduce inappropriate friendliness; at T1:

She seems to be indiscriminate; but it doesn't always feel real or genuine; I need to "un-train" this behaviour. She is learning not to hug strangers. I talk through "boundaries" and the rules of social interaction.

At T2:

She used to kiss anybody but now makes a better distinction. I've explained "personal space" and who is family and who is not. This seemed to help.

At T3:

Much more appropriate friendliness to strangers. No more worries.

But several children were still causing their parents considerable concern in relation to strangers. One control group parent said, at T1:

She is indiscriminate in who she attaches to, she gets between other children and their mothers, and latches on to girls of her sister's age. We find talking to her, praising and cuddling works best.

At T2:

In the supermarket will go off with other women, but only (when) in family groups; but rarely comes into contact with other strangers.

At T3:

> *But she still went off with a woman in the playground. I explained she mustn't go off with other people, but didn't labour the point.*

Another control group parent said at Time 3:

> *She talks to anybody but especially people with dogs; (the other day she) ran off after some horses; would just wander off with anyone. We have explained about danger but she just doesn't see it.*

One theme emerged from the parental interviews which we had not set out to ask about. Eleven parents (30%) reported that their children exhibited extremely controlling behaviour, which they found particularly difficult to manage, and in many ways very irritating. As one described it:

> *She is not exactly a naughty child, but she is very controlling and this has many of the same effects, as she spends a lot of time disputing what I say or suggest. It is very exhausting.*

It is accepted that many adopted children show this type of behaviour (Golding, 2007), the origins of which may vary from child to child. For some, to be "in charge" was probably the only way to survive parental neglect:

> *She is still very anxious and likes to be in control: for instance, we must explain the day's plans and stick to them. She is very upset by even slight variation.*

For others, being in charge represented their attempts to protect younger siblings; they were used to ordering other children's lives. Some children had, in effect, been in charge of their own birth parents or their siblings – the "parentified" child:

> *We now realise that her need to be in control is linked with necessity of trying to look after her younger (sibling): it is now less (T3), but she still doesn't like to comply with our suggestions or requirements.*

His controlling behaviour is very marked and persistent: wants to know everything and interrupts grown-ups' conversations. We are sure this is because he had to know what his mother was up to.

Parents also varied in which behaviour they described as "controlling". For some parents, it was the child's determination to direct family plans, and a complete inability to behave in an accommodating way towards the needs of other people. Serious rages and tantrums often followed from parents insisting on conformity to family values the child was not familiar with, like getting to school on time.

Conclusions

Although some of the problems in these complex domains were rated as improved by the parents over time, there was not a great deal of evidence that the improvement took place to a greater degree in the intervention groups. However, parents in the combined intervention group were more likely to say that they were responding differently to emotional distress and were less angry in relation to misbehaviour compared with the control group.

It is widely recognised that although children may show rather similar behaviour, the origins of that behaviour may lie in circumstances that are almost unique to each child. For example, children's violent behaviour may emerge from being the victim of violence or from having witnessed violence, or from having been brought up with no guidance on other strategies for reasonably asserting oneself, or from never having known that relationships can be negotiated through kindness. In one family, the older brother had been cared for by a grandmother for the first two years of his life, but the younger brother had only experienced care from his drug-addicted mother who was prone to violent rages; only the younger brother exhibited violent aggression in the adoptive family.

These unique early experiences will also influence how the children respond to their parents' efforts to improve their behaviour or encourage more appropriate relationships. The trust arising from spending time in their first secure family will also influence how the children learn their new patterns of behaviour within and outside the family. The parents nearly all felt that they had been successful in having made small improvements in these three key domains, as witnessed in the results from the Visual Analogue Scales. Nevertheless, a number of parents remained extremely worried about how their children were going to negotiate relationships outside the family in future years. The interventions (both the parenting advice sessions and the other forms of help available to the control group parents) undoubtedly helped them to make important improvements, and provide a strong argument for such help to be available at a much earlier stage in the placements. The need to provide encouragement to parents when their child's behaviour changes only slowly is one reason why access to specialist services is important (see Chapter 11).

Summary

- All the children were reported as showing serious aggression and other forms of "misbehaviour" at T1. By T3 only one child was said to be no longer showing serious "misbehaviour".
- Intervention group parents were more likely than the controls to have adopted different strategies to deal with "misbehaviour".
- Parents in the intervention groups reported that they had changed aspects of their parenting but that change was slow for their children.
- Inappropriate behaviour towards strangers was common at T3 in both the combined intervention group and the control group children, and a major cause of parents' anxiety.

11 The families' access to further specialist support services

In Chapter 8 we discussed the cost effectiveness of supplying the experimental parent advice sessions and other support services to the adoptive families. In this chapter we present the material which emerged from the third research interview in which we asked all parents about the details of the specialist services they had received or sought. For those in the intervention group, these services were additional to the advice sessions, about which we had asked separate questions. In a follow-up letter sent to all the parents after the third interview, we asked for additional information on how long they had had to wait for the provision of a service after first judging that they or their child needed it, and whether they were content with that timing.

Unlike clinical drug trials, in which access to the other forms of "treatment" may largely be eliminated or controlled, it was an ethical agreement within the present study that both the parents and the local authorities were free to pursue other services for the families if they deemed them necessary. It was therefore important to examine which other services had been used, and in particular to see whether the control group had received anything comparable to the ten weekly, home-based interventions provided to the two intervention groups. In addition, given the very positive response by parents to the advice sessions provided within the research, we wanted to know how useful any other services had been.

Access to specialist services

In the third interview, detailed questions were asked about the receipt in the previous six months of any specialist services that were designed specifically to meet the needs arising from the child's placement (see also Chapter 8). In other words, this would not include routine services like attending the dentist or optician, data on which had been collected in each research interview and added to the costs of services analysed for

Chapter 8. The specialist services might have focused on the child, the whole family or the parents alone. Questions included who had asked for and/or arranged these services, what the service consisted of, how long it had continued, who had decided to end the provision, and whether the parents rated it as useful or not.

We have already seen that many parents were taken aback by the severity of their child's problems (Chapter 4), and that they felt the preparation, even though warmly appreciated at the time, had often not equipped them to deal effectively with these problems. Drawing on the responses to the follow-up letter, it appeared that parents in both the combined intervention group and the control group thought that they could have done with specialist help almost as soon as the child was placed with them (see Tables 11.3a and 11.3b below).

Some examples may be useful: In the first interview, (T1) a control group parent had said:

We could do with some help over the temper tantrums: why she does it. Why is she so reluctant to say "goodbye" or "thank you"? We are sure she has feelings she is concealing and cannot express.

At the second interview, this parent again said:

We could do with help with strategies to tackle her behaviour. Her social worker doesn't seem to be interested in her. We'd like some help with whatever damage her past has done. Although we think she is doing OK, we'd like the seal of approval that we're doing OK, so it would be helpful if the social worker came. As it is, she seems totally disorganised and it seems she only contacts us when there are boxes to be ticked.

This family received no extra help. At T1, a parent in the combined intervention group had said:

We saw problems straight away (2003): constant aggression, thumping other people; jealousy of people around him.

At T3, they said:

By September 2006 we saw a lot of symptoms of attachment disorder which we had noticed from the start, but things came to a head in August. We arranged an appointment with a child psychologist to discuss what he currently needs, so we have no official diagnosis yet. We have had to ask for outside help due to both myself and my wife getting to breaking point with him. We love him dearly but find his behaviour, particularly at home and towards his sister, increasingly difficult.

Data from the third interview revealed that 23 families out of 37 in the trial had used at least one specialist service which was focused on issues around the placement and the needs of the family members. There was no difference between the control group and the combined intervention group in the extent to which these extra services were used. Parents had been involved in initiating these services themselves (10 cases), or in collaboration with the child's school (two cases) or their social worker (six cases). In the other five cases their social workers had suggested the service to the parents. Again, there was no obvious difference between the control group and the combined intervention group in whether parents initiated contact with the specialist services. Providers included post-adoption support workers (6) or family social worker (2), educational or clinical psychologists (4), specialist teachers (2), psychiatrists (6) or courses from adoption organisations (3). Table 11.1 shows the main issues that the parents understood were being addressed by the specialist service for the index child (some children had more than one service). Some services were delivered in the child's school, and were set up to improve behaviour or enable the child with grossly delayed learning to catch up.

Table 11.1
The index child's problems targeted by special services

Targeted behaviour	To be addressed by specialist service	Not identified as problem; family did not access services
Aggression/anger	13	10
Peer relationships	5	18
Anxiety, fearfulness	7	16
Hyperactivity and/or attention deficit problems	4	19
Sexualised behaviour	1	22
Attachment problems	10	13

The specialist services were recorded if it was clear that they were designed to address the post-placement problems presented within the family; this meant that the child was not always the only focus of the help (Table 11.2).

Table 11.2
Family members who were receiving special services

Service provided for	Number of families
Parent(s) only	7
Index child only	10
All the children	2
Other child in family	1
Whole family	3

Four index children had only one session with the specialist service which was usually in the form of a consultation or assessment; some parents were waiting for the outcome before the next steps – if any were needed – could be taken. For seven children, the services were still ongoing or daily (the latter were largely school- and classroom-based). Services for parents included one-off consultations or recruitment onto special courses. For example, one intervention group parent was offered a special service by her social worker:

> *There was an incident in November when my social worker jumped to the conclusion that I was using wrong tactics [to control the child's aggression] but this had the effect of getting me in on a [CBT] course run by county.*

At times it was thought best to provide for the index child only, but sometimes services for the index child were made available only with other children in the family. A control group parent said:

> *As CAMHS [Child and Adolescent Mental Health Services] were not willing to provide the service we required, the children's social worker did some individual sessions with them and one session with both of them.*

Timeliness of services

A constant theme at the time of the third interview was the struggle to get timely help. A number of families had wanted a particular service that did not materialise and frustration was expressed in the interviews at having to wait for their social worker to provide or organise more help. It may have been the case that the social workers had been trying to fix appointments with specialist services, but the services could not be supplied. If so, the parents were not aware of this, as they would have told us in response to specific questions. Several parents complained about the lack of post-adoption services that could easily be accessed by the family themselves, but accepted that their local authority might have to agree payment. The follow-up letter particularly probed the timeliness of services and the satisfaction with eventual timing of the referral.

In Tables 11.3a and 11.3b we present the results from the follow-up letter case by case (each case is referred to by the research ID). From this it can be seen that several families reported that more than one service had been requested, and eventually provided, for different problems.

Twenty-four parents responded to the follow-up letter which had gone to all 37 parents in the study. Replies came from all except one of the 23 families we already knew [from T3 interviews] had received further services; we subsequently learnt that this family had moved house. In addition, replies came from two other families simply confirming that they had not accessed further services within the timescale of the research study. Among these respondents, parents in 12 of the 19 intervention group families identified 22 problems (10 problems had been apparent since placement) for which they had extra services, waiting on average nearly 14 months. Ten of the 18 control group parents reported extra services for 17 problems (four problems apparent since placement or the pre-placement introduction stage); they waited on average 10½ months. Little can be deduced from these differences as the numbers are so small. However, it is striking that altogether the parents had identified 14 major problems as soon as the children were placed, which they felt they needed help with, but worryingly waited an average of 17½ months before they received an appropriate service. Set against this sorry picture it must be noted that two families got immediate help.

However, it is not therefore surprising that there were many complaints from parents about being left on their own to tackle major problems that they felt they could not manage. This was evident in both the control group and in the combined intervention group. For example, at T1 (i.e. before receiving the parent advice sessions) a parent in the intervention group said:

It feels like all the effort goes into arranging the adoption [as opposed to post-adoption]. We were led to believe that support would always be available, but it isn't.

At T3 the same parents said:

The County Council social workers never return calls. We have had no services at all. We would like a visit maybe once a month from someone like the [research study] parent adviser.

Two families in the control group commented:

We've had nothing – it feels very final being cast off at adoption without any support.

And:

I have had to fight for every piece of support. We expected practical help from the social worker, but got sympathy instead. Not very helpful!

A single working parent in the intervention group struggled to find the right person within her local authority who could help her:

My own social worker retired directly after the Adoption Order was granted and her replacement was useless as she did not know us. It took nine phone calls to find the right person to speak to [in the post-adoption service] and when I found her she was excellent, but why was I not given the right number from the start?

Another couple said:

We asked for help because of his inability to form relationships with peers, and his aggression. He has been seen since placement by his social worker. By the time we saw the local "Family Team" we had sorted the issues ourselves, and they offered us nothing new. The team we saw was not very child friendly and the environment was also child unfriendly. We were pleased he never attended.

Parents sometimes reported that the timing of these services appeared very unresponsive to the family's needs, and they felt they were more to do with the organisation of the provider than with their own problems (courses starting and ending to suit several families, not just theirs, or the length of waiting lists in specialist centres). For example:

We had funding to go to major attachment specialist, but – six months since we last saw you – we are no further forward with this plan. However, we met [a social worker in another project] and she is connected to this centre so we hope that her approach is consistent with what we wanted in the first place. We are happy with this, as we sorely needed some support and feel comfortable with her.

Overall, 20 families had accessed 37 separate specialist services between them (combining the data in Tables 11.3a and 11.3b). They reported that they were content with the timing of 18 (48%) services and not content with delays experienced waiting for the other 19 (52%) services. For 16 identified problems, a service had been provided within six months, for nine problems within a year, but for the rest of the problems (12–32%) families had waited more than 12 months before they had access to the specialist service they considered would help.

We investigated whether there were any differences between the combined intervention and the control group families in the speed with which they accessed the services. Table 11.3a shows that for only 12 (54%) of the 22 problems cited by the intervention group parents were they content with the time taken to provide the special service, and for only seven (34%) problems did they express satisfaction with the service provided. Table 11.3b shows the results for the control group parents, who said they were content with the waiting time for six (35%) of the 17 problems they had identified (one family commenting that they had paid for it themselves). These control group families said they were satisfied with what was provided to meet six of the 17 problems; for the other 11 problems they were not happy with the service.

Sometimes, however, even though problems have been noted by professionals as well as parents, help is often not provided:

He needed help in talking about his past circumstances and his adoption. This was identified by his social worker and was recorded in the report to Panel, the Care Plan and the Adoption Support Plan (March '05). His social worker tried to refer him to CAMHS, but they declined to take the case. CAMHS eventually saw us in November '05, but again declined to see our son or assess his needs. In January '06 they offered help to us but again not to our child. The case was raised by senior adoption workers and CAMHS suddenly offered an assessment for the whole family. We had reached the point where we said we wouldn't adopt unless there was some support in place.

This point was made by other adoptive parents as well, reluctantly recognising that their only way of persuading their authority or their PCT to clear the expenditure was to threaten to send the child back into the care system.

One of the important issues raised by parents was that, by the time they were asking for specialist help, the advice or therapy was often urgently needed. In other words, they had tried to tackle problems themselves for a while and only when they felt the child's needs (or those of other family members) were beyond their capabilities did they ask for help. For example, one family in the combined intervention group reported at T3 that there were still some outstanding problems that could not have been addressed in the parent advice sessions, but remained urgent. When faced by delay, the solution for some families was to pay for private services, a route not open to all.

Intervention group parents, two-and-a-half years after the child's arrival in the family, said:

> We needed to make faster progress with getting the statement [of special educational needs] ready for the school so we paid for a private consultation with a psychologist who diagnosed reactive attachment disorder. There is a plan to get her a course of "sensory integration" to deal with her hyper-vigilance. We are now on a six month waiting list for CAMHS to review the post-adoption support package.

The issue that should be a cause of grave concern was that some parents were reduced to threatening not to go ahead with the placement if they could not have proper support. A control group parent said, at T2:

> We are having a really hard time just now; it has reached crisis point and we feel we need to have help. We are considering whether we are the best placement for (child) but feel now that it would be the same wherever she is placed. We feel desperate as a family.

At T3 they said:

> We are still postponing applying for an adoption order, three months at a

time, to see the funding for the therapy. We feel that if we finalise the adoption, we will be out of the loop, and left on our own. Social services say they will fund the therapy after the adoption, so why not fund it now when we need it. All the family feels frustrated as we feel that finance is the issue, not the child's needs.

A single parent in the intervention group commented:

He was physically aggressive with peers at school and with my nephews – I noticed it about six months after he arrived. Three months later, the post-adoption counselling service talked to the teachers. I had to push this very hard at review meetings and I think this might not have been forthcoming if the placement wasn't under threat – the breakdown was a real possibility. Consultation was only available on a monthly basis but what was required was more intensive contact, preferably weekly; partly to help me cope with his unusual behaviour.

Other parents took their complaints to higher levels. As an example of the level of frustration felt by parents, one father said:

We waited two years to see the educational psychologist. The school said there was no problem and also told us: 'We don't "do" special needs until Year 2. [For the same child, it took a year to get a CAMHS appointment] '. . . but we still didn't get any therapy for his angry outbursts until we put him on medication – two years later. We wrote to our MP who wrote to the heads of social services in the two authorities. The placing authority admitted they had done nothing, and our authority said it was not their responsibility. Meanwhile we were stuck in the middle.

How useful were the services?

The third research interview revealed quite a lot of criticism of the helpfulness of the services that had been provided. Parents in 13 of the 23 families receiving special services said they were satisfied or very satisfied with the outcome. The remaining parents reported that the services their child or family had received were not particularly helpful.

Among the 13 families who were satisfied with the services they received were four who had attended the *It's a Piece of Cake?* course, financed by their local authority. One family said: 'It validated how we felt as parents and gave us some more ideas'. However, the most frequent reason given by the parents for finding a specialist service which met their needs was that it offered individual, not group, work: ten families emphasised this, and seven mentioned the choice of topics being appropriate for them and their children, rather than being a standard programme. This compared with only two families saying that there had been advantages in meeting other adopters. In part, this response validated the approach used in the research RCT – that parents would prefer to have a service focusing on their family alone.

Information from the third interview and the follow-up letter showed that nine families were referred to CAMHS, but their experiences varied markedly, not least in the length of time taken to get the appointments. Five control group families waited an average of nearly 18 months after identifying the problems. Four intervention group families waited an average of 15 months, although one family was very promptly referred by an educational psychologist.

The parents' reports of how useful CAMHS was also varied. Some families reported that they did not feel that the issues within adoptive families or the needs of adopted children were sufficiently well understood within the CAMHS teams. One family had three appointments with the local CAMHS, but no diagnosis was offered to them. They were advised that the child had made good progress, and so no further interventions were offered. Meanwhile, their own experience of the child at home was that she still had major behaviour problems. In another family, a specialist psychotherapist assessment led to a diagnosis of an attachment problem, but no further help was forthcoming.

The issue of the "threshold" for providing a service emerged several times. For example, another intervention group parent said at T1: 'We asked for help with binge eating but were told it was too minor a case for any intervention.' At T3 these parents said that their handling of the child had changed radically ('We put it down to the parent adviser'), their understanding of the child had deepened, and most problems had disappeared. But that does not overcome the possibility that their original request for help was perfectly valid.

One control group family attended an attachment therapy centre for assessment, which had been paid for by the local authority, and which they knew had been very costly, but when they received a report after a long wait, they felt it did not tell them anything they did not already know. In other words, for these parents no extra advice was available.

The single most frequently cited reason for not finding a service useful was that the topics chosen by the provider were not appropriate for their family – some parents felt they had not been properly listened to by the specialists. One mother, attending a first consultation with CAMHS, felt so patronised by the therapists that she declined to go back, subsequently contacting a post-adoption worker who (she felt) was much more understanding of the family's needs.

Of course it is possible that the purposes and processes of a particular service were not always explained fully enough to parents, or they did not understand the explanations so that their expectations were out of kilter with the therapy offered. For example, one control group parent said:

Then there were the music therapy sessions: we were very disappointed – he was just banging drums. We thought we would get an experienced specialist.

An intervention group parent commented:

He attended an art therapy at our local CAMHS – but I don't see it's done him any good. I was very disappointed; there was no analysis, it was never explained to me what it was about, why they did things, what they perceived, or anything. I chose to sit in the sessions so I had someone to talk to but that was my choice and I didn't have to; nothing was shared with me. He liked playing in the sand.

Additionally, there was scope for considerable disagreement between therapists and parents:

We have been told by the therapist that (the child) is "happy", but we aren't happy with that at all. We feel we need more help to unblock her emotions. (Control group parent)

The frustration with getting children's needs properly assessed is shown in this next example:

We needed help with dealing with uncontrollable behaviour, tantrums and violence which had been there since September 05; we were offered the "Parent/Child Game" in May 06. The staff who were trained to run this were judgemental and (appeared to have) no understanding of the special needs of adopted children. They spent much of their time trying to convince us that our daughter did not have an attachment disorder, though they had no medical or psychiatric training. When we eventually saw a psychiatrist (February 07), she was immediately diagnosed with severe attachment disorder. (Our daughter) is now receiving weekly therapy and the violence is much reduced.

There were some real successes as well: one single mother had been very satisfied with the CAMHS and educational psychologist services which had provided individual attention for her daughter. She reported that the child 'had been able to come to terms with a lot of her anger and feelings of rejection'. One intervention group couple had a series of monthly appointments focusing on the parents alone and discussing ways of parenting a child exhibiting rages, along with controlling and oppositional behaviour. This support was designed to be "unlimited" and the parents were reassured by this.

Of course, in this study we were not able to ask the specialists for their views of the child's progress, so to that extent there is only the parents' perspective on the "success" of any given service. However, support for enhancing their parenting skills and providing therapy for their child when their own efforts could not meet the child's needs is an essential part of post-adoption work, so it is right to take seriously the parents' views of success or lack of it.

Conclusion

This chapter has concentrated on the support that parents received in relation to the adoptive placement, and the finding that a large proportion of parents did not feel that the family's needs had been appropriately met. It needs to be remembered that these families were selected for the study because of the high level of their children's problems. Nevertheless, it is noticeable that a high proportion of the parents had waited an inordinate time for specialist services for their children, and sometimes had been forced into themselves paying for a service which their local authority or Primary Care Trust (PCT) should have provided. In the third research interview, parents had already expressed very real concern about getting help that they were certain would have made a considerable difference to their child's integration in primary school, the acquisition of friends, and happiness at home. The responses to the follow-up letter confirmed that some parents were obliged to wait long periods for services, and that they were very disappointed and sometimes angry with the lack of timely support. The post-adoption support services appeared to be very patchy, and this forms the background to the high level of appreciation of the parent advice sessions received by the combined intervention group. There were other services which met the families' needs, but the general impression is that these were seldom provided when they were needed and sometimes only if the parents threatened not to continue the placement.

Summary

- The children and families in this study used a wide range of support services but in general waited for many months for access to a service which they had wanted much earlier.
- The delay in getting help was a severe burden for some families. It appeared that many families struggled to solve their own problems and only asked for help when it was urgent. The belief that the crisis would be met by the swift provision of a service was not borne out.
- Many parents complained that the services were not suited to the needs of their child and family.
- In particular, there was considerable concern at the delays before a

Table 11.3a
Satisfaction with the timing of post-adoption support – combined intervention group

Case ID	Problem	Time until problem noticed	Time to receiving help	Type of support	Satisfaction with wait	Satisfaction with support
1	Aggression	From placement	1 year	Own social worker	Yes	No
1	Attachment	From placement	4 years	Child psychologist	No	No
1	Lack of friends in school	From placement – getting worse	4 years	SENCO	Yes	Yes
1	Respite care	July 07	2 months	Respite scheme	Yes	Yes
16	Poor bonding	March 03	18 months	CAMHS	Yes	No
16	Poor social skills	March 03	18 months	CAMHS	Yes	No
20	Extreme anger	From placement but getting worse	Immediate	Private play therapist	Yes	Yes
21	Aggression	March 04	2 years	Clinical psychologist	No	No
21	Extreme non-compliance	March 04	2 years	Clinical psychologist	No	No
23	Extreme aggression	From placement	1 year	Psychotherapist	No	No
25	Extreme aggression	Summer 05	3 months	Post-adoption team	Yes	Yes

Case ID						
25	Parents' own needs	Summer 06	Immediate	Counsellor at work	Yes	Yes
28	Behaviour at school	May 06	No delays	Educational psychologist, social worker & CAMHS	Yes	Ongoing
29	Multiple	Summer 06	2 months	NSPCC counsellor	Yes	Yes
31	Reactive attachment disorder	From placement	18 months	Clinical psychologist	No, crisis needs swift attention	No
31	Behaviour problems	July 06	3 months	Clinical psychologist	Yes	Yes
32	Aggression & behaviour at school	From placement	8 months	Family Futures assessment		No
32	Ditto	From placement	12 months	Local authority parenting programme	No	No
32	Other behaviour	Oct 06	12 months	Family Futures	No	No
35	Speech & language	From placement	3 months	Local speech & language unit	Yes	No
35	Emotional and behaviour problems	From placement	2 years	CAMHS	No	No
35	Sensory integration	Jan 07	8 months	Occupational therapist	No	No

7 The case ID has been retained in this table to indicate the fact that some families asked for more than one service

Table 11.3b
Satisfaction with the timing of post-adoption support – control group

Case ID[a]	Problem	Time until problem noticed	Time to receiving help	Type of support	Satisfaction with wait	Satisfaction with support
2	Aggression Social isolation	From placement	2 years	'Social worker family team'	No	No
6	"Behaviour"	July 04	2 months	Paediatrician	No	No
6	Poor school performance	Summer 04	2 years	Educational psychologist	No	No
6	Aggression, hyper-arousal	Summer 04	3 years	CAMHS	No	n/a
10	Problems re peers	September 06	1 month	School counsellor	Yes	No
10	Severe educational delay	June 07	2 months	Private tutor	'Yes; we paid'	ongoing
12	Parental "concerns"	nil	nil	n/a	n/a	n/a
18	Violent tantrums	Spring 05	6 months	Senior social worker 'Coping with Kids' course	Yes	Yes
18	Need for more parenting support	November 04	2 months	Mothers' Union facilitator	Yes	Yes
18	Child rejecting parents	August 06	1 month	Senior social worker and SENCO	Yes	Yes

27	Extreme violence & aggression	August 05	6 months	Social worker	No	No
27	Attachment disorder	August 05	18 months	CAMHS psychiatrist	Yes	Yes
30	Multiple but service to parents	Pre-placement	18 months	CAMHS	No	No
30	Multiple	Pre-placement	20 months	Social worker	No	Yes
33	Non specific disorder	From placement	Intermittent	Information meetings for adoptive parents	n/a	n/a
34	Tantrums etc problems	December 05	11 months	CAMHS	No	No
37	Attachment & multiple	July 06	6 months	CAMHS	No	Yes

[8] The case ID has been retained in this table to indicate the fact that some families asked for more than one service

specialist service could be found, and sometimes there was concern about whether the "specialists" were fully aware of the particular needs of adopted children.

- There was a widespread feeling that, when they needed to talk to someone about their adopted child's often serious problems, it would be most helpful to be able to do that at least as quickly as access from a GP to a hospital consultant.

- There was also a good deal of admiration at the help that some social workers and some specialist services were providing; looked at overall, however, it was clear that it was patchy and unpredictable, with different services being provided for the same problems and long waiting times. There was no way of assessing whether this was a "postcode" problem.

12 Conclusions and implications

Interpreting the key findings

This study has examined the effectiveness of parenting advice provided to adopters facing serious challenges from their children's behaviour within 21 months of placement. It is based on the experiences of adoptive parents in 15 local authorities in England and four families recruited from Adoption UK. The central message to take away from the results of this trial is that, although no differences were apparent between the intervention group and the control group regarding a reduction in the *children's psychosocial problems* in the subsequent six months, greater changes in *aspects of parenting* were recorded for the intervention group.

In the current study no statistically significant differences were found in the children's behaviour before and after intervention, or between the combined intervention group and the control group. The high initial level of the children's psychosocial problems persisted regardless of the passage of time and the parenting advice interventions. The mean SDQ Total Difficulties score dropped only a little from the first research interview (baseline) to the final research interview nine months later (six months post-intervention) and nearly equally in both groups (combined intervention group: 18 to 17; control group: 19 to 18).

This might be explained as a consequence of profoundly adverse pre-adoption histories. The children in the study had experienced maltreatment, separation from birth families, time in care, often with multiple changes of placement, and then a relatively late placement in an adoptive family. We have seen that experiences in care differed between the children entering the study with high SDQ scores and the children who did not come into the study because they had low SDQ scores. In particular, if the adoptive placement was after the age of five years, and there had been a substantial length of time in care, the children were significantly more likely to have high SDQ scores when screened for the study. Other risk factors may have been present but not captured in this trial, for example, genetic risk, pre-natal exposure to toxins and peri-natal hazards. It must also be remembered that these children were selected into the trial because, in the view of family social workers and/or parents, they had a high level of psychosocial problems. It might therefore seem over-optimistic to expect these difficulties to reduce substantially in a relatively short time. Although this may be seen as a disappointing outcome for the children, it may be useful in indicating the limits of a brief parenting intervention to effect major change in this selected group of children.

The parenting advice sessions (interventions) took place when the children were still within the first 21 months of placement. Perhaps the beneficial influence of a longer period of stable, positive family life would be necessary to see noticeable change. Furthermore, some effects of earlier maltreatment might not readily be remedied, even when parents were helped to develop their parenting skills. It is also possible that one of the reasons why these children had high SDQ scores in the first place may have been because they were more genetically vulnerable or more susceptible to adversity. In turn, this may have led to them being less responsive to any therapeutic aspects of the new adoptive environment. We have concluded that the children in the study showed little change, but the sample was chosen in order to test the interventions in the context of severe problems and so it is important that the results of the trial are not generalised to all placements of children in this age group.

Of course, the comparison of average SDQ Total Difficulties scores masked changes in either direction within the groups. For example, we have seen in Chapter 8 that, although some children improved markedly in the intervention group, some got worse. By contrast, in the control group, some got worse but some improved, even in the absence of the experimental intervention. Clearly, many other factors contributed to outcomes apart from receiving or not receiving the parent advice sessions.

On the basis of the standardised Parenting Sense of Competence (PSOC) measure and of feedback from the adopters, it appears that the parents had a greater capacity for change than the children. Significant differences existed between the groups of parents at six months follow-up on the PSOC indicating that Satisfaction with the Role of Parenting rose after receiving advice sessions, while the Satisfaction of the control group fell slightly. This was true despite the fact that the level of difficulty of the children in both groups remained almost the same, at least within the time scale of the research study. For the combined intervention group, raised satisfaction may be seen as a better platform on which to stand when looking to the future of the placement.

Two possible explanations may be offered for the lack of change in the children. First, any growth of understanding and development of enhanced parenting strategies may take time to be absorbed and acted upon so that effects on the child may not be seen until much later. Perhaps this is more clearly illustrated in the parents' reports of whether they had changed their strategies for dealing with problems in three key domains: emotional distress, misbehaviour and distorted personal relationships. Tracking their reports of the children's behaviour at three time points showed that progress was often very slow, but that many parents felt they were using techniques that would encourage change in the end. The parents' capacity for incorporating new ways of helping their child was far ahead of change in the children. Second, as we have noted above, given the extent of the pre-placement ill effects on the child's psychosocial functioning, it may take far longer than six months of enhanced parenting for the child's behaviour to change noticeably.

So, to summarise the trial more formally, and in terms of our original hypotheses:

- The prediction of outcome on the children's psychosocial problems did not hold, as improvement was no greater in the combined intervention group than in the control group six months after intervention.
- The prediction held that, although little improvement was evident in the children, change was very similar in the "behavioural" and "educational" groups at six-month follow-up. However, numbers were too small for statistical comparison when controlling for baseline measures.
- The prediction held that Satisfaction with the Role of Parenting showed more positive change in the combined intervention group at six-month follow-up than in the control group.

Cost-benefit analysis

Most RCTs of psychological and social interventions in community samples lack cost analyses. In the current study, it was possible to collect information on most of the standard services received by the families and the specialist services provided for the adopted children or their parents. The results show that the combined intervention group had higher costs over the follow-up period, but only when including the cost of the parent advice sessions. We have seen that these additional costs attached to the parenting advice sessions did not "purchase" significant changes in the children's mental health measured on the SDQ, but did result in significantly greater satisfaction by parents in their parenting role. This evidence may be important, although only long-term follow-up studies of larger samples will prove the point. However, it is likely that this satisfaction with the role could lead to future placement stability. As outcomes for parents were improved in terms of increased satisfaction, it is a value judgement as to whether a cost of £731 per unit improvement in satisfaction in the short term or £337 in the longer term represents good value for money. Evidence from this study suggests that, for a relatively modest investment in post-adoption support, parents report an improvement to their satisfaction with their role.

Comparison with other studies

These findings also need to be placed in the context of other recent parenting studies where advice was given to parents with "difficult" children. The earlier literature review showed that group-based interventions with struggling birth parents in the community can be successful in changing the children's behaviour, whereas the three recent UK studies of foster parenting (Minnis *et al*, 2001; McDonald and Turner, 2005; The Hadley Centre, 2007) did not show such positive changes in the children. It is possible that the community parents lacked consistency and disciplinary strategies, but that the effects on their children were not so grave that they were likely to be taken into care: such problems as did exist could be addressed and remedied relatively quickly. The challenges facing adopters of ex-care children are likely to be of a different order. In addition to the effects of the very poor parenting that led to the decision to take them into care, these children will also have experienced many changes of household and loss of contact with members of their families. Our study confirms, consistent with other studies, that substantial change in the children's psychosocial problems is unlikely to occur in the short term.

By way of comparison, the mean problem scores in the Maudsley Adoption and Fostering study of children placed in middle childhood were virtually static over the first year of placement (Quinton *et al*, 1998, Table 8.8, p 120). Nearly half remained above the cut off during the first year, although this sample was not screened for high difficulties.

However, the present study shows that not only did the parents respond positively to the interventions, as has been noted in other studies (McDonald and Turner, 2005), but also that their satisfaction with the parenting role rose significantly in the combined intervention group. We suggest that this is due to the much more intensive, one-to-one, tailored intervention in our study compared with group-based interventions. The parents frequently drew attention to one particular advantage of the parent advice sessions in the current study: *they were able to talk exclusively about the problems presented by the index child*. Interestingly, this aspect of the advice sessions filled the gap that nearly all the parents had been aware of in their pre-placement training sessions: that any discussion of the problems of ex-care children could only be theoretical until the child arrived in their household.

Whereas the two UK foster care trials employing group-based interventions probably had too little power to effect substantial change in the children, Fisher and Kim's recent US trial (2007) claims to have shown a significant reduction in avoidant, and increase in secure, behaviour in the foster children. However, this effect was achieved by means of much greater professional input. This included a team allocated to each case, pre-placement training for the foster careers, a post-placement daily support and advice line and weekly foster carer meetings, and behaviour specialists together with weekly therapeutic playgroup sessions for the children. Their sample was also different in being fostered rather than adopted, the age range was three–five years, slightly younger than our sample, and also not selected for a high level of problems. This amount of staff resource is likely to be far beyond what most post-adoption services in the UK are able to offer. If the effective results can only be obtained with a replication of this resource level, then this may diminish its relevance for the UK context. The trial presented here has indicated that modest gains could be obtained for modest cost.

Qualitative findings are perhaps harder than the quantitative to condense simply. However, a great deal was gained in understanding the character of the two interventions, the process of change and practice issues by gathering detailed feedback from both the advisers and the parents. We learned what was most and least useful in the topics covered in the manuals and the process of help giving and help receiving. The parents almost universally responded positively to the interventions. Those who had struggled to have their concerns heard by professionals, or who had failed to gain access to appropriate services, were especially appreciative. The weekly, home-based, structured advice sessions were, in most cases, reported to be much more intensive than the help given beforehand and the parents praised highly the skills of the parent advisers. One aspect of the advice service that stood out was the benefit of *working through* problems with the same trusted adviser week by week. This stood in contrast to the generalised parenting advice most families had received before placement of their child.

The advisers provided thoughtful feedback to the research team on using the manuals, their contents, appropriateness and limitations. We learned that the manuals work best when focused solely on parenting challenges and behaviour. Different forms of intervention would be needed for broader couple and family relationship problems and psychological difficulties that may surface for the parents. The advisers included in their comments strong support for the aspect of the manuals devoted to the benefits of relaxed time for play, but found the manuals less helpful in relation to aggressive and dangerous behaviour.

Advisers found that the adopters received the parenting interventions differently. Some were slower to comprehend and benefit from the advice and to turn it into enhanced parenting, while others implemented the advice immediately and often saw a rapid and positive response from the child. In many cases, the advisers felt they were helping the parents to use what they already knew, but to implement it to maximum effect.

We have learned a good deal about how a home-based parenting programme can best be delivered to this group of parents and that some changes come hard even when the parents are well motivated. The advisers showed sensitivity towards those parents who found it difficult to reveal their concerns and disappointments despite their best efforts at parenting a challenging child.

It is extremely important to note that the manuals should not be used by inexperienced practitioners. The intervention was by no means a mechanistic delivery of a programme. The advisers used their empathic and communication skills, especially in managing the strong feelings expressed by the adopters. They also used their extensive experience of working with foster and adoptive families and their accumulated knowledge of the many disadvantages experienced by ex-care children.

Differences between the interventions

The trial design provided the opportunity to compare and contrast the two interventions – at least via the qualitative data, although the small numbers limited the statistical comparison. Both interventions were highly valued and it appears that gaining understanding was valued as much as behavioural advice. However, some differences emerged in the adopters' responses. The parents in the behavioural group said they were helped to carry through the advice consistently and persistently while the education group parents valued the opportunity to stand back and review and reach a better understanding of the problems with the assistance of a knowledgeable and experienced practitioner.

Lessons to be drawn about conducting pragmatic RCTs

This study raised several important issues in relation to conducting a pragmatic trial of a structured, complex intervention. We remain convinced of the value of randomised controlled trials in social intervention despite the numerous difficulties of execution. The first concern was about recruiting participants into an RCT. We stress that this is not an issue for social care research alone. Ward *et al* (1999) discuss the methodological, ethical and practice difficulties encountered in managing a trial of brief psychotherapy in general practice. They examined common issues like the reluctance of some practitioners to become involved in research, especially when their organisations are undergoing change. They also point to the difficulties that may arise in maintaining momentum in the recruitment process and to developing and sustaining good researcher/ practitioner relationships. It is important not to underestimate the need to engage an agency fully with the research, not just at senior level, but more especially with the front line practitioners and their line managers.

Four main sources of difficulty arose in raising a large sample for this study. The first was the necessary research ethics committee instructions on the way we approached the families. This meant that we had to rely entirely on social workers as "gatekeepers" in the first stage of recruitment, and it was clear to us that co-operating with the study presented a difficulty to some individuals and some placement teams. This restriction caused us increasing concern when the flow of referrals was too slow. It was clearly designed with the aim of protecting the privacy of the research participants and preventing them from receiving "cold calling" from researchers, but in reality it took out of our hands a possibly more effective recruitment of the sample. Had we been given permission to approach the adopters without any intervening agency, we feel sure we could have raised a larger sample and thereby produced more secure findings, and we question whether any adverse effects would have resulted for the adopters. We look forward to these issues being fully debated in order that research designed to bring benefit is not needlessly hampered.

Second, the demands of the research design on sampling criteria reduced the numbers of eligible families even before consent was asked for. Third, a large proportion of local authorities approached chose not to participate, or agreed to collaborate but produced SDQs from a low proportion of the eligible cases. Fourth, many parents of children with high SDQ scores chose not to participate. A small number of parents gave the reasons why they would prefer not to join the study, but for those who did not answer, we could only speculate on the reasons (see Appendix 6).

It is likely that some adoptive parents prefer initially to try to solve the problems without external help, or that some were already receiving or hoping to receive a similar specialist service. Parental attributions may have played a part, leading parents to the view that the child's problems are an inevitability that "only time will heal", or that weekly visits will not be potent or lengthy enough to meet the family's needs. For other parents, the fact that the offer of help was based on random allocation may have deterred them, or they may have seen the timetabling of parent advice sessions as too demanding. This latter reason was provided by a few of the parents who declined to participate. Under-recruiting should not necessarily be seen as a research shortcoming as adopters may have many reasons for not participating in an intervention study, whether or not justified.

Strengths and limitations of the study

Most pragmatic RCTs in community settings have strengths and weaknesses and this one is no exception. On the limitations side, the planned sample size was impossible to achieve even when the number of participating authorities was increased.

In addition, there was under-representation of black and minority ethnic families in the study. Nine London boroughs, all with large black and minority ethnic populations, were approached but either they declined to join the study or initially agreed to participate but did not then produce any cases. Several of the participating authorities covered urban areas with large black and minority ethnic populations, but there were no referrals of adoptions within those populations. As we have noted above, in some authorities only a minority of the eligible families were approached to complete the screening questionnaire. We were unable to determine whether large numbers of families had been "missed" or whether their social worker was taking a decision not to ask them to participate. If the latter, the ethical issues associated with social workers taking the decision not to ask parents if they would like to join a research study needs attention. However, among those parents whose children had high SDQs, about half did not finally join the study. Our sample is not therefore fully representative of all current local authority placements and this affects its external validity: that is, the extent to which our results can be generalised to other adoptive placements, and even to other placements with seriously disturbed children.

We must accept the limitations of a relatively small sample size and that this cannot therefore be considered a full-scale RCT. The trial unfortunately shared the same fate as many social intervention RCTs in under-shooting the target size, needing an extension and facing more obstacles to recruitment than anticipated (see the STEPS study: Campbell *et al*, 2007). The small sample means that, beyond the main outcomes, other effects are hard to detect and Type II errors may result: that is, failing to detect differences that are there and which could be evident with a larger sample. A small sample raises doubts about equivalence of the compared groups, although a check on sample characteristics did, in fact, show reasonable similarity on about a dozen characteristics (see Appendix 5). In the light of this, we conclude that this trial, in only achieving a sample size comparable to a pilot study, requires a larger sample replication before the results can be used as more than a pointer for changing practice in post-adoption support.

We discussed in the methods section the difficulty of reliably measuring children's psychosocial problems by questionnaire. In addition, despite its considerable importance to the families, we did not have a reliable measure of attachment difficulties at the screening stage or thereafter except through parent feedback. Independent observations or video recordings of the adoptive family would perhaps have strengthened the study and may have allowed us to examine progress in translating the interventions into observation of "enhanced parenting". However, there would have been practical difficulties in doing this with such a geographically spread sample and we thought it might have cut our participation rate. We were also disappointed that the low return of teacher questionnaires meant that we could not use these data in the quantitative analysis. Finally, in conducting the follow-up, we remain ignorant of what longer-term effects there might be beyond six months after the parent advice sessions ended.

Despite these drawbacks, the trial largely achieved its aim of recruiting adoptive families from local authorities and of using a truly experimental design with supervised parent advisers using manuals. Fully describing the interventions (see Appendix 7) allows them to be implemented reliably and replicated in further research. The study used a tightly defined sample with regard to age at placement and type of placement, with children then selected for a high level of problems. Virtually all interventions ran for the full ten weeks without drop-outs and no bias occurred through sample attrition at either of the post-intervention research follow-ups. This was not a volunteer sample of adopters and fathers were involved in advice session wherever possible. Overall, there was negligible missing data which contributed to the internal validity of the trial. A small trial with complete data is to be preferred to a large trial with missing data.

Translating the findings into practice

How should the findings from the study be taken forward? As some evidence has emerged in support of satisfaction with the parenting advice and of positive changes in parenting, it seems reasonable to encourage this approach to be developed further. First, if greater experience of employing the manuals can be gained, the interventions can be refined to increase their relevance and effectiveness, profiting from additional feedback from adopters and advisers. Our experience of organising the delivery of manual-based parent advice was generally very positive. The parent advisers said they liked using the manuals and found them highly relevant to the problems faced by these families. We have learned from the adviser and adopter feedback what was most valued and what was missing in the programmes and are in a better position to know how much material is suitable for each session. As both manuals were equally appreciated, as neither showed superior results, and as adopters generally wanted both "understanding" and "strategies", there is a strong case for combining the manuals into a single document. Second, this intervention was provided as a standard package to all the adoptive parents in the trial. Prior assessment of the profile of adopters' parenting strengths and difficulties could lead to the advice being more accurately targeted at identified areas.

When considering tailoring the intervention, the question will arise as to how faithfully the manuals have to be delivered in order to replicate the positive findings of this study. Clearly, the basic principles, as set out in the manuals, must be adhered to and as much of the content as possible covered. Straying too far from the interventions as employed in the trial increases the likelihood of different outcomes. However, within these acknowledged parameters, there must, of course, be some flexibility in the offer to individual families. It might be possible, for example, to start each course with a session devoted to discovering the main issues within the family, and deciding, with the parents, which behavioural or educational aspects they would like to prioritise.

A future challenge will be to integrate these parenting interventions into current practice. Adoption agencies may wish to consider how to implement such intervention programmes in accord with their current resources and priorities. Pressures of time, staffing resources and commitment may conspire to weaken any attempts at local implementation of the intervention. A long standing dilemma has been the feasibility, within the local authority setting, of protecting more structured, intensive social work against a wide range of other and often more immediate demands. Aspects of the trial have highlighted what expertise is needed and what common challenges advisers might face; this could be an argument for employing experienced social workers who no longer want to work full-time. Post-qualifying social education will have its part to play in the development and initiating of approved training courses for parent advisers.

If an evaluation study were to be repeated, the sample size would have to be larger to allow for more definitive, statistically sound conclusions to be drawn, with a longer time scale and more sensitive measures of outcome. Future trials of adoption support could demonstrate whether other approaches, for example, Filial Therapy (Ryan, 2007) or the Story Stem approach (Steele, Hodges and Kaniuk et al, 2003), can be effective. We hope the study, although mindful of its limitations, will be of use to providers and commissioners of adoption support services in being able to refer to an advice programme to adoptive parents that has been subjected to a test of its effectiveness.

The relative simplicity of the logic underlying RCTs belies the complexity involved in their planning and conduct and the analysis and interpretation of data. (Bower and King, 2000)

References

Achenbach T. M. and Edelbrock C. S. (1983) *Manual for the Child Behavior Checklist*, Burlington, VT: University Associates in Psychiatry

Adcock M. and White R. (1998) *Significant Harm: Its management and outcome*, Croydon: Significant Publications

Adoption Agencies Regulations (2005), London: The Stationery Office

Argent H. (1985) 'Opportunities in adoption', *Adoption & Fostering*, 9:2, pp 17–20

Barth R. and Berry M. (1988) *Adoption and Disruption: Rates, risks and responses*, New York: Aldine de Gruyter

Batchelor J. (2008) ' "Failure to thrive" revisited', *Child Abuse Review*, 17, pp 147–159

Beecham J. and Knapp M. (2001) 'Costing psychiatric interventions', in Thornicroft G. (ed) *Measuring Mental Health Needs*, London: Gaskell

Beesley P., Hutchinson B., Millar I. and de Sousa S. (2006) *Preparing to Adopt: A training pack for preparation groups*, London: BAAF

Berwick R. (2007) *Is Improvement Science?* Annual Great Ormond Street Lecture, 26 September 2007

Boutron I., Moher D., Altman D., Schultz K. and Ravaud P. (2008) 'Extending the CONSORT statement to randomized controlled trials of nonpharmacological treatment: explanation and elaboration', *Annals of Internal Medicine*, 148, pp 295–309

Bower P. and King M. (2000) 'Randomised controlled trials and the evaluation of psychological therapy', in Rowlands N. and Goss S. (eds) *Evidence Based Counselling and Psychological Therapies: Research applications*, London: Routledge

Campbell M. K., Snowdon C., Francis D., Elbourne D., McDonald A. M., Knight R., Entwistle V., Garcia J., Roberts I. and Grant A (2007) 'Recruitment to randomised trials: strategies for trial enrolment and participation study – The STEPS study', *Health Technology Assessment*, 2007, 11:48, pp 1–123

Corby B. (2006) *Applying Research in Social Work Practice*, Maidenhead: Open University Press

Corney R. H. (1981) 'Social work effectiveness in the management of depressed women: a clinical trial', *Psychological Medicine*, 11, pp 417–423

Crnic K. A. and Booth C. L. (1991) 'Mothers' and fathers' perceptions of daily hassles of parenting across early childhood', *Journal of Marriage and the Family*, 53, pp 1043–1050

Curtis L. (2007) *Unit Costs of Health and Social Care*, Canterbury: PSSRU, University of Kent

Dance C., Rushton A. and Quinton D. (2002) 'Emotional abuse in early childhood: relationships with progress in subsequent family placement', *Journal of Child Psychology and Psychiatry*, 43, pp 395–407

Davies H. and Spurr P. (1998) 'Parent counselling: an evaluation of a community child mental health service', *Journal of Child Psychology and Psychiatry*, 39, pp 365–376

Department for Education and Skills (2005) *Practice Guidance on Assessing the Support Needs of Adoptive Families, Adoption and Children Act, 2002*, Nottingham: DfES Publications

Department of Health (1998) Local Authority Circular, *Adoption: Achieving the right balance*, London: Department of Health

Department of Health (2000) *Adoption: A new approach*, White Paper, London: The Stationery Office: Cm 5017

Department of Health (2003) *Adoption Support Services (Local Authorities) (England) Regulations*, London: HMSO

De Wit, D. J., Lipman E., Manzano-Munguia M., Bisanz J., Graham K., Offord D. R., O'Neill E., Pepler D. and Shaver K. (2007) 'Feasibility of a randomized controlled trial for evaluating the effectiveness of the Big Brothers Big Sisters community match program at the national level', *Children and Youth Services Review*, 29, pp 383–404

Festinger T. (1986) *Necessary Risk: A study of adoptions and disrupted adoptive placements*, Washington: Child Welfare League of America

Fisher P., Burraston B. and Pears K. (2005) 'The early intervention foster care program: permanent placement outcomes from a randomised trial', *Child Maltreatment*, 10, pp 61–71

Fisher P. and Kim H. (2007) 'Intervention effects on foster preschoolers: attachment-related behaviours from a randomized trial', *Prevention Science*, 8:2, pp 161–170

Gardner F., Burton J. and Klimes I. (2006) 'RCT of a parenting intervention in the voluntary sector for reducing child conduct problems: outcomes and mechanisms of change', *Journal of Child Psychology and Psychiatry*, 47:11, pp 1123–1132

Gibaud-Wallston J. and Wandersman L. P. (1978) 'Development and utility of the parenting sense of competence scales', Paper presented at the annual meeting of the American Psychological Association, Toronto

Goodman, R. (1997) 'The Strengths and Difficulties Questionnaire: a research note', *Journal of Child Psychology and Psychiatry*, 38, pp 581–586

Goodman R. (2001) 'Psychometric properties of the Strengths and Difficulties Questionnaire (SDQ)', *Journal of the American Academy of Child and Adolescent Psychiatry*, 40, pp 1337–1345

Goodman R., Ford T., Simmons H., Gatward R. and Meltzer H. (2000) 'Using the Strengths and Difficulties Questionnaire to screen for child psychiatric disorders in a community sample', *British Journal of Psychiatry*, 177, pp 534–539

Goodman R., Ford T., Corbin T. and Meltzer H. (2004) 'Using the Strengths and Difficulties Questionnaire multi-informant algorithm to screen looked-after children for psychiatric disorders', *European Child and Adolescent Psychiatry*, 13:2, pp 25–31

Goodman, R. and Scott, S. (1999) 'Comparing the Strengths and Difficulties Questionnaire and the Child Behavior Checklist: is small beautiful?' *Journal of Abnormal Child Psychology*, 27:1, pp 17–24

Gould N. (2006) 'An inclusive approach to knowledge for mental health social work practice and policy', *British Journal of Social Work*, 36:1, pp 109–125

Harrington R., Cartwright-Hatton S. and Stein A. (2002) 'Annotation: randomised trials', *Journal of Child Psychology and Psychiatry*, 43:6, pp 695–704

Harrington R., Kerfoot M., Dyer E., McGiven F., Gill J., Harrington V., Woodham A. and Byford S. (1998) 'Randomized trial of a home-based family intervention for children who have deliberately poisoned themselves', *Journal of the American Academy of Child and Adolescent Psychiatry*, 37:5, pp 512–518

Johnston C. and Mash E. (1989) 'A measure of parenting satisfaction and efficacy', *Journal of Clinical Child Psychology*, 18:2, pp 167–175

Logan J. and Hughes B. (1995) 'The agenda for post-adoption services', *Adoption & Fostering*, 19:1, pp 34–6

Lowe N., Murch M., Borkowski M., Weaver A., Beckford V. and Thomas C. (1999) *Supporting Adoption: Reframing the approach*, London: BAAF

Macaskill C. (1985) 'Post-adoption support: is it essential?', *Adoption & Fostering*, 9:1, pp 45–9

Mathai J., Anderson P. and Bourne A. (2003) 'Use of the Strengths and Difficulties Questionnaire as an outcome measure in a child and adolescent mental health service', *Australasian Psychiatry*, 11:3, pp 334–337

Maxwell G. (1993) 'Physical punishment in the home in New Zealand', (Occasional paper no 2), Wellington, NZ: Office of the Commissioner for Children

McDonald G. and Turner W. (2005). 'An experiment in helping foster-carers manage challenging behaviour', *British Journal of Social Work*, 35, pp 1265–1282

McMunn A., Bost L., Nazroo J. and Primatesta P. (1997) 'Psychological well-being', Chapter 10 in Prescott-Clarke P. and Primatesta P. (eds) *Health Survey for England, 1997: Young people's report*, London: The Stationery Office

Minnis H, and Devine, (2001) 'The effect of foster care training on the emotional and behavioural functioning of looked after children', *Adoption & Fostering*, 25:1, pp 44–54

Minnis H., Pelosi A. J., Knapp M. and Dunn J. (2001) 'Mental health and foster care training', *Archives of Disease in Childhood*, 84:4, pp 302–306

Mulcahy J. (1999) 'The value of post-adoption services', *Adoption & Fostering*, 23:2, p 6

Netten A., Rees T. and Harrison G. (2001) *Unit Costs of Health and Social Care*, Canterbury: PSSRU, University of Kent

Ohan J. L., Leung D. W. and Johnson C. (2000) 'The parenting sense of competence scale: evidence of a stable factor structure and validity', *Canadian Journal of Behavioural Science*, 32, pp 251–261

Olds D., Sadler L. and Kitzman H. (2007) 'Programs for parents of infants and toddlers: recent evidence from randomized trials', *Journal of Child Psychology and Psychiatry*, 48:3/4, pp 355–391

Pallett C., Scott S., Blackeby K., Yule W. and Weissman R. (2002) 'Fostering changes: a cognitive-behavioural approach to help foster carers manage children', *Adoption & Fostering*, 26, pp 39–48

Pawson R. and Tilley N. (1997) *Realistic Evaluation*, London: Sage Publications

Phillips R. (1988) 'Post-adoption services: the views of adopters', *Adoption & Fostering*, 14:2, pp 32–36

Puddy R. and Jackson Y. (2003) 'The development of parenting skills in foster parent training', *Children and Youth Services Review*, 25:12, pp 987–1013

Quinton D., Rushton A., Dance C. and Mayes D. (1998) *Joining New Families: A study of adoption and fostering in middle childhood*, Chichester: Wiley and Sons

Roy P., Rutter M. and Pickles A. (2000) 'Institutional care: risk from family background or pattern of rearing?', *Journal of Child Psychology and Psychiatry*, 41:2, pp 139–149

Rushton A. (1989) 'Post-placement services for foster and adoptive parents: support, counselling or therapy?', *Journal of Child Psychology and Psychiatry*, 30:2, pp 197–204

Rushton A. (2003a) 'Support for adoptive families: a review of current evidence on problems, needs and effectiveness', *Adoption & Fostering*, 27:3, pp 41–50

Rushton A. (2003b) 'Local authority and voluntary adoption agencies' arrangements for supporting adoptive families: a survey of UK practice', *Adoption & Fostering*, 27:3, pp 51–60

Rushton, A and Dance, C. (2002) *Adoption Support Services for Families in Difficulty: A literature review and UK survey*, London: BAAF

Rushton A. and Dance C. (2006) 'The adoption of children from public care: a prospective study of outcome in adolescence', *Journal of the American Academy of Child and Adolescent Psychiatry*, 45:7, pp 877–883

Rutter M. (2006) *Genes and Behaviour: Nature-nurture interplay explained*, Oxford: Blackwell Publishing Ltd

Ryan V. (2007) 'Filial therapy: helping children and new carers to form secure attachment relationships', *British Journal of Social Work*, 37, pp 643–657

Sar B. (2000) 'Preparation for adoptive parenthood with a special needs child: role of agency preparation tasks', *Adoption Quarterly*, 3:4, pp 63–80

Scott S. (2008) 'An update on interventions for conduct disorder', *Advances in Psychiatric Treatment*, 14, pp 61–70

Scott S. and Lindsey C. (2003) 'Therapeutic approaches in adoption', in Argent H. (ed) *Models of Adoption Support: What works and what doesn't*, London: BAAF

Scott S., Spender Q., Doolan M., Jacobs B. and Aspland H. (2001) 'Multi-centre controlled trial of parenting groups for child anti-social behaviour in clinical practice', *British Medical Journal*, 323, pp 194–8

Selwyn J., Sturgess W., Quinton D. and Baxter C. (2006) *Costs and Outcomes of Non-Infant Adoptions*, London: BAAF

Slade M. and Priebe S. (2001) 'Are randomised controlled trials the only gold that glitters?', *British Journal of Psychiatry*, 179, pp 286–287

Social Services Inspectorate (2000) *Adopting Changes: Survey and inspection of local councils' adoption services*, London: The Stationery Office

Steele M., Hodges J., Kaniuk J., Hillman S. and Henderson K. (2003) 'Attachment representations in newly adopted maltreated children and their adoptive parents: Implications for placement and support', *Journal of Child Psychotherapy*, 29, pp 187–205

Sturgess W. and Selwyn J. (2007) 'Supporting the placements of children adopted out of care', *Clinical Child Psychology and Psychiatry*, 12:1, pp 13–28

The Hadley Centre (2007) *Evaluation of Adoption UK 'It's a Piece of Cake?' training programme*, Bristol: The Hadley Centre, School of Policy Studies, University of Bristol. www.bristol.ac.uk/sps/research/fpcw/hadley

Ward E., King M., Lloyd M., Bower P. and Friedl K. (1999) 'Conducting randomised trials in general practice: methodological and practice issues', *British Journal of General Practice*, 49, pp 919–922

Webster-Stratton C. (2003) *The Incredible Years: A trouble shooting guide for parents of children aged 3–8*, Toronto, ON: The Umbrella Press

Webster-Stratton C. and Hancock L. (1998) 'Training for parents of young children with conduct problems: content, methods and therapeutic processes', in Schaeffer C. E. and Briemester J. M. (eds), *Handbook of Parent Training*, New York: Wiley, pp 98–152

White C., McNally D. and Cartwright-Hatton S. (2003) 'Cognitively enhanced parent training', *Behavioural and Cognitive Psychotherapy*, 31, pp 99–102

Wind L., Brooks D. and Barth R. P. (2006) 'Adoption preparation: differences between adoptive families of children with and without special needs', *Adoption Quarterly*, 8:4, pp 45–74

Woolf N. (2000) 'Using randomised controlled trials to evaluate socially complex services: problems, challenges, recommendations', *Journal of Mental Health Policy and Economics*, 3, pp 97–109

Zosky D., Howard J., Livingston-Smith S., Howard A. and Shelvin K. (2005) 'Investing in adoptive families: what adoptive families tell us regarding the benefits of adoption preservation services', *Adoption Quarterly*, 8, pp 1–23

Appendices

1. Advisory group for enhancing adoptive parenting

2. Adviser and adopter feedback forms

3. The measures

4. Letters, information sheets and consent forms for parents

5. Intervention and control groups compared post randomisation

6. Barriers to participation

7. The Parenting Manuals

Appendix 1

Advisory group for enhancing adoptive parenting

Professor Roy Parker, Chairman
Centre for Social Policy, Dartington,

Sharon Witherspoon
Deputy Director, The Nuffield Foundation

Monica Duck
Director, The Post Adoption Centre, London

Dr Danya Glaser,
Department of Psychological Medicine
Hospital for Sick Children, London

Elaine Dibben
Professional Adviser Adoption Team
Department for Children, Schools and Families

Dr Morven Leese
Health Service & Population Research Department
Institute of Psychiatry

Dr Paul McCrone
Health Economist, Health Services Research Division
Institute of Psychiatry

Professor Geraldine McDonald
Commission for Social Care Inspection

Professor Stephen Scott
Department of Child & Adolescent Psychiatry
Institute of Psychiatry

Dr John Simmonds
Director of Policy, Research and Development
British Association for Adoption & Fostering

Professor Marjorie Smith
Co-Director, Thomas Coram Research Unit
Institute of Education, London

Caroline Thomas
Department of Applied Social Science, University of Stirling

Caroline Murphy
Clinical Trials Unit, Institute of Psychiatry

Research Directors
Dr Alan Rushton,   a.rushton@iop.kcl.ac.uk
PO 32, Health Services Research Division
David Goldberg Building
De Crespigny Park, London SE5 8AF

Dr Elizabeth Monck   e.monck@ioe.ac.uk
Thomas Coram Research Unit
27/28 Woburn Square, London WCIH 0AA

Appendix 2

Adviser and adopter feedback forms

Weekly feedback from parents advisers

Research code number . . . .
Child's initials/DOB . . . .
Number of session . . . . Date . . . .

What was the main issue the parents talked about in this session?

_____

_____

Did the session achieve its aims?

_____

_____

If not, why not?

_____

_____

What worked well in the session?

_____

_____

What didn't work well and why?

_____

_____

If you think this was a particularly good session, please say what happened

_____

_____

If the adopters decided to drop out, please say why they did so and how many sessions were completed

_____

_____

Weekly feedback from adopters

Code number . . . .
Number of session . . . .
Date . . . .

How easy to understand was the topic discussed this week?

_____

_____

What did you find most useful in this session?

_____

_____

What did you find least useful?

_____

_____

What did you find difficult/challenging in this session?

_____

_____

How can you apply what you have learnt?

_____

_____

Any other thoughts or feelings you have had?

_____

_____

_____

_____

Enhancing adoptive parenting RCT – Summary of data collection

Domain	Measure	Sources of information	Measured when?
Child measures			
Child's psychosocial difficulties	Strengths and Difficulties Questionnaire (SDQ) and impact scale	Adoptive parents Teachers	Caseline (T1), immediately post-intervention (T2), 6 months post-intervention (T3)
	Post placement problems (9-items) (PPP)	Adoptive parents	T1, T2, T3
	Expression of Feelings Questionnaire (EFQ)	Adoptive parents	T1, T2, T3
	Analogue scales on how far the child has progressed re emotional distress, mis-behaviour and attachment	Adoptive parents	T3 only
Adoptive Parent measures			
Changes in parenting	Interview-based assessment of initial and enhanced parenting style	Adoptive parents	T1, T2, T3
Parenting competence	Parenting sense of competence scale	Adoptive parents	
Parental challenge	Daily Hassles	Adoptive parents	
Satisfaction with additional intervention	Parental feedback questionnaire (PFQ)	Adoptive parents	
Other data collection			
Child's background	Protocol for file searching	Adoption agency records	Before first interview with adoptive parents
Costs	Client Service Receipt Inventory	Adoptive parents	T1, T2, T3
Preparation and training for adoptive placement	Reearch interview	Adoptive parents	T1
Adoption support services provided alongside additional family advisers (social, medical, educational)	Interview based – measure: content, quantity and quality of the ongoing standard service	Adoptive parents	T2

Appendix 3

The measures

Appendix 3.1

Parental Sense of Competence Scale

Please ring the score that reflects how much you
agree or disagree with the questions below

		Strongly agree				*Strongly disagree*	
1.	The problems of taking care of a child are easy to solve once you know how your actions affect your child, an understanding I have acquired	1	2	3	4	5	6
2.	Even though being a parent could be rewarding, I am frustrated while my child is his/her present age	1	2	3	4	5	6
3.	I go to bed the same way I wake up, feeling I have not accomplished a whole lot	1	2	3	4	5	6
4.	I do not know why it is, but sometimes when I'm supposed to be the one in control I feel more like the one being manipulated	1	2	3	4	5	6
5.	My mother (father) was a better mother (father) than I am	1	2	3	4	5	6
6.	I would make a fine model for a new parent to follow in order to learn what s/he would need to know in order to be a good parent	1	2	3	4	5	6
7.	Being a parent is manageable and any problems are easily solved	1	2	3	4	5	6

8. A difficult problem in being a parent is not knowing whether you are doing a good job or a bad one   1   2   3   4   5   6

9. Sometimes I feel like I'm not getting anything done   1   2   3   4   5   6

10. I meet my own personal expectation for expertise in caring for my child   1   2   3   4   5   6

11. If anyone can find the answer to what is troubling my child, I am the one   1   2   3   4   5   6

12. My talents and interests are in other areas, not in being a parent   1   2   3   4   5   6

13. Considering how long I've been a parent, I feel thoroughly familiar with this role   1   2   3   4   5   6

14. If being a parent of a child were more interesting, I would be motivated to do a better job as a parent   1   2   3   4   5   6

15. I honestly believe I have all the skills necessary to be a good mother/father to my child   1   2   3   4   5   6

16. Being a parent makes me tense and anxious   1   2   3   4   5   6

17. Being a good mother/father is a reward in itself   1   2   3   4   5   6

Office coding only

S Scale   [   ]

E Scale   [   ]

Appendix 3.2

Parental Satisfaction Questionnaire   Child's ID [   ]

Please put a tick next to the answer that best fits your views

1. **Since the start of the parent adviser's visits, have the problems with your child changed?**

   Problems are much worse   [   ]
   Problems are somewhat worse   [   ]
   They are the same as before   [   ]
   They are better than before   [   ]
   They are much better than before [   ]

   Any comments?

   _____
   _____
   _____

2. **Was the help from the parent adviser what you expected?**

   Yes [   ]
   No   [   ]

   Any comments?

   _____
   _____
   _____

3. **Do you feel your parent adviser accurately understood the nature of the problems in the child or family?**

   Not at all   [   ]
   To some extent   [   ]
   Quite well   [   ]
   Completely   [   ]

   Any comments?

   _____
   _____
   _____

4. **Did the advice offered by the parent adviser make sense to you as a way of meeting the problems you had identified?**

Not at all   [   ]
To some extent [   ]
Quite well   [   ]
Completely   [   ]

Any comments?

_____
_____
_____

5. **Did you feel that you understood the reasons for the kind of help your parent adviser offered?**

Not at all   [   ]
To some extent [   ]
Quite well   [   ]
Completely   [   ]

Any comments?

_____
_____
_____

6. **Do you think the advice was helpful?**

Not at all   [   ]
To some extent [   ]
Quite well   [   ]
Completely   [   ]

Any comments?

_____
_____
_____

7. Have you sought help elsewhere for the same problem?

Yes [ ]
No [ ]

Any comments?

_____
_____
_____

8. Did the original problems –

Get worse   [ ]
Stay the same   [ ]
Get a bit better   [ ]
Mostly clear up   [ ]
Clear up completely?   [ ]

Any comments?

_____
_____
_____

9. If the problems stayed the same, did you:

Feel that the visits of the parent advisor were a waste of time?   [ ]

Come to feel better about or feel more able to cope with the   [ ]
problems?

Any comments?

_____
_____
_____

10. If a friend of yours had a similar problem (with their child) would you recommend this service to them?

Yes   [   ]

No   [   ]

Any comments?

_____

_____

_____

Name(s) of parent(s) who completed this questionnaire

. . . .

. . . .

Date. . . . .

THANK YOU FOR PROVIDING THIS INFORMATION

Appendix 3.3

Post-placement problems

Please give your answers based on how you see your child, bearing in mind the last three months.

Please show how often each problem occurs for your child

		Never	Sometimes	Often	Very often	Always
1.	Behaves as if not part of the family	☐	☐	☐	☐	☐
2.	Needs to control others	☐	☐	☐	☐	☐
3.	Is excessively independent	☐	☐	☐	☐	☐
4.	Keeps others at a distance	☐	☐	☐	☐	☐
5.	Shows little trust in others	☐	☐	☐	☐	☐
6.	Manipulates others	☐	☐	☐	☐	☐
7.	Shows excessive fears	☐	☐	☐	☐	☐
8.	Is rejecting towards new mother	☐	☐	☐	☐	☐
9.	Is rejecting towards new father	☐	☐	☐	☐	☐

Appendix 3.4

Expression of Feelings Questionnaire

SECTION A: Children express their feelings to different degrees and in different ways. Please tick the box on each line which best describes your child.

	Not at all	Not too much	Somewhat	Very much	Entirely
1. How openly does your child express feelings?	☐	☐	☐	☐	☐
2. How openly does your child express anger?	☐	☐	☐	☐	☐
3. How openly does your child express fear?	☐	☐	☐	☐	☐
4. How openly does your child express frustration?	☐	☐	☐	☐	☐
5. How openly does your child express affection?	☐	☐	☐	☐	☐
6. How openly does your child express sadness?	☐	☐	☐	☐	☐
7. How openly does your child express pain?	☐	☐	☐	☐	☐
8. How openly does your child express pleasure?	☐	☐	☐	☐	☐
9. How appropriately does he/she express anger?	☐	☐	☐	☐	☐
10. How appropriately does he/she express fear?	☐	☐	☐	☐	☐
11. How appropriately does he/she express frustration?	☐	☐	☐	☐	☐
12. How appropriately does he/she express affection?	☐	☐	☐	☐	☐
13. How appropriately does he/she express sadness?	☐	☐	☐	☐	☐
14. How appropriately does he/she express pain?	☐	☐	☐	☐	☐
15. How appropriately does he/she express pleasure?	☐	☐	☐	☐	☐
16. To what extent does he/she talk to you about how he/she is feeling?	☐	☐	☐	☐	☐

SECTION B: Children vary in their behaviour when upset, angry or seeking attention. Please tick the box that is closest to describing your child.

	Not at all	Not too much	Somewhat	Very much	Entirely
17. Often seems to be bottling things up	☐	☐	☐	☐	☐
18. When upset or angry, is tearful	☐	☐	☐	☐	☐
19. When upset or angry, seeks comfort	☐	☐	☐	☐	☐
20. When upset or angry, becomes withdrawn	☐	☐	☐	☐	☐
21. When upset or angry, becomes aggressive	☐	☐	☐	☐	☐
22. When upset or angry, becomes destructive	☐	☐	☐	☐	☐
23. Takes less than 15 minutes to recover	☐	☐	☐	☐	☐
24. Takes 15–30 minutes to recover	☐	☐	☐	☐	☐
25. Takes more than 30 minutes to recover	☐	☐	☐	☐	☐
26. Likes to be comforted	☐	☐	☐	☐	☐
27. Pushes me away or ignores me if I try to comfort	☐	☐	☐	☐	☐
28. Behaviour when upset/angry is difficult to handle	☐	☐	☐	☐	☐
29. Behaviour when upset or angry bothers me	☐	☐	☐	☐	☐
30. Will ask for attention, as required	☐	☐	☐	☐	☐
31. When seeking attention, will make physical contact	☐	☐	☐	☐	☐
32. When seeking attention, will join in with activity	☐	☐	☐	☐	☐
33. When seeking attention, will misbehave	☐	☐	☐	☐	☐

	Not at all	Not too much	Somewhat	Very much	Entirely

34. When seeking attention, will complain of illness
□　　□　　□　　□　　□
35. When seeking attention, will use facial expressions
□　　□　　□　　□　　□

SECTION C: Children differ in the amount of affection they like to give and receive. Please tick the box that best reflects the relationship between you and your child.

36. Shows me a lot of affection
□　　□　　□　　□　　□
37. Likes to be hugged or cuddled
□　　□　　□　　□　　□
38. Can seem immature in wanting cuddles
□　　□　　□　　□　　□
39. Can seem too mature in wanting or giving affection
□　　□　　□　　□　　□
40. Affection shown does not seem genuine
□　　□　　□　　□　　□
41. An easy child to feel close to
□　　□　　□　　□　　□
42. I feel my child trusts me
□　　□　　□　　□　　□
43. I feel my child cares about me
□　　□　　□　　□　　□
44. I feel my child has positive feelings towards me
□　　□　　□　　□　　□
45. I feel we have a very good relationship
□　　□　　□　　□　　□

SECTION D: Finally, here are some contrasting statements that describe different behaviours. Please tick the box on each line that most closely reflects your child.

46. Much too trusting
□　　□　　□　　□　　□
47. Lacking in trust
□　　□　　□　　□　　□

	Not at all	Not too much	Somewhat	Very much	Entirely
48. Overly attention seeking	☐	☐	☐	☐	☐
49. Very shy or reserved	☐	☐	☐	☐	☐
50. Over-friendly with strangers	☐	☐	☐	☐	☐

Appendix 3.5

Strengths and Difficulties Questionnaire: Parents 4–16

For each item, please mark the box Not True, Somewhat True or Certainly True. It would help us if you answered all items as best you can even if you are not absolutely certain or the item seems daft! Please give your answers on the basis of the child's behaviour over the last three months.

Child's initials only. . . . .

Child's date of birth. . . . . Male/Female

	Not True	Somewhat True	Certainly True
Considerate of other people's feelings	[ ]	[ ]	[ ]
Restless, overactive, cannot stay still for long	[ ]	[ ]	[ ]
Often complains of headaches, stomach aches or sickness	[ ]	[ ]	[ ]
Shares readily with other children (treats, toys, pencils, etc)	[ ]	[ ]	[ ]
Often has temper tantrums or hot tempers	[ ]	[ ]	[ ]
Rather solitary, tends to play alone	[ ]	[ ]	[ ]
Generally obedient, usually does what adult requests	[ ]	[ ]	[ ]
Many worries, often seems worried	[ ]	[ ]	[ ]
Helpful if someone is hurt, upset or ill	[ ]	[ ]	[ ]
Constantly fidgeting or squirming	[ ]	[ ]	[ ]
Has at least one good friend	[ ]	[ ]	[ ]
Often fights with other children or bullies them	[ ]	[ ]	[ ]
Often unhappy, down-hearted or tearful	[ ]	[ ]	[ ]
Generally liked by other children	[ ]	[ ]	[ ]
Easily distracted, concentration wanders	[ ]	[ ]	[ ]
Nervous or clingy in new situations, easily loses confidence	[ ]	[ ]	[ ]
Kind to younger children	[ ]	[ ]	[ ]
Often lies or cheats	[ ]	[ ]	[ ]
Picked on or bullied by other children	[ ]	[ ]	[ ]
Often volunteers to help others (parents, teachers, other kids)	[ ]	[ ]	[ ]
Thinks things out before acting	[ ]	[ ]	[ ]
Steals from home, school or elsewhere	[ ]	[ ]	[ ]

	Not True	Somewhat True	Certainly True
Gets on better with adults than with other children	[ ]	[ ]	[ ]
Many fears, easily scared	[ ]	[ ]	[ ]
Sees tasks through to the end, good attention span	[ ]	[ ]	[ ]

Overall, do you think that your child has difficulties in one or more of the following areas:

Emotions, concentration, behaviour or being able to get on with other people?

No difficulties	Yes, minor difficulties	Yes – definite difficulties	Yes – severe
[ ]	[ ]	[ ]	[ ]

If you have answered "YES", please answer the following questions as well:

How long have these difficulties been present?

Less than a month	1–5 months	6–12 months	Over a year
[ ]	[ ]	[ ]	[ ]

Do the difficulties upset or distress your child?

Not at all	Only a little	Quite a lot	A great deal
[ ]	[ ]	[ ]	[ ]

Do the difficulties interfere with your child's everyday life in the following areas?

	Not at all	Only a little	Quite a lot	A great deal
Home life	[ ]	[ ]	[ ]	[ ]
Friendships	[ ]	[ ]	[ ]	[ ]
Classroom learning	[ ]	[ ]	[ ]	[ ]

	Not at all	Only a little	Quite a lot	A great deal
Leisure activities	[ ]	[ ]	[ ]	[ ]

Do the difficulties put a burden on your family as a whole?

	Not at all	Only a little	Quite a lot	A great deal
	[ ]	[ ]	[ ]	[ ]

Signature . . . .

Date . . . .

Print name [please] . . . .

Mother/father (please specify) . . . .

Thank you very much for your help.

Appendix 3.6

Options for correcting child's "misbehaviour" shown to parents in each home interview

PARENTAL OPTIONS TO DEAL WITH MISBEHAVIOUR

Which of the following actions have you found yourself taking in the last month to deal with your child's misbehaviour?

a) Explained or discussed why s/he should not do it
b) Told him/her off
c) Threatened a punishment
d) Made him or her go without something or miss out on something
e) Made him or her go to their room or somewhere else on their own for less than 5 minutes
f) Made him or her go to their room or somewhere else on their own for more than 5 minutes
g) Found yourself bribing him or her
h) Shouted or yelled at him or her
i) Pushed or shoved or shaken him or her
j) Smacked him or her with your hand
j) Anything else?

Appendix 4

Letters, information sheets and consent forms for parents

Parents' consent form for contacting school, nursery or playgroup

I understand what is contained in the information sheet and I have a copy to keep.

I give permission for the research team to contact the teacher/carer of my child named below. I understand this contact will only be for the completion of the Strengths and Difficulties Questionnaire and information on attendance. I understand that the information collected is strictly confidential and will be used only for research purposes.

Name of teacher/nursery staff . . . .

School address: . . . .

. . . .

I know that if there are any problems, I can contact either of the research directors.

Dr. Alan Rushton   Dr Elizabeth Monck
PO32   Thomas Coram Research Unit
Health Services Research Department   27/28 Woburn Square
De Crespigny Park   London WC1H 0AA
London SE5 8AF
Tel: 0207 7848 5068   Tel: 020 7612 6957

I freely consent to the research team contacting the above teacher/carer for the purposes of the research only.

Name of parent(s) Please print . . . .

Signature(s) . . . . Date . . . .

. . . . Date . . . .

Dr. Alan Rushton,
PO32
Research Unit
Health Services Research Department
De Crespigny Park
London SE5 8AF
Tel: 0207 848 5068

Dear adoptive parent,

A research study comparing types of support for adoptive families

We are writing to ask if you would be willing to help other adoptive parents by agreeing to take part in an important new national research study.

The local adoption service is helping us with the research, which looks at the best ways of supporting families with a newly adopted child. We know that most adopters would like some extra help, but we need to know more about what kinds of support and advice is most helpful.

With your help we will be able to find the best way to offer vital support to other adoptive parents in the future.

We are enclosing an Information Sheet with more details of the research, which, because of its importance is supported by the government.

If you think you might like to take part, please fill in the enclosed form marked **'YES'** and send it back to us in the stamped addressed envelope. The form asks for your name and phone number. We will ring you back at a time convenient for you, and answer any questions you may have. Only then will we ask whether you want to take part.

If you decide that you do not want to hear any more about the research, please fill in the form marked **'NO'** and post it to us in the envelope provided. On this form we only ask you to put the date, the local authority where you live and your own initials: please do NOT put your full name or address.

If you choose not to take part, or want to withdraw from the research at any stage, this will have no consequences for the family social work or any specialist services that you may receive.

We hope you will be able to help us with this important work, and look forward to hearing from you.

Yours sincerely,

Dr Alan Rushton: Research Director
Dr Elizabeth Monck: Research Director

encl: Information leaflet Consent forms [2 copies of each] Stamped addressed envelope

Dr. Alan Rushton,
PO32
Research Unit
Health Services Research Department
De Crespigny Park
London SE5 8AF
Tel: 0207 848 5068

Information Sheet for Parents

Why is this research study important?

Adoption does not always run smoothly. Adopted children often have problems that can be very hard for their parents to manage. So the aim of this research study is to test different ways of supporting parents. With your help, the study will provide vital information about how best to provide support to parents during the first months after adoption.

What happens if I agree to take part?

If you agree to take part, you will be offered one of three different types of support package, on a random basis. All three aim to make adopted family life run as smoothly and successfully as possible for you and your children. We don't know which support package works best – that is the point of the research, after all – but we do know that all three are helpful.

What is the help on offer?

A short summary of the three support packages is set out below. But remember, all parents who take part will continue to receive all the help and support normally provided by their local authority. The support described below is extra to that provided by your local authority.

SUPPORT PACKAGE A

Parents assigned to this group will receive a programme of help for 10 sessions. A specially trained parent advisor will visit parents at home over a period of 10 weeks, at times and on days that fit in with the family's needs. The support will focus mainly on managing children's difficult behaviour.

SUPPORT PACKAGE B

Parents in this group will also be offered a special 10-session programme from trained parent advisors, who will visit the family home at times and on days that suit the family. This programme also lasts 10 weeks, but it aims to help parents understand how the child's past has led to their current problems and how the ways in which parents act can help the child.

SUPPORT PACKAGE C

Like parents receiving support packages A or B, parents in this group will receive all the services normally provided by their local authority. However, they will not receive extra specialist support straightaway. Instead, after nine months, they will be offered the chance to choose either support package A or support package B.

It's an important principle of this research study that parents taking part are allocated to one of the above three groups – A, B or C – at random. You won't be able to choose which group you are in, but we do know that all three types of support have proved helpful to other parents.

What will I have to do?

If you decide to take part in the study, you will be visited three times by one of our researchers: once when you first join the study, once again about three months later, and for the third and final time six months after that.

The first research interview will last about one and a half hours. We will ask you about any problems you have and what help you are already getting. The second and third visits should be shorter. We will ask how your child is getting on and what changes, if any, you have made in the way you deal with problems.

If you do agree to take part in the study, we will also get some basic information about your child's background from social services files before the first research interview. This is so we won't have to take up so much of your time at the first interview.

Will anyone else be involved?

At the first research interview, we will ask your permission to approach your child's teacher or nursery staff to fill in a simple behaviour questionnaire. The teacher will not be told about the particular focus of the study, so your confidentiality is assured.

If you agree, we will also ask the teacher to fill in the questionnaire again at the time of the second and third research interviews. This is so we can track the changes in your child's achievements at school as well as at home.

The researchers will only ever want to see you as the parents; they will not need to speak to your children.

What if I want to drop out?

You are free to drop out of the study at any time. Just tell your local researcher, or if you prefer, tell us.

Will everything be confidential?

Yes. As researchers, we work to the highest ethical standards. We will not tell anyone outside the research team about any personal information. All our researchers and parent advisors have been cleared by the Criminal Records Bureau and have special permission from the Secretary of State to have access to adoption files.

What if I have more questions?

We will be happy to answer any of your questions at any time. If you want more information now to help you decide whether to take part in the study, or if you have any questions during the study itself, we will always be happy to speak to you. You can contact either of us on the phone numbers below.

Dr. Alan Rushton,
PO32
Health Services Research Department
De Crespigny Park
London SE5 8AF
Tel: 0207 848 5068

Dr Elizabeth Monck
Thomas Coram Research Unit
27/28 Woburn Square
London WC1H 0AA
Tel: 0207 612 6945/6957

YES

FIRST CONSENT FORM FOR PARENTS

This form confirms that you would like to talk to one of the research directors, or your local researcher to find out more about the research.

IT DOES NOT COMMIT YOU TO JOINING THE RESEARCH STUDY

Name(s) of adoptive parent(s)

Telephone number(s)

Best time(s) of day to be contacted

Best day(s) to be contacted

I/we understand what is contained in the information sheet and I/we have a copy to keep. I/we understand that personal information is strictly confidential and used only for research purposes. We have been told that this information is kept securely. I/we know that if I/we do not take part in the study or drop out later I/we will still receive all other services to which I/we or my child is entitled.

Dr. Alan Rushton,
PO32
Health Services Research Department
De Crespigny Park
London SE5 8AF
Tel: 0207 848 5068

Dr Elizabeth Monck
Thomas Coram Research Unit
27/28 Woburn Square
London WC1H 0AA
Tel: 0207 612 6945/6957

NO

FIRST CONSENT FORM FOR PARENTS

Thank you for thinking about the Helping Adoptive Parents Study

This form confirms that you do NOT want any more information about the research at this stage.

YOU CAN GET IN TOUCH WITH US LATER IF YOU DECIDE TO JOIN THE RESEARCH STUDY

Initials only of adoptive parent(s) Please do not give your full name

Reasons

Local authority adoption service

Today's date

I/we understand what is contained in the information note and I/we have a copy to keep. I/we understand that personal information is strictly confidential and used only for research purposes. We have been told that this information is kept securely, including this form, and shredded at the end of the study. I/we know that our decision not to take part in the study will make no difference to our family receiving all other services to which I/we am/are entitled.

Dr. Alan Rushton,
PO32
Health Services Research Department
De Crespigny Park
London SE5 8AF
Tel: 0207 848 5068

Dr Elizabeth Monck
Thomas Coram Research Unit
27/28 Woburn Square
London WC1H 0AA
Tel: 0207 612 6945/6957

Appendix 5

Intervention and control groups compared post-randomisation

	Interventions	*Controls*
Child variables		
Boys	53%	47%
Girls	47%	53%
mean age at placement (months)	70	65
Minority ethnic (dual heritage) child	3	2
Mean SDQ score pre-intervention: social worker	17.8	18.4
Mean SDQ score pre-intervention: adopters	18.6	20.2
Adopter variables		
Single parents	(6) 67%	(3) 33%
Two parents	(11) 42%	(15) 58%
Same sex parents	2	2
"Well prepared" by placing agency	8 (44%)	10 (56%)
"Not well prepared/mixed" feelings	9 (53%)	8 (47%)

Appendix 6

Barriers to participation

Question:
Why might adoptive parents whose child/ren has/have substantial difficulties (screened using the SDQ) decline the offer of a free parent support service delivered as part of a randomised trial?

Parents feel they can cope:
1. Parents prefer initially to try to solve the problems without outside help
2. Content with routine services or already receiving, or hoping to receive, a similar specialist service

"It will work out"
3. "Time will heal"
4. Inertia/procrastination – it is easier to do nothing – especially via letter of invitation – maybe different if direct contact by researchers?

Parents cannot cope but don't see parent adviser visits as potentially helpful
5. Parental attributions – weekly visits by a professional will not be thought potent enough, lengthy enough or sufficiently relevant to meet needs
6. Beliefs about the origin of the problems e.g. inevitability because of genetic inheritance?
7. Low expectations that anything will change

Reluctance to be involved in [any] research
8. Reluctance to accept randomisation – especially given the "routine service" possibility (but participation rates are low in many medical trials and in free parenting programmes)
9. Parents see potential difficulty in timetabling home and research visits
10. Non-specific unwillingness to have a weekly visitor to the home

Appendix 7

The parent adviser manuals

Intervention A – Cognitive behavioural approach
Intervention B – Educational approach

Research directors:

Dr Alan Rushton, Institute of Psychiatry, King's College London

Dr Elizabeth Monck, Thomas Coram Research Unit, Institute of Education

Practice consultants: Dr Helen Upright and Mary Davidson

Enhancing placement stability:
Introduction to both interventions

Policy background

Significant changes have been planned for the field of adoption. Increased effort is to be made to move children from the care system into family homes; to recruit more adopters to offer children a permanent home and to strengthen ongoing post-placement support services following implementation of the Adoption and Children Act 2002.

In 1999, about 4,000 older children were adopted in England and Wales and about half of these were looked after children. Since then, there has been a 25 per cent increase in ex-care adoptions to an annual total of 3,400.

Current targets are to increase by at least 40 per cent the numbers of looked after children adopted by 2004/2005. In light of this, there should be a significant rise in new placements, often of children with considerable difficulties who have been waiting a long time for a suitable family. It is therefore an opportune time to be investigating how best to support these newly created placements.

The aim of the study is to test whether carefully prepared interventions designed to enhance existing parenting capacity, and delivered in the early months of the placement, have beneficial effects on the placed children, on the new parents, and on the stability of the placements. In order to answer this question adequately, both the experimental interventions need to be devised and controlled by the research team in order to offer the best possible intervention. The interventions will therefore need to be:

a) delivered in a standardised way that can be replicated in future;
b) delivered according to best practice principles; and
c) grounded in existing knowledge about adopters' satisfactions and dissatisfactions with support services.

a) Standardised interventions

- The interventions will be home based, each session lasting about 60 minutes and arranged at the convenience of the family and their child-care routines and will involve both parents if appropriate/possible.

- Both interventions will be based on a structured and manualised programme but will not be driven by a rigid menu. They will be individualised and sequenced according to the family's pressing needs. The session agenda and sequence should allow for priority to be given to urgent issues.

- The interventions will be time limited (8–10 sessions). It must be clear to the families that the research-related interventions will have to end after 10 weeks and requests for continuing help will have to be referred back to the family's support worker. Carefully planned endings are therefore important. Time for reviewing and reinforcing messages is important.

- Efforts should be made to keep the sessions focused on enhancing parenting. If the conversation strays into a range of other topics, the adviser should politely curtail these and steer a way back to parenting issues.

- Both intervention groups will receive regular handouts and summaries to reinforce important messages (e.g. children do still need to be nurtured even though they act to push the carer away).

- The research intervention is necessarily focused and limited to parenting tasks and is not intended to cover all the varied aspects of placement support (e.g. practical, legal, financial help and contact arrangements).

- The aim of the interventions is to assist with current difficulties. If these prove beneficial, it is also hoped that the gains will endure beyond the interventions. However, there cannot be a single intervention that will suffice for all problems. These brief interventions may not be capable of benefiting all the children or enhancing each of the parents' skills. Different or more intensive interventions may be needed later.

- Advisers in both interventions will need to be aware of the parents' developing relationship with the child. Despite the agency's initial assessment of parenting capacity, the new mother and father may respond very differently to the child once placed in their home. The nature of the parents' reactions to the new child, particularly the growth of positive feelings and the way the child's behaviour is "read" and interpreted, may be a critical feature of the early months. Finding ways of helping the parents to reflect on what is happening in the new relationship, and maintain their warmth and their level of engagement and responsiveness with the children may be crucial.

b) Best practice

- The interventions will be delivered by experienced adoption or family workers with good communication skills who will be additionally trained to implement the programmes.
- The parent advisers will possess the classic characteristics of empathy, warmth and genuineness.
- The parent advisers will be supervised and supported by the practice consultants, who will also be concerned to maintain fidelity to the programme content and structure.
- The attitude of the adviser towards the parents is important. The aim is to empower rather than to prescribe.
- The interventions will be non-discriminatory and culturally sensitive. Adoptive parents will be recruited from different class, ethnic and educational backgrounds and may hold different views about parenting, discipline, talking about personal feelings, attitudes towards professionals, etc. It will be important to respect these differences when advising on parenting behaviour.
- Maintaining good relationships with the local authority adoption unit or placing agency is very important. Others will be involved in the adoption support, especially the family support worker and the child's social worker. It is likely that the child's social worker will retain case responsibility up until the adoption order is granted. The parent adviser needs to be aware of this and to liaise effectively.
- Possible sources of friction with the responsible social workers might be clashes of home visiting appointment times, providing contradictory advice, duplication of roles, unhelpful competitiveness between

interveners and "splitting" by the family of the two or three workers.

- Some intended adoptions will be contested and the new parents may be looking for support for their case to the family adviser. It should be made clear that this is not part of the role.

- Child protection concerns. In the event that the new parents reveal aspects of their parenting that appear abusive, suspicions of significant harm to the child must take precedence over confidentiality. Any action to make a referral should first be discussed with the supervisor.

c) Learning from adopters' views as service users

- The process of engagement with the new parents is extremely important and can easily deter them if the approach is misjudged.

- It is important to be aware of all the family members and their names; in some cases this might include birth children and other foster, adoptive or step-children.

- It may be best to begin with finding out about the family and building trust and developing a relationship before moving too swiftly on to parenting strategies.

- For the parents, admitting to difficulties may run the risk of seeming to be unsuitable parents. The advisers will need to be aware that admitting to problems may be seen as incurring a risk. Adopters can experience inappropriate blame if problems persist and may feel uncomfortable about accepting help. They may need help to be released from this.

- Adopters are sensitive to interventions being pitched at an inappropriate level. Some will be experienced parents; some will not have been parents but will have parenting/child care experience; and some will have parenting experience although it may not have prepared them for looking after ex-care children. The advisers need to be able to adjust their style accordingly.

Enhancing adoptive parenting: Parent adviser manual

Intervention A – Cognitive behavioural approach

Research Directors:

Dr Alan Rushton, Institute of Psychiatry, King's College London

Dr Elizabeth Monck, Thomas Coram Research Unit, Institute of Education

Practice consultant: Dr Helen Upright

January 2004

Acknowledgements

This cognitive-behavioural programme has adopted many of the principles of behaviour management developed by Carolyn Webster-Stratton (1994). Webster-Stratton's research has shown the effectiveness of this model in reducing behaviour problems in young children. Given the effectiveness of this model, a similar structure has been used, with additional principles that are specific to adoptive families.

Reference
Webster-Stratton C. (1994). *The Incredible Years: A trouble shooting guide for parents of children aged 3–8*, Umbrella Publishing: Ontario

This is an abbreviated version of the parenting manuals. Exercises, role plays and scenarios for discussion are not included, nor are handouts and homework. A full version of the manual is available from the authors.

SESSION 1

Introduction

Aims:
- To find out about the child's history and challenging behaviours.
- To introduce the programme to the parent.
- To discuss the parent's expectations.

This intervention has been specifically designed for children from care placed in adoptive homes. In this session, parent advisers begin by discussing the child's background history with the adoptive parent, and then move on to discuss their child's behaviour, including the child's strengths and any inappropriate behaviours.

Parents have an opportunity to discuss these behaviours and tell the advisers how they feel. This leads to a discussion on how the parents currently respond to these inappropriate behaviours and the parents share with the adviser what techniques have been helpful or not.

Following this introduction, the adviser discusses the adoptive parent's expectations of the intervention, including what they would like to gain from the programme, and explaining that the programme will help them learn effective behaviour management strategies which will help reduce some of the inappropriate behaviours of their child. Specific goals are identified (for example, reducing temper tantrums).

Advisers then introduce the **parenting pyramid**, and explain that a different level of the pyramid will be focused on in each session, beginning with play and working up to consequences and problem-solving. It is stressed that the order of these is important, as they focus on developing attachment relationships and building up positive relationships, only after which can other behaviour management strategies be implemented.

SESSION 2

Using positive attention to change behaviour

Aims:
- To provide information regarding children's behaviour and attachment.
- To highlight links between parental beliefs about problem behaviour and parental management.
- To help the parent make links between their feelings and their child's behaviour.

In this session, advisers review the problem behaviours previously identified by the adoptive parent and try and define them as specifically as possible, rather than using vague terms. The adviser explains that such labels can be negative and can, in turn, lead parents to anticipate negative behaviour because this can make parents behave in ways which actually encourage negative behaviours.

The adviser explains how thoughts can influence feelings and behaviour, and invites the parent to consider how their own behaviour can influence a child's behaviour. Advisers then help parents to understand children's behaviour, explaining that, although parents often focus on one factor to explain their child's behaviour, in reality there are many. These could include an abusive and neglectful background in the child's birth family, before they were adopted; peers and school influence; parental physical and mental health; and others. Each such factor can lead children to behave in very different ways, for example, children who have experienced abusive or neglectful backgrounds might exhibit very controlling behaviours or have a tendency to be very independent. The adviser encourages the parent to identify which one factor the parent can quickly change to alter the child's behaviour – the parent should indicate that it is their own behaviour which is the easiest and quickest factor to alter.

The adviser then discusses with the parent the idea that most of children's behaviour is aimed at gaining attention from their parents, and many children want attention all the time. This is impossible for any parent to provide and so, children learn which behaviours get most attention and then exhibit these most often. Children prefer to receive negative attention than to receive none at all, and this is illustrated with an everyday example of a child being shouted at because they have done something naughty. The adviser helps the parent understand the difference between the limited attention that good behaviours generally get, and the considerable attention that inappropriate behaviours receive. Therefore, there is a need for the parent to start providing attention to the positive behaviours and removing attention from the inappropriate ones.

SESSION 3

Play

Aims:
- To review the homework tasks set last week.
- To introduce the concept of play and its importance for establishing positive relationships and effective behaviour management.

The start of the session provides an opportunity to review the previous week's homework, and advisers discuss the parents' thoughts and feelings and how these influence their child's behaviour.

This session is about play and its value. Advisers should begin discussion on play, questioning how often the parents play with their child and whether or not they enjoy it. Advisers explain that sometimes children can be rejecting during play, and the reasons for this.

Advisers discuss why play is important for children in their development and relationship-building, and that it also provides top quality one-to-one attention to the child. This is particularly good at developing attachment relationships with children who have been neglected or who have experienced multiple placements in the care system, and "special play" can help break down the child's barriers to building relationships with their adoptive family.

Advisers encourage the parent to select a particular kind of play –

creative activities which are particularly good for increasing attachment, especially those involving touch, for example, playing with toys in the bath, having fun blowing bubbles, face-painting, etc. The parent is asked to practise such play with their child for about 10–20 minutes a day. The importance of having a regular playtime slot is emphasised, and the adviser also makes clear that play is not conditional on the child's behaviour and should not be withdrawn. To have this dedicated playtime together ensures at least one positive interaction between parent and child every day. The parent is asked to keep a record of their play sessions. The adviser should explain to the parent that their child will probably not be used to adults being involved in their play, and may not be comfortable with this to start with.

SESSION 4

Verbal praise

Aims:
- To review tasks set for last week.
- To introduce the concept of using praise to increase positive behaviours and develop children's self-confidence and self-esteem.

This session begins with a review of practising play – the child's response, the parent's response, etc. If the parent has encountered a specific problem, this is discussed in depth with the adviser, who can begin to consider what the parent could do to improve the play.

This session is concerned with verbal praise and why it is important. Advisers should find out what the parent praises their child for and how often; the child's response to being praised; and the parent's feelings about praising their child.

The adviser explains the importance of praise, including in increasing children's confidence and self-esteem; increasing appropriate behaviour; and helping the child develop a positive self-image. Children who have been in care may have poor self-esteem, and may not respond well initially to positive messages from adults, but advisers should stress that praise is very good at improving the frequency of appropriate behaviours and that, by praising children, parents are providing them with attention for appropriate behaviours. This means that children are likely to repeat these behaviours in order to continue to gain attention. Advisers explain to parents that praise should not be reserved only for special achievements, but for any behaviour that they would want to see repeated – this can be difficult, as human beings are generally programmed to look for the negatives rather than the positives. Advisers explain to parents how to make praise as effective as possible:

- The praise should be specific so the child knows what they are being praised for.
- The praise should be positive, taking care not to slip in a negative remark.
- It is useful to praise children for starting to do a good behaviour.
- Praise should be delivered immediately after a particular behaviour has happened.
- Praise should be sincere and enthusiastic.

The adviser discusses why some children may reject praise and therefore how important it is to continue praising, as eventually the rejection will subside. Advisers also discuss when praise may be difficult, for example, if a child has been challenging all day, but highlight that this is probably the most important time to praise the child, so that the child can notice the difference between the attention they get for appropriate behaviour and lack of attention for inappropriate behaviour. Advisers should spend time with the parent identifying specific behaviours which they can praise. Advisers should explain to the parent that the child may not be used to being praised, and may not respond well initially.

SESSION 5

Praise and rewards

Aims:
- To review homework tasks set for last week.
- Introduce the concept of using rewards as a way of increasing appropriate behaviour.
- Distinguish rewarding from bribing.

The session begins with reviewing the main concepts of praise and looking at parent's records of using praise, its effect on the child's behaviour and how using praise made the parent feel. Advisers also check that the parent is still playing with their child.

This session is about different ways to reward children: one way is by using verbal praise, and another is to use a physical object. The adviser explains that both types of reward are useful and ideally, verbal praise should be used all the time and physical rewards selectively, when the parent wants to increase the frequency of a particular behaviour. Advisers help parents think about what physical rewards they could use, for example, sweets, toys, extra TV time. They also discuss the difference between a bribe and a reward. A bribe is a treat given before the desired behaviour has occurred, and is unhelpful because it actually encourages negative behaviour. There is no guarantee that the appropriate behaviour will occur. A reward is given after the child has done the appropriate behaviour. Advisers should again emphasise to the parent that children who have been adopted from care may not be used to being praised or rewarded, and may not respond well initially.

The adviser introduces the parent to the use of star charts. The adviser asks the parent to identify one particular behaviour for the chart. The behaviour should be specific, and not too difficult for the child to achieve, for example, if the child never gets dressed, the identified behaviour would be for the child to put some of their clothes on rather than get completely dressed. The adviser emphasises that rewards need to be small and frequent; that stars should never be removed once given; and that stars should be given immediately after the behaviour has occurred.

The adviser helps the parent to identify what behaviour they could tackle by using the star chart, and how the parent can explain the star chart to their child.

SESSION 6

Clear commands and boundaries

Aims:
- To review last week's homework
- Introduce the general skills required for parents to set limits and boundaries
- Help the parent communicate better with their children using clear commands

Advisers should discuss the successes and difficulties the parents have experienced using rewards and star charts, and should check that the parent is still playing and praising.

The adviser explains that adults give such frequent commands to children that it is unsurprising that most are not acted upon – parents of children with behavioural problems give 40 commands every half-an-hour! The adviser explains that giving lots of commands does not necessarily increase a child's compliance, as it is difficult for the parent to always enforce the child's obedience. However, boundaries can be set around children's behaviour, and are important – many children in care will not have had boundaries set for them.

Family rules are a good way of increasing children's compliance, as rules can become habits. Advisers can help parents identify rules to introduce.

Advisers discuss how commands are issued so as to increase children's compliance. Effective commands need to be: clear and specific; one command at a time; gain the child's attention; given in a calm, firm voice using child-friendly language; positive, short explanations and not containing questions. Advisers should explain to the parent that their child may not be used to consistency and abiding by rules, and so may take time to respond to family rules.

SESSION 7

Ignoring

Aims:
- To review last week's homework
- To introduce the ignoring technique to reduce inappropriate behaviours

Advisers should discuss the successes and difficulties of using commands and setting boundaries. Advisers should also review the parent's use of strategies and techniques learnt so far.

Advisers discuss how parents have previously used ignoring, and whether they have found this effective and what can make ignoring difficult. Advisers explain that ignoring is useful for reducing inappropriate behaviour because it removes attention from the difficult behaviours. It can only work if the parent continues to play and praise the child, as the child then receives a balance between gaining positive attention and having attention removed.

Advisers discuss which behaviours can be ignored, including those which are not harmful or dangerous. Advisers then discuss the main principles of ignoring: don't look at the child; don't speak to the child; don't touch the child. Advisers discuss the importance of remaining calm and of using ignoring consistently. Once the child is quiet, it is important to praise the child – in this way, the child can distinguish between inappropriate and appropriate behaviour.

Advisers should warn that many parents find that when they first start to use ignoring, the child's behaviour can get worse before it gets better – this is because the child is testing the parent. Advisers discuss with the parent what they can do to ensure that their ignoring is successful, and the strategies and techniques they can use.

SESSION 8

Consequences

Aims:

- Review of last week's homework
- To help the parents inform their child of what behaviours are expected of them and the consequences of their actions
- To introduce consequences as an alternative strategy to manage harmful and dangerous behaviours

Advisers discuss the successes and difficulties of using ignoring, and also review the parents' use of strategies and techniques learnt so far.

Advisers ask the parent about their child's most dangerous behaviours and how they currently manage them. Advisers point out the disadvantages of smacking and that smacking can have particular negative connotations for children who have been abused, as it can bring back traumatic memories and can be very rejecting. Smacking should therefore be avoided when managing the behaviour of adopted children, and alternative strategies used, including problem-solving and consequences.

Advisers should explain that consequences are designed by the parent as punishment to fit the crime, for example, the consequence of a child breaking one of their toys is that they can no longer play with it. Consequences are best used for particularly difficult problems, when the parent should decide, before the event, how they are going to respond to a child's inappropriate behaviour.

The adviser should explain that most of children' inappropriate behaviours are not dangerous and therefore can be managed by using ignoring. However, consequences can be used for dangerous or harmful behaviour, for example, hitting others or breaking things. Advisers also stress the importance of continued use of play and praise so that withdrawal of privileges is balanced with receiving attention for appropriate behaviours.

Advisers discuss the aspects of consequences to ensure that they are implemented appropriately. Consequences must be fair and immediate; must be followed through; must be appropriate and non-punitive. The "if . . . then . . ." rule could be useful in introducing a consequence. The parent should have realistic and age-appropriate expectations of their child.

The adviser should help the parent identify which behaviours to use consequences for, and what these should be.

SESSION 9

Time-out and problem solving

Aims:
- To review last week's homework
- To introduce time-out as an alternative strategy to physical punishment for the management of harmful and dangerous behaviours
- To enable the parent to help their children think of solutions to their problems and perceive which solutions are most effective

Advisers should review the parents' successes and difficulties with the use of consequences and should review their continued use of strategies and techniques learnt so far.

Advisers should describe time-out as another strategy which can be used to manage poor compliance and dangerous behaviours. However, it should be used with care, and may not always be an appropriate technique to use with children who have been adopted from the care system, as many of them have had neglectful experiences and time-out could bring back traumatic memories or make them feel neglected.

The adviser discusses how to conduct time-out successfully. For example, if an inappropriate behaviour occurs, the parent should give a warning and if the warning is not complied with, take the child to the designated time-out place. Once there, the parent explains to the child why they are in time-out, how long they are going to be there, and when the child will be allowed to come out of time-out. If the child runs out of time-out, the parent should calmly return the child, and if the child refuses to go to time-out, the parent should warn them that a privilege will be removed if they do not comply. Advisers should discuss where time-out should be – the preferred place is the bottom step of the stairs. Once the child is out of time-out, the parent should immediately try to praise the child, for reasons explained in previous sessions.

Time-out can be very difficult to implement. Emphasise that the parent needs to be consistent and to follow time-out through to the end.

Advisers explain that children tend to respond to their problems by screaming or hitting out, simply because they do not know any other way. Parents need to help their child learn more effective ways to resolve problems, to learn adaptive ways of coping with difficult situations which will help them avoid conflict and make it easier for them to maintain relationships. Advisers should help the parent practise problem-solving by using the problem-solving model above and role-playing.

SESSION 10

Review

Aims:
- To review last week's homework
- To review all the strategies covered during the programme
- To problem solve any final concerns

Advisers should review the parents' successes and difficulties with the use of time-out, consequences and problem-solving, and should also review their use of other techniques and strategies learnt so far.

Advisers should help the parent identify why each strategy is useful, and the main principles of each one. They should provide parents with specific feedback about which strategies they have used well, and highlight specific examples of their progress.

At this point, it is important that advisers recap the parenting pyramid and emphasise the importance of the parent continuing to use play and praise, so that the child continues to receive attention for their positive behaviours.

Enhancing adoptive parenting

Parent adviser manual

Intervention B – Educational approach

Research directors:

Dr Alan Rushton, Institute of Psychiatry, King's College, London

Dr Elizabeth Monck, Thomas Coram Research Unit, Institute of Education

Practice consultant: Mary Davidson, Adoption Adviser, Surrey County Council

March 2004

Introduction for parent advisers to the educational manual

The parent advisers delivering this manual will be working to a sequence of structured topics but they will need a certain amount of up-to-date background knowledge of child development. They will especially need to know about the consequences of child maltreatment (see MacMillan and Munn, 2001) and attachment theory to help the parents to have a better understanding of the child's difficulties. Here are some ideas to consider.

The process of distorted development

A more complex model of child development has emerged over the last ten years or so through research in the field that is now called "developmental psychopathology". The model applied in the field of child care practice had been very environmentalist in the past: that is, it has been concerned mostly with the adverse effects of poor or hostile parenting on children and, by contrast, the belief in the beneficial effects of stable, nurturing environments. However, concern has shifted somewhat in relation to the kinds of adverse events that affect development and their consequences for well-being. For instance, drug and/or alcohol abuse in pregnancy, an increasingly common phenomenon, may have adverse effects *in utero*, that then persist. Furthermore, such effects often occur in combination with other factors like poor diet, smoking and the mental state of the mother. Consequently, the child born in these circumstances may already have neuro-developmental problems. The child may then have poor parenting in the early years with further negative effects on emotions and relationships – operating at both biological and psychological levels (see Glaser, 2000).

For some adopted children, the difficulties they have could have been inherent in them throughout. A child born with a difficult temperament is likely to be harder to care for and in some cases may evoke negative parenting behaviour, particularly if their parents already face several other stressors like unemployment or a complete lack of local/family support systems. It is sometimes the case that the "difficult" child is the straw that breaks the camel's back. In a minority of cases, this may lead to abuse, rejection or ejection from the family home. The point is that the child placed for adoption may be carrying difficulties that originate from a variety of sources. For example, the presence of abuse in a child's history is likely to be highly influential on development but may not explain current behaviour by itself. Other adversities prior to the abuse; the child's characteristics (age, sex, intelligence) and response to the event (sensitivity, flexibility); subsequent insecurity; poor relationships and multiple moves in care may all accumulate and interact to produce the current effect. Therefore, suggestions that everything is explained by a single event or circumstance should be avoided.

Distorted patterns of relating

Parent advisers should remind themselves of the key elements of attachment theory in "thinking about the child" past and present. Attachment theory is, of course, a large and growing topic but advisers should be aware of the concepts more closely related to adoption, for example, the development of care seeking and exploration in infants; the importance of a secure base; parenting styles and psychological problems in parents that work against the formation of secure attachments; short- and long-term consequences of separation from the main caregiver; types of insecure attachment; regulations of feelings and internal representations of the self and significant caregivers. Bacon and Richardson (2001) have produced a readable but extensively referenced overview for practitioners.

Much more has been written about the development of insecure attachment than the growth of a fresh attachment with a new carer (but see Hughes, 1998). There is considerable enthusiasm in some quarters for therapies to promote fresh attachment, although academic writers tend to be very cautious about whether we really know what to do, what is the rationale for it and what positive effects can be expected (see O'Connor and Zeanah, 2003). It is unclear how adoptive parents contribute to the long-term course of attachment difficulties in their children, although it is likely that the daily occurrences of family life over time which encourage mutual positive feelings are the most influential contributors to the development of secure attachment.

The process of developmental recovery

This educational intervention is intended to assist the parents in helping the child to achieve normal development. We were probably more optimistic ten years ago about outcomes for abused children, who were subsequently adopted, hoping that a child's natural resilience and a loving, stable home would repair the damage. Follow-up studies and clinical evidence show that, although some children do indeed make a good recovery, many children only recover slowly and some problems may persist throughout and beyond childhood. The Maudsley adoption studies have shown that children in continuing placements, even after an average of six years in the adoptive home, can still have considerable problems compared with non-adopted children (Rushton and Dance, 2004). It would, in effect, be unrealistic to think that a child loses forever his or her painful memories; their shadow at least will probably persist, and problems like "emotional dysregulation" are not likely to become "regulated" simply with change of circumstance or via short-term professional interventions.

Conveying "understanding" to adopters

What level of "understanding" should the parent advisers themselves possess? How is this "understanding" of the child's development to be conveyed by the parent advisers? It would be realistic to convey to the parents that we by no means possess a complete understanding of the origin of problems: our theories are often inadequate and contradictory and the research evidence is so often lacking. It would be good for the advisers to be relieved of the burden of thinking they have to produce definitive answers. It would be more appropriate to discuss and reflect together with the parents on how the puzzling behaviour might best be interpreted. In many cases, it will be useful to see a pattern of behaviour as adaptive in the previous abusive situation (e.g. by withdrawal, hypervigilance or distractibility) but which remains and is now dysfunctional in the new environment. As Dr Danya Glaser says: 'The child's developing brain is adversely affected by early negative experiences, but when the child moves to a new placement the brain doesn't know it.'

Reliable knowledge of the major pre-placement circumstances and events in the child's life should help in enhancing understanding which, in turn, should reduce the parents' impatience, bewilderment or dashed expectations. They should, with increased insight, be able to devise parenting strategies more rationally and consider new approaches if the usual methods are failing.

Preparatory reading for the educational intervention

Bacon H. and Richardson S. (2001) 'Attachment theory and child abuse: an overview of the literature for practitioners', *Child Abuse Review*, 10, pp 377–397

Brodzinsky D., Lang R. and Smith D. (1995) 'Parenting adopted children', Chapter 8 in Bornstein M. (ed) *Handbook of Parenting* (Vol. 3). Mahwah, NJ: Lawrence Erlbaum

Glaser D. (2000) 'Child abuse and neglect and the brain – a review', *Journal of Child Psychology and Psychiatry*, 41, pp 97–116

Glaser D. (2002) 'Emotional abuse and neglect (psychological maltreatment): A conceptual framework', *Child Abuse & Neglect*, 26, pp 697–714

Howe D. (2003) 'Adopted children's behaviour and development in childhood and adolescence', in Gupta R. and Gupta F. (eds) *Children and Parents: Clinical issues for psychologists and psychiatrists*, London: Whurr Publishers

Hughes D. (1998) *Building the Bonds of Attachment: Awakening love in deeply troubled children*, Northvale, NJ, Aronson.

Macmillan H. and Munn C. (2001) 'The sequelae of child maltreatment', *Current Opinion in Psychiatry*, 14, pp 325–31

O'Connor T. G. and Zeanah C. H. (2003) 'Attachment disorders: assessment strategies and treatment approaches', *Attachment & Human Development*, 5:3, pp 223–244

Rushton A. (2004) 'A scoping and scanning review of research on the adoption of children placed from public care', *Clinical Child Psychology and Psychiatry*, 9:1, pp 89–106

Rushton A. and Dance C. (2004) 'The outcomes of late permanent placements: the adolescent years', *Adoption & Fostering*, 28:1

Rushton A., Mayes., Dance C. and Quinton D. (2003) 'Parenting late placed children: The development of new relationships and the challenge of behavioural problems', *Clinical Child Psychology and Psychiatry*, 8:3, pp 389–400

This is an abbreviated version of the parenting manuals. Exercises, role plays and scenarios for discussion are not included, nor are handouts and homework. A full version of the manual is available from the authors.

SESSION 1

Introduction

Aims:
- To find out about the child's history and challenging behaviour
- To introduce the programme to the parent, and give them the handout and the loose-leaf folder
- To discuss the parent's expectations of the ten weeks of advice

This intervention has been specifically designed for children from care placed in adoptive homes. In this session, the advisers begin by discussing the adopted child's background history with the adoptive parents, any difficult or inappropriate behaviour the child exhibits and how this makes the parent feel. The adviser explains that, during the sessions, a gradual unravelling process will hopefully help the parent to make sense of the child's behaviours.

The adviser discusses the parent's expectations of the programme and what they might gain from the course, explaining that the child's life history and past experiences will be considered as possible root causes for their behaviour, with suggestions for how the parent can improve this behaviour.

The structure of the course – a series of seminars with handouts provided – will be explained by the adviser, with parents reminded that the course is not tailored to fit the behaviour of any one specific child, but that the lessons learned should be broadly applicable to every child.

SESSION 2

Understanding insecurity

Aims:
- To find out how having a child placed for adoption is working out for them.
- What expectations have they brought to adoption?
- What expectations has the child brought?
- How much 'baggage' is there around for both?
- Do they understand the nature of the task being asked of the child and of them?

Advisers should discuss the effects of insecurity on children in the care system – primarily, lack of attachment to caregivers, and difficulty or inability in forming attachments. Attachment difficulties may manifest in obvious ways, such as over-familiarity with strangers, excessive coolness, or excessive demands, but may also result in other forms of difficult behaviour.

The adviser should ask the adoptive parent to review their knowledge of their child's placement history, and to use this context to understand why this history may have taught their child not to grow too attached to any carer. They should discuss what the parent can do to reinforce the idea of permanency for the child.

The adviser and parent should discuss: whether the child shows symptoms of insecurity; whether progress has been made since the child joined them; whether the child's world outside the home is helping or hindering this; how the parent's views of the child's behaviour might have changed in the light of attachment theory; and how the parent can help the child to talk about and come to terms with the good and bad parts of their past.

SESSION 3

Parents undersanding their own reactions to children's disturbed behaviour

Aims:
- To help them understand their reactions – deal with guilt, puzzlement, exasperation etc.
- To examine their own backgrounds and how that may be contributing to how they react.
- If there are two parents, how their parenting may have to "meet in the middle".
- How children learn to "press the buttons" that produce a familiar [abusive] reaction from adults, and how they will have to learn new "buttons" to produce reactions from their parents that they will gown to enjoy and find rewarding.

Advisers should review the parents' understanding of attachment and attachment difficulties from the previous session.

In this session, advisers will be discussing the importance of parents considering and understanding their own parenting behaviour and reactions to their adopted child's behavioural difficulties. The adviser and parent should discuss the parent's background and childhood experiences, and how these can affect parenting skills. Points to consider include: how parenting can be affected both by the parent's early experiences and by their personality; if there are two carers, whether they had very different early experiences with their parents, and how this affects their own parenting styles; and whether they are confusing the child with different parenting messages, and how these differences could be used as a strength.

The adviser should discuss with the parent how adoption can cause difficult or overwhelming emotions for adoptive parents, and how this experience may differ from parenting birth children. Encouraging the parent to describe any successes they have had with their child and the strategies they have found useful can impress upon them how far they have come. The adviser should explain the hierarchy concept: as people find it difficult to make more than two major life changes successfully at any one time, the parent should prioritise what urgently needs to change for them and the child over what can wait.

SESSION 4

Understanding how "bad" experiences affect learning and behaviour

Aims:
- Helping them make sense of their child's difficulties
- Providing a "linkage" between the past and present in regard to learning and behaviour
- Looking at their child's strategies and their own.

The start of the session provides an opportunity to review the previous week's work, and for advisers to review the importance of parents being aware of their parenting style and understanding how their child's behaviour can affect them.

This session is about how a child's past experiences can shape their present behaviour, and the importance of control to abused and neglected children. Advisers should begin by explaining how trivial difficulties and relatively minor behavioural problems can be more upsetting to daily life with an adopted child than more serious but infrequent emotional traumas. Getting ready for school on time, frequently losing possessions, never sitting still and eating food too slowly or quickly are all common infuriating behaviours that can disrupt the bonding process between parents and children.

The adviser should also discuss with the parent how people outside the home experience the child – at school, with other family members, etc – and whether difficulties with "social learning" and social boundaries or educational problems are affecting the child's ability to settle into their new family.

The adviser should stress the importance of control to children who have been abused or neglected. For these children, having control, looking after themselves and not allowing parents or carers to be in charge may have been a vital survival strategy. The parent may need to help their child to gradually let go of this behaviour and to trust parents to care for them successfully before their behaviour can change.

SESSION 5

Understanding how "bad" and broken relationships affect social development

Aims:
- Understanding seemingly immature behaviour
- Emphasising past deficits in the child's upbringing
- How continual severance of early attachments has affected development

The session begins by reviewing the subjects covered in the previous sessions, with advisers ensuring that parents understand the importance of attachment, and the way in which their parenting style and the child's behaviour are both affected by past experiences.

This session looks at the effects of previous relationships on children's current behaviour and social development. Immature behaviour is common among children who have had difficult early experiences. The adviser should discuss with the parent how they view such behaviour: was immature behaviour in adopted children explained to them before they adopted? Are they making unfair comparisons between the behaviour of their child and others in their peer group who have not had the same difficult early years?

This behaviour can be caused by a child's early experiences and previous relationships. However, such behaviour may also have a use for the child: children learn through play and re-enactment, and "becoming" a baby or toddler again may be helping the child to learn how to forge new relationships.

Parents should also be aware that a child's early experiences may mean that they interpret adults' behaviour in unexpected ways: a child may not have the emotional intelligence to distinguish between being asked to do something, e.g. put away their toys, and being punished, e.g. having their toys taken away.

Advisers should stress the importance of unmet early needs on children's behaviour: how this has affected who the child is today, and how parents can help to change this situation.

SESSION 6

Survival strategies and defensive reactions – the outward show

Aims:
- To find out the "buttons" children are pressing to worry or infuriate parents
- To try to understand why the children do it.
- Is what you see, what you get?
- What their behaviour might really mean.

The session begins by advisers and parents reviewing the subjects covered in the previous sessions.

This session examines the survival strategies and defensive reactions that abused or neglected children often use. Advisers begin by describing some common behaviours by which children display their survival strategies: emotional immaturity; disruptive behaviour and non-compliance; emotional withdrawal; and fear, anxiety and anger. Advisers should stress that although parents may feel that such behaviour is aimed at annoying them, in fact the child may be acting out internalised feelings in a "cry for help". The parent should be encouraged to reflect on the reasons that may lie behind these behaviours.

In the light of this, the adviser should help the parent to reappraise the child's past experiences and consider what survival strategies the child may have learnt during this time that they are still using in their adoptive home. Behaviour that may display these strategies can range from a simple fear of the dark to more complex fear of failure.

Advisers should discuss with the parent what the child's behaviour may really be trying to say, and consider how the parent can teach the child new coping mechanisms that are a more accurate reflection of how the child is feeling now.

SESSION 7

Expression and control of feelings

Aims:

- To build upon what they have learned and reflected upon from Sessions 5 and 6.
- They have hopefully identified some of the causes of their child's behaviour; explore how understanding of these causes may help both them and the child?
- With (hopefully) this new knowledge and insight, how do they think they can help the child negotiate his or her way around the wider world?

The session begins by advisers and parents reviewing the subjects covered in the previous sessions, particularly how early relationships and experiences can affect children's behaviour, and lead to the use of survival strategies.

Advisers should explain that, because of the non-prescriptive nature of the programme, this session cannot give parents particular ways to respond to their children to help them express and control their feelings. Instead, the session aims to help parents to develop their own strategies, based on what they have learned and tailored to their own child.

The adviser should encourage the parent in thinking about how they may already have helped their child to "reframe" their thoughts and interpret adult behaviour in more appropriate ways. What behaviour may the child have learnt from neglectful carers, and how could this be "reframed" to suit their current situation? Advisers should stress that some behaviours may take longer to "reframe" than others.

Parents should also be encouraged to help teach their child to express their emotions in more socially acceptable ways. Advisers should suggest that parents liaise with the child's school and the parents of the child's friends, etc, to help with this.

SESSION 8

Understanding how children develop new relationships

Aims:
* Helping parents to understand the 're-invention' process that adoption requires of children
* Why a child needs to retain the 'good' aspects of their original identity and how to build them up
* How the child may be rationalising their fears and not letting the past go.

The session begins by advisers and parents reviewing the subjects covered in the previous sessions.

Advisers should begin the session by discussing how the parent feels their relationship is developing with their child. Is this relationship the main benefit that the parent sought from adoption, and has it been satisfied? How difficult has it been for the child, whose past moves may have taught them that relationships last only until they are moved again?

The adviser should help the parent to realise how difficult it may be for an adopted child to develop new relationships, particularly if they are expected to lose all contact with their past when they are adopted – wiping out the past cannot teach children how to trust. Parents should give their child the opportunity and permission to talk about their past, visit former foster carers or places in which they previously lived, etc. If this is not logistically possible, working with a life story book or photographs can also help.

Above all, children should be given the opportunity for discussion. The adviser should reassure the parent that, in time, the parent will learn to instigate conversation with their child about the past, and also learn to "seize the moment" when the child is receptive. Talking about the past can help the child to move on and learn to trust, but during this process painful memories may need to be revisited, similarly to counselling for bereavement or divorce. But rather than formalised therapy, the parent should try to create a conducive home environment in which the child can heal. In discovering what their child may find difficult about their relationship, the parent can formulate ways to help them trust that are mutually beneficial.

Advisers should note that therapists have divided views about the benefits of recalling past abuse, and that new research indicates that this may re-traumatise the child. Such counselling is best undertaken by mental health professionals.

SESSION 9

Surviving in the wider world

Aims:
- A recognition that the contents of the programme have not been just about them and their child
- How the child's functioning affects day-to-day life
- How their child and they as parents are being judged.

The session begins by advisers and parents reviewing the subjects covered in the previous sessions.

This session should be primarily used to allow the parents to express and normalise their feelings about adoption now, compared with their initial hopes and fears when they first started the process. What has the impact been on the family of "parenting in a goldfish bowl", with relatives, friends and social workers judging their actions? Is their child subject to unfair peer group comparisons by the wider world?

Advisers should concentrate on the relationship between the parents and child, and the wider world. Parents should be encouraged to help the child to decide what information they share with others, and how to be selective about what they tell and to whom they tell it. Are they and their child able to discuss adoption with the wider world on a "need to know" basis? Are cover stories permissible and how do the parents construct them? What help do they receive from their social worker?

Advisers and parents should discuss the changing nature of adoption and general public attitudes towards it. The concepts of "bad blood" in an adopted child's birth family, or of adoption as a total cut-off from a child's past are still widely held concepts, although the parents should have already found that adoption today is very different. However, they may have come into contact with people, including professionals like teachers or doctors, who still hold these outdated perceptions, and may well be "re-educating" others on a daily basis. The adviser should discuss the importance and also the difficulty of this task, and suggest how parents can best approach it.

SESSION 10

Concluding thoughts

Aims:
- An evaluation of what has been learned over the past nine sessions.
- Is there any session or particular issues that parents failed to understand fully and would like further clarification upon?
- Have any questions been thrown up by the material that haven't yet been dealt with?
- A reminder about the aims of the project: a test of the usefulness of advice given to parents.

Just as Session 1 was a "getting to know you" session, Session 10 will be a leave-taking, clarifying the work that has been undertaken and any problems or confusion that parents may still have, and acknowledging the way in which advisers and parents have worked together.

The non-prescriptive nature of this intervention model will probably have to be reiterated by the advisers, as parents may see this session as an evaluation of their progress and that of the child. Advisers should reassure parents that judging their progress is not the intention.

Advisers should end by thanking parents for their co-operation and wishing them and their children well for the future.

Index

Compiled by Elisabeth Pickard

abused children 98, 99
  vignettes 124, 127, 129
adopted children, arrival in
  placement 57–60
adopter-based interventions 15–16
Adoption Agencies Regulations 47
Adoption and Children Act 2002 1,
  11–12
adoption preparation 47–62
  content and quality 4, 50–1
  parenting training needs 53–5
  relevance 54–60
  views on 41, 43, 49, 50–7
adoption records *see* case files
adoption support services 11–17
  effectiveness 15–17
  legal requirement 1, 12
  literature review 14
Adoption Support Services
  Regulations 2003 12
Adoption UK
  in recruitment for study 34, 64
  self-help 13
  support services 123
  see also It's a Piece of Cake?
    course
*Adoption:Achieving the Right
  Balance* 11
adoptive parents 2
  expectations and reactions to a
    child's arrival 57–60, 105
  feedback from 90–108
  feedback on 107–8
  interviews with 50
  satisfaction with preparation
    52–4
  SDQ at screening 65–8

SDQ results 82, 83, 86
support services 11–14
  specialist services 152–65
adoptive placements
  early days 57–60
  intervention timing 25–6
aggression
  dealing with 140–1, 142
  not in manuals 104
  at placement 58–9
  vignettes 126, 129, 130
anger
  dealing with 100
  at placement 58
  pre-placement training lack 56
  vignettes 127–8, 131
attachment difficulties 16, 61,
  144–6
  management 16
  of parents 29–30
  pre-placement training lack 56
  questions on 40
attachment formation 101–2
attachment relationships, play and
  28

behaviour, questionnaires on 44–5
behaviour management
  parenting behaviour 27–30
  support for strategies 3
  understanding the behaviour
    30–3
behavioural problems 14
  construction of meaning 30
  deterioration 130–1
  parenting changes 142
  post-adoption needs 1

N.B. This index does not cover the appendices.

255

pre-placement training lack
53–5
questions on handling 40
study results 132–3, 171–3
bias, elimination of 18–20
birth family problems 70–2
see also substance abuse;
violence
black and minority ethnic (BME)
children 5, 179
boundary setting 16, 28–30, 97
British Association for Adoption
and Fostering (BAAF)
on parenting preparation 47
on post-adoption support 9

case/control design 19
case files 35, 39–40, 69–72
case vignettes 104–5, 121–33
challenging behaviour 61, 132
Child and Adolescent Mental
Health Services (CAMHS)
costs 115, 116, 118
satisfaction with 128, 164
shortcomings 13, 123, 156,
159, 163–4
waiting times 160, 161, 162
child-based interventions 15
child-based measures, results 82–8
child-based questionnaires 2–3,
44–5
Child Behaviour Checklist (CBCL)
36
client satisfaction, with advice
sessions 43
Client Service Receipt Inventory
42–3
cognitive behavioural intervention
27–30, 96–8
costs 111–20
study design 2–3
study results 177
commands, specific techniques 93,
97

community parenting programmes
16
complexities, case vignette 104–5
conduct problems 14, 16
in study 36–7, 65–7
confidence-building, for parents
92, 95–6
conflicting viewpoints 104–8
consequences, strategy 98, 122,
123
consultants, involvement in trial 26
control group 2, 35–6, 45
case vignettes 127–31
costs 111–20
delay in help 21
ethical limitations 5
parenting changes 138–9,
145–6, 147
post-adoption support 168–9
study results 173
controlling behaviour 129–30
coping styles, of children 32–3
cost-benefit analysis 42–3, 173–4
cost-effectiveness 1–2, 4, 110–20
cost issues, in RCTs 20–1

Daily Hassles questionnaire 2, 41,
76
disinhibited attachment 125
dual heritage children 101, 130–1

economic costs see cost-benefit;
cost-effectiveness
education support, for children
114–19
educational interventions 98–101
results 93–4
study design 30–3, 35
vignette 104–7
educational psychologists 161, 162,
164
Effect Size 3, 75
Efficacy as a Parent 75–6
emotional distress 135–9

emotional problems
  of adoptive parents 107
  in EFQ 44
  improvements 83, 84
  on initial SDQs 66, 67
  post-adoption needs 1
  vignettes 127–8
emotional strain, on parents 53, 59
expectations of adopters 50, 95
Expression of Feelings
  Questionnaire (EFQ) 2, 40,
  44–5
results 84, 87

Family Centre support 130
family interviewers, selection and
  training 38–9
family problems, in adoptive
  families 102, 103
family profiles, in study 34, 69
family support worker, delivery of
  interventions 22
financial support, information on
  47, 49
foster care
  length of time pre-adoption 6,
  70
  placement moves 6, 70, 129,
  132, 171
    vignettes 122, 127
  studies on 174–5

gender differences, on initial SDQs
  65–7
general practitioners (GPs) 42–3
  costs of care 111, 116
group meetings, pre-adoption
  preparation 51

help-seeking issues 5–6, 13, 102,
  103
homework, in study 94, 95
honeymoon period 59–60
hyperactivity 36–7, 65–7

hypotheses 38, 89
  study results 173

ignoring strategy 28, 29, 98
  vignettes 124, 126
inattention 36, 92
Incremental Cost-Effectiveness
  Ratio (ICER) 111
independent providers (of support)
  13
index child 39, 155, 175
  specialist services for 154, 155,
  156
indiscriminate friendliness 14, 40,
  125, 127, 129
  dealing with 135, 143–50
intervention groups
  case vignettes 122–7
  post-adoption support 166–7
interventions
  features and aims 27
  outcomes 74 –89
  selection for study 25–6
  timing of 25–6
interviewers, selection and training
  38–9
interviews 37–8, 40–1
It's a Piece of Cake? course 5, 13
  parenting changes 145–6
  satisfaction with 162

legal issues, parenting training 47,
  49
lessons learned 93–5, 177–9,
  181–2
literature review, adoption support
  services 14
local authorities
  collaboration in study 24, 34–6,
  63–4
  funding for specialist services
  159–61, 165
  information from files 32–3
  legal obligations 12

see also case files
logical consequences strategy 28, 30

maltreated children 45, 133
manuals 2, 5, 6, 26
    delivery of interventions 22, 96
    future use of 181
    usefulness 176–7
    views on 6, 7
    weaknesses 103–4
Maudsley Adoption and Fostering study 48, 60, 133, 175
measures, in study 41–5
mental health problems
    birth parents 71
    in-care children 11
misbehaviour 40
    improvements 83, 84
    parenting techniques 43–4, 135, 140–3

negative feelings of parents 29–30, 59, 102, 105
negative parenting approaches 3, 6, 97
neglected children 98, 122
    vignettes 122, 124, 125, 127, 129
Nuffield Foundation 12

older children 1, 2, 11
outcomes of interventions 74–89
overactivity 14

parent advisers 26–7, 33, 106–8
parent-based questionnaires 2–3
parent satisfaction, with parenting advice 3
parental care, dysfunctional in birth family 71–2
"parentified" children 149–50
parenting advisers
    feedback from 90–108

praise for 126
parenting changes, six-month follow-up 3
parenting Daily Hassles measures 2, 41, 76
parenting interventions 2, 45
    advice sessions
        client satisfaction 43
        costs 110–11
        feedback on 91–5
        lack of time 92, 103–4
    costs 111–20
    for emotional distress 136–9
    future use of 182
    for inappropriate relationships 143–50
    individualised needs 53–5
    for misbehaviour 140–3
    outcomes of 132–3
    resistance to 104–6
    satisfaction with 3, 77–81
    selection for study 25–6
    study results 177
    timing 25–6
parenting quality 27
parenting satisfaction 6–7, 172–3, 174
Parenting Sense of Competance (PSOC) 2, 42, 75–6
    improvements 3
    study results 172–3
parenting skills and attitudes
    measures of 41–4
    study results 171–3
parenting style
    changes 93–6
    reviewing in advice sessions 92–3
parenting techniques 43–4
    changes in use 142
    need for training 48
parents see adoptive parents
Parents' Satisfaction Questionnaire 43

parents self-report measures 75–81
peer relationship problems 37,
  65–7
physical affection (hugs/cuddles)
  136–9
  difficulties with 144–7
placement changes 70
placements *see* adoptive
  placements; foster placements
play
  attachment and 28, 101–2
  importance of 93
  parenting skill 96
  vignettes 124, 126
post-adoption services 154,
  156–61, 165
post-adoption worker 22
Post-Placement Problems (PPP)
  questionnaire 3, 45, 85
pragmatic trials 177–9
praise
  parenting skill 28–9, 93, 96–8
  for parents 95, 96
  vignettes 124
pre-placement adversities 6–7, 121
  case file information 39–40,
    69–72
  and outcomes 85
  symptoms and behaviour 44–5
  understanding the behaviour
    30–1, 52–3, 94, 95, 99–101
preparation for adoption see
  adoption preparation
psychosocial interventions, ethical
  issues of trials 20–1
psychosocial problems 15
  measurement of 180
  selection criteria 36–7
  study results 171–3

qualitative analysis 1–2, 90–108,
  176
  cost-effectiveness 110–20
Quality Protects initiative 9

quantitative research results 74–88,
  135–51
questionnaires 2–3, 41–5

randomised controlled trial (RCT)
  design 19
  ethical issues 20–1
  lack of understanding about 35
  lessons from 177–9
  in USA 16
  validity 21–4
Reactive Attachment Disorder 126
recruitment into sample 2–3, 4–5,
  34–6, 63–8
  refusal to participate 64, 68
regulating relationships 135,
  143–50
rejection
  of adopters 127
  by birth parents 71–2, 99, 100
  vignettes 122, 124
relationship building 101–2
relationship problems 14, 44–5
  dealing with 143–50
  see also indiscriminate
    friendliness; regulating
    relationships
resilience 72
  lack of 132
risky behaviour see indiscriminate
  friendliness
routine services, standard questions
  on 42

same-sex adopters 2, 101
sample for study 2–3
  recruitment problems 179
  selection 24
  size limitations 4–5
Satisfaction measures, of adoption
  support 2
Satisfaction with the Parental Role
  75–6, 85
  costs and 113, 120

school, access to specialist services
154, 155
screening, study participants 63–70
screening questionnaire, selection of
36–7
secure attachment, adoption aim 9
self-awareness, of parents 103,
105–6
self-help groups 13
service costs 110–20
siblings 102
significant difference, between-
groups analysis 75–6
single parent adopters 2
vignettes 92, 122, 158, 161,
164
skills-based parenting needs 61
social workers
access to specialist services
154, 156
delivery of interventions 22
inadequacies 153
as parent advisors 26
in recruitment to study 179
SDQs at screening stage 65–8
in setting up study 35
unhelpful 123, 125, 126
use of manuals 2, 5
socially undiscriminating behaviour
see indiscriminate friendliness
special time 93, 96
specialist services
access to 152–6
costs of 4, 110, 114–19
mapping 12
standard questions on 42
timeliness of 156–69
Strengths and Difficulties
Questionnaire (SDQ)
completed by parents 65–8, 71,
72, 82, 83, 84, 85, 86
completed by social workers
65–8
costs and 113

in sample selection 2–3
at screening 64–9
selection of 36–7
study results 171–2, 174, 178
study design 18–25
study methods 2–3, 25–33
study results 3–4, 171–81
lessons learned 177–9,
181–2
study strengths and limitations 4–5,
179–81
substance abuse, birth parents 71,
122, 127, 130
support groups, post-adoption 13
support services, legal requirement
1, 12
symptoms, questionnaires on 44–5

tailored parenting education 2–3
teachers, views in SDQ 41
time out 28, 30, 123, 142
Total Difficulties score, screening
questionnaire 36–7
results 171–2
trial registration 19–20
trusting
by children 150–9
EFG score 84
by parents 102, 103

United States (US)
foster care trials 175
parenting clinic 27
post-adoption support 15, 16

validity, of the trial 21–4
violence in birth family 71, 125
case vignette 122
Visual Analogue Scales (VAS) 3, 45
results 82–4
use in interviews 40
voluntary adoption agencies (VAAs)
13, 25